BUSH
for the
BUSHMAN

Need
"The Gods Must Be Crazy"
Kalahari People Die?

by
John Perrott

Beaver Pond Publishing & Printing
Greenville, Pennsylvania

Library of Congress Cataloging-in-Publication Data

Perrott, John, 1932-
  Bush for the Bushman : need "the Gods must be crazy" Kalahari people die?
/ by John Perrott.
      p.   cm.
  Includes bibliographical references and index.
  ISBN 1-881399-04-4 (pbk.) : $14.95
  1. Kung (African people)—Social conditions. 2. Kung (African
people)—Government relations. 3. Kung (African people)—Social
life and customs. I. Title.
DT1058.K86P47   1992
960'.04961—dc20   92-11105
                                                                      CIP

Beaver Pond Publishing & Printing
P.O. Box 224
Greenville, Pennsylvania 16125

Table of Contents

COVER CAPTIONS AND CREDITS

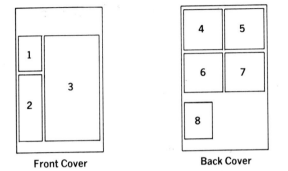

Front Cover **Back Cover**

1 Rock paintings, Tsodilo Hills, of rhinos which haven't been known there in recorded memory. —*JP*

2 Noishay hunting. —*JP*

3 Older unattached woman decked out in her 'Sunday finery'—ostrich eggshell chip necklaces. —*BG*

4 Bushman women foraging. Wild game skin kaross of girl on right has tail up—on other days it was observed tail down. —*JP*

5 Victoria Falls with rainbow, the 'end of the world', where the Bushman in *The Gods Must Be Crazy* went to dispose of the 'evil' Coke bottle. —*JP*

6 Rough-hewn Okavango mokoro. —*BG*

7 A sturdy wild Bushman in scant attire. —*JW*

8 John R. Perrott, the author. —*IP*

Dedication

To Qui and his small band of Kalahari hunter-gatherers,
may they endure.

Ninety percent of any profits from this book
will go to
organizations actively supporting
the survival of the San and their culture.

Acknowledgements

Many people have helped me with this book. They know who they are, and they know I am grateful. I do not feel it necessary to list all their names.

I have had help, however, that must be mentioned. As an amateur blundering into a field for experts, I have been welcomed and encouraged by established authorities who have tried to tolerate my errors and gone far out of their way to assist me. Dr. Robert Hitchcock of the University of Nebraska talked to me at length and sent me a large quantity of material out of his personal files. Dr. Megan Biesele, who is presently out in the field where the action is with the Nyae Nyae Development Foundation in Windhoek, but mostly up in Bushmanland, talked to me extensively and provided invaluable background material. John Marshall gave me fresh insight, in particular pointing out that it would not be fruitful to concentrate on a few hundred remaining truly wild Bushmen, and forget about tens of thousands that have attempted the transition into modern civilization, not always successfully. All the preceding is not to imply that these people endorse my views or my book. If there are errors or misjudgements, they are mine.

I want also to mention people who took considerable trouble to read and critique the entire manuscript: Aunt Lewan Collings, Harriet Bowlus, Patsy Givins, Peter Comley, Alan Warhaftig, Connie Dowling, Valerie Watson and Hilary Dennison. Debbie Ryder and Jasper McKee not only assisted in the laborious word processing, but added advice, insight and encouragement.

All my colleagues of the group led by Dr. Jack Wheeler, who visited the Kalahari Bushmen, were helpful and encouraging. A special mention goes to one of our seven, Jim Reed, who was responsible for the creation of the eighteen minute video, *In Search of the Bushmen*, to further the 'Save the Bushman' effort. Unfortunately, Jim did not survive to see the book published.

SOUTHERN AFRICA

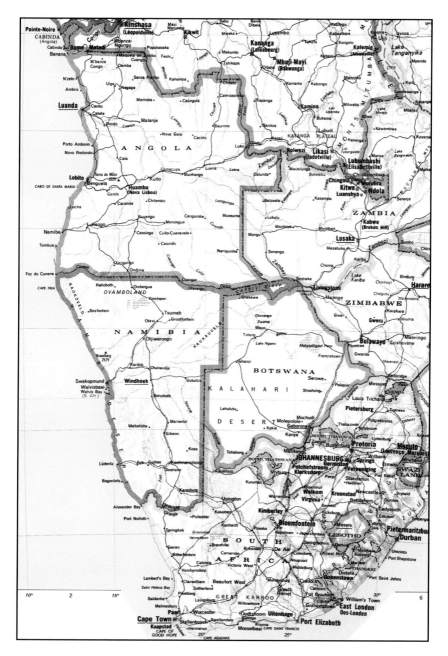

From **Rand McNally New Century World Atlas**
Copyright 1991 by Rand McNally. R.L. 92-5-47

The Bushman's fire is his real home—he lives and sleeps next to it. The '90 second People's' flimsy shelter is almost a decorative backdrop. —WT

Clan takes a breather during gathering expedition. These two pictures show entire 12-member clan (plus Keeme). —WT

—1—
Prologue

At the dawn of history, the Bushmen possessed all the land—bush—in the whole of southern Africa. They viewed their bush like water and air, as their gifts from God; inappropriate for individual or private ownership. Then more advanced people who thought differently arrived and dispossessed the Bushmen. Today the Bushmen have none of their bush left.

A week of my sixteen years in Africa was spent visiting a small clan of still nomadic Kung San hunter-gatherers, known commonly as the Bushmen of Africa, *'The Gods Must Be Crazy'* people. This tale grew out of that experience. The twelve people, two brothers, their wives and children and two other unattached women, were living in a remote area of the Kalahari desert in conditions very like those of their, and all our, ancestors of 10,000 years ago. This clan represents possibly the most primitive people remaining in the world today. Genetic researchers at the University of California Berkeley, using blood samples and DNA "fingerprinting", have recently announced these Kung as the oldest surviving humans. There are but a few hundred hunter-gatherers left living in their traditional ways. Perhaps 70,000 ethnic San eke out a living in southern Africa, having been dispossessed of their traditional lands and culture. Of these, the luckier ones are janitors, cattle herders and laborers. Dispossession has left many others as beggars, prostitutes and thieves. It is not so many years ago, into the twentieth century, that Bushmen were legally classified as animals and literally hunted down for a bounty.

There are, or were until recently, fifty-eight aboriginal hunter-gatherer peoples left in the world: most of the earth's aboriginal peoples were wiped out long ago. Those few who survive are in constant peril.

Few modern people have been able to meet traditional Bushmen on

1

their own turf. The San are a shy people by nature and have learned through generations of contact that whites often bring only death. The onrush of modern technology, combined with the present political turmoil in southern Africa, contribute to the destruction of the Bushman's way of life and of the people themselves. The days when the San could fade deeper into the bush and find safety are gone. Even their arid thirstland Kalahari haven is coveted by herders and miners and game conservationists, and the San lack the education and political skills necessary to lobby effectively for their own share of the African bush.

When I went to the Kalahari it was with a vague wish to see these people, to learn something of their way of life, to add to my lexicon of African lore. But I came away committed to attempting to find a way to help the Bushmen continue their way of life. They changed me, and now I want to change you, to make you, the reader of *Bush for the Bushman*, aware of their plight.

Back in prehistory we were all hunter-gatherers, living in small groups or clans. The evolution of man through the agrarian revolution starting 10,000 years ago led to the first discovery of planting and domestication and herding of animals. This allowed and led to people concentrating in one place, dwelling in villages and developing tribal and chieftain systems. As human and livestock populations increased there was a need for more land and so people organized together to usurp and control the land of others.

Hunter-gatherer clans tend to be small and distributed in such a way as not to overuse an area of sparse resources. Nomadic clans practice seasonal convergence at a water source during the dry season and disperse over their whole range during the wet season, following the seasonal availability of veld food and wildlife movements and migrations. There are loose kinship ties between clans but no central authority, no paramount chieftain or tribal leader, no Chaka Zulu. Foraging clans are more or less leaderless and, as they keep their population down, they do not need to expand their territories; nor do they have a large sedentary village population from which to raise an army. Around the globe the more advanced tribal societies of the post-agricultural revolution period have aggressively searched for more land and have overrun, assimilated and annihilated the small nomadic clans of hunter-gatherers. Examples of this phenomenon can be found in the whites of Australia over the Aborigines, America's white settlers over the Plains Indians and the white and black pastoralists in southern Africa over the San.

Two milestones mark man's transition away from the stone age hunter-gatherer way of life—the agricultural revolution and the industrial revolution. The traditional San are one of the few cultures yet to take those two monumental steps down the road of human development. Ten thousand years ago, when the world was occupied only by hunter-gatherers, there were no more than ten million people on earth! Today there are over five billion people living an agropastoral or an advanced industrial way of life. The hunter-gatherers have been reduced to a few thousand. Is it any wonder that the very few remaining nomadic people are losing out in the battle for land?

Yet in recent years concrete events in Australia and Canada suggest that it is possible to effect positive change for primitive peoples. In Australia in the 1970's the government made an abrupt change in policy. After almost two centuries of genocide and dispossession, they returned land to the Aborigine hunter-gatherers, as a result of the public's change of heart, ensuing outcry and political action. The politicians will move on behalf of a people, if they hear the public demanding it.

In Canada late in 1991, after 15 years of negotiations, the government announced the creation of a territory encompassing one fifth of Canada's land mass primarily for the Inuit, their traditionally nomadic igloo building, arctic dwelling hunter-gatherers.

You will see as you read on that the Australian Aborigines' and Canada's Inuits' Commonwealth cousins in the Kalahari are not so fortunate. Governments there are continuing to dispossess the Bushmen of the last of their African bush.

But Australia and Canada are flourishing modern societies with informed and participating populations that have insisted that their governments reverse past wrongs and grant their respective aboriginal peoples rights to their ancestral lands and the power to manage them.

The political entities that hold sway over the San in Botswana and Namibia are struggling democracies with populations that themselves are just moving into modern times. These young governments will need practical models and concerted pressure, then assistance from people the world over if they are to grant the San what they need—the land and water necessary first to survive, then to permit a handful to continue in their traditional ways. And they will need help in finding a means to provide the San with the autonomy and the political voice that they must have if they are to survive and prosper in their chosen way of life. If the San choose to move into the modern world they will require active assistance from a variety of sources. This book is an effort on their behalf.

I don't claim to be a writer, and would be much more comfortable building a pipeline to the moon than writing a book. It has been an arduous task for me. But it is a labor to which I am committed, and I am not sorry that I have temporarily put the rest of my life on hold in order to undertake it. I hope that the book will convince you that these gentle, beautiful people deserve the rights that we take for granted and that you will use your influence to help them get those rights. I am going to take you through the experience as it happened to me, which means that I must begin at the beginning. Come, let me take you to Africa.

Even as a youngster I always had a yen for Africa. I grew up enchanted by names like Mozambique, Tanganyika, Bechuanaland, Angola, Kilimanjaro, Ngorongoro Crater and the exotic people and animals who lived there. My family lived on a cattle ranch overlooking the Pacific Ocean in northern California, a backwater isolated from the post war progress of the cities and towns. Our parents encouraged us to learn about the wider world and to get an education that would prepare us to meet it. Early on I read Gunther's *Inside Africa*, which provided a mass of information on that mysterious continent of Africa, but also raised a thousand new questions. In my university days during the '50s I followed with avid fascination the Kikuyu's Mau Mau insurrection then going on in Kenya, leading to its independence. Each week I religiously read the African section of *Time* for details about the Mau Mau and to find out more about the dark continent, following the winds of change and freedom sweeping across that part of the globe. African aficionado Hemingway was my idol and I read all his books, including *The Green Hills of Africa*.

After getting my engineering degree from Cal Berkeley, I worked on highways with the State of California while awaiting my call up for military service. When I finished my tour of duty in Florida in the Navy's Pensacola flight training program, three of my flying buddies and I went on a junket to Cuba, our own Hemingway-like adventure. We got involved, taking sides in heated bar and restaurant debates of the then ongoing revolution, favoring Castro in the hills, over Batista in power. Mikey, our guide and driver who had worked as Hemingway's personal driver, frightened us into a 3 a.m. exit out of Pinar del Rio, to avoid a before daylight visit he expected from Batista's brutal henchmen. Clear of town, we stopped at a remote cafe for breakfast, and ran into Hemingway and his wife Mary out on a Sunday drive into the boondocks. This only whetted my appetite for further adventure; maybe, even Africa!

Military service behind me, wanderlust led me to apply to several international engineering and construction companies. After a year of having my resume put on file, I was surprised and elated at a job offer from the giant Bechtel Corporation. As luck or the fates decreed the assignment was on a pipeline in Africa. Little did I know then that Africa was to be my home for over half of the next thirty years, building pipelines around the world. But before I was to see the exotic southern and central areas of Africa I had dreamed about, I had to serve several hard years in the Sahara. After all, that's where the oil was, and the pipelines were to be built.

After five years of seven-day weeks in Algeria, Tunisia and Libya, I was rewarded with a break from the Sahara, a short assignment in the San Francisco home office. But where did I go first? Deeper into Africa, to Kenya to hunt and visit the parks. I stayed for forty-five days of hunting, highlighted by the shooting of a lion which had just killed and was eating a man near where the maneaters of Tsavo had stopped Kenya's railroad construction at the turn of the century. I stayed on and visited Kenya and Tanzania's game parks, and it was with reluctance that I departed Kenya for the States. I had relished my first real taste of the enchanting Africa I had dreamed about. At the time it looked likely to be my one and only such trip. I left prepared to live the rest of my life as an anticlimax.

Luck was with me, and after only a few months in San Francisco it was discovered that while I wasn't head office material, I had proved very skilled at "getting the job done" at remote sites, so I was sent back to Libya. We were putting new oil fields on line and building cross country pipelines to the coast and offshore tanker loading facilities. In Libya I heard of a project in Tanzania and Zambia to build a pipeline to move petroleum products from Dar es Salaam on the Indian Ocean to Zambia's copper belt. Could I break out of the company's Sahara horsecollar and get to black Africa? I made my interest in the project known to the higher-ups but didn't hold out much hope; I was a rough and ready type, without the tact and finesse to get what I wanted from the head office. Imagine my joy at receiving orders to report in Dar es Salaam, Tanzania ... Hemingway hunting country!

I set out to learn Swahili so that I could make it on my own in the bush. I worked my way through the complicated and restrictive process required to obtain gun and hunting licenses and then organized my own four-wheel drive vehicles. Whenever there was time when I didn't have to be out on the pipeline I was off deeper into the bush, learning about and photographing the people, animals, country and hunting. East Africa is blessed with an Eden of game parks and I covered hundreds of kilometers visiting them, never tiring of returning again and again. At the end of pipeline construction I disappeared into the remote bush for three months of daylight-to-dark hunting and photographing, including visits to the Masai Steppes where Hemingway had hunted, the setting for *The Green Hills of Africa*. It was a glorious time; I was young and hungry to experience Africa.

My interest in Africa has only grown with the years. I am drawn by any opportunity to explore a new corner, discover a new park, see new game, or other primitive cultures. In 1971 I was in the wilds of New Guinea, but after that assignment returned not to the United States but went back to Tanzania for the dry season, the best three months of hunting. Then, reporting back in San Francisco, my very next assignment was two more years in Zambia and Tanzania increasing the product pipeline's capacity. Again, all the spare time that work allowed was spent in the bush, and at the end of that assignment I faded into the remotest bush for three more months. I got enough of hunting and gave it up entirely in 1973, but I never got my fill of Africa.

When I decided in 1988 to retire after thirty years of fulltime employment, part of the lure was the chance to be free to continue searching out new African destinations. It was just prior to my retirement that Dr. Jack Wheeler entered the picture. I was heading up a major pipeline project over the Andes in Colombia when the mail pouch brought me a published schedule of Dr. Wheeler's 1986 adventure travel trips. From this exotic list I wanted most to join Jack's Africa trip taking a group to visit with Savimbi behind the lines of Angola, but that trip fell at a critical stage of the Colombian project and I couldn't get away. Instead, later in the year with the pipeline completed and delivering oil, I joined Dr. Wheeler in Beijing for a three week overland trip across the roof of the world.

Tibet had only recently been opened to outsiders after being off limits since the Chinese invaded in 1950. Jack took us where no tourist had yet gone, including a thirty-two mile high-altitude walk around Mount Khailas, sacred to the Hindu and Buddhist alike. Jack and I shared a love of exotic locales. We had both been to Uhuru Point, the 19,340 foot summit of Mount Kilimanjaro on the border between Kenya and Tanzania. Neither of us was interested in posh accommodations. We wanted adventure and were dedicated to finding it.

In Kasgar in Chinese Turkestan, our discussions turned to one of several trips Jack was planning, this one to the Kalahari to camp with nomadic Bushmen. On his earlier clandestine trip into Angola Jack had met Peter Comley, a young South African operating game viewing safaris out of Maun in the heart of the Kalahari. During that meeting Jack had engaged Peter to undertake the difficult assignment of trying to find some still wild Bushmen and keep tabs on them until Jack's party could fly over and join them in a remote corner of Botswana largely uninhabited and untouched by modern civilization.

The Kalahari Bushman trip brewed while I was sent to work on bidding pipelines in Argentina, from where I was able to join Jack for yet another three week overland trip across Tibet in 1987. We passed through Lhasa to the base of Everest and out through Nepal. We were in Lhasa in October when the first of the recent uprisings by the Tibetans, pleading to the world for their independence from their Communist Chinese oppressors, resulted in death to several Chinese and more Tibetans. It was a difficult trip in which seven of the party of twelve headed for the exit in Lhasa, while only five of us remained to tough out the full itinerary.

In the spring of 1988 I joined Dr. Wheeler on a visit to the North Pole. 'Action Jack' is listed in the *Guinness Book of World Records*, under "Parachuting Records, Most Northerly" for his April 15, 1981 sky dive landing at the North Pole. The arrangements for the Kalahari trip were solidifying, and at the Pole I told Jack to count me in. I couldn't pass up this opportunity to revisit Africa.

Finally, in the summer of 1988 (winter in the Kalahari), it was on. I was going back to Africa after too many recent years elsewhere—- Borneo, Saudi Arabia, Colombia, Peru, and Argentina. My last Africa visit had been during an R & R from Saudi in 1984, when I had gone on a two week French Club Adventure overland camping trip through Mali and Niger, including Timbuktu in the deep Sahara to visit Touaregs, Dogons and other Niger river peoples.

I like traveling with Jack Wheeler. He's not a shiney-hiney, memo-producing PhD., but rather one that visits the world's remotest corners in pursuit of his great curiosity for first-hand knowledge of geography and people. Jack's undergraduate work at UCLA was in anthropology. The further off-the-beaten track and the more difficult the trip, the more probable Jack will tackle it. If he'd lived in another time he might have traveled with Columbus or Lewis and Clark. Jack is a professional traveller and has written a book, *The Adventurer's Guide* (1976). His first-hand campfire stories are fascinating.

Jack has a special thing for aboriginal people. He has studied and visited first-hand many lost and ancient cultures, be it the Inuit of the north, the Aborigines of Australia, or now the Kalahari Bushman. At a young age Jack lived with head hunters in the Ecuadorian regions of the Amazon, and later joined anthropological groups that made first contacts with previously undiscovered peoples in the Amazon Basin and New Guinea. He doesn't waste time organizing luxury bus tours to the Eiffel Tower.

Jack admitted there was a risk in the Kalahari Bushman undertaking. There are only a very few true nomadic hunter-gatherers left, and their history has taught them to avoid all strangers, black or white. There was a long delay while Peter made trips to the bush to make contact with the few who knew these elusive people's movements and could assure a reasonable chance of putting us in contact with a small clan who had never been in close contact with European types before. But there were no guarantees. It was possible to travel to the Kalahari and spend time with Bushmen but they would be sedentary people who had been forced to give up the old hunter-gatherer ways. This isn't what Jack wanted. He suspected that there were still pristine San living in the remote regions of the Kalahari, clothed in skins and hunting with poisoned arrows, and he meant to see them if he could.

I wasn't worried about the risks—this was an opportunity not to be missed. I had egged Jack on to undertake the trip when the subject was discussed on our two Tibet trips. I wanted to be back in Africa and was willing to take my chances, even if we didn't find the still nomadic San we sought. Being in Africa, and the search, was enough for me.

I had one more job for my old employer, as a consultant to find a route for a Shell gas pipeline across the Andes from the Amazon drainage to the Pacific at Lima, which if and when built would be the highest altitude major pipeline on earth. It took two months to establish the route, then to prepare a detailed construction plan and estimate, shoehorned in between the North Pole and the Kalahari. Then I was going back to Africa!

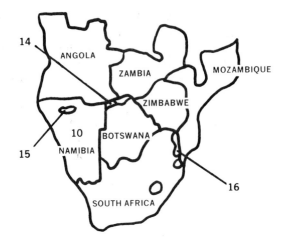

Seven Nations of Southern Africa

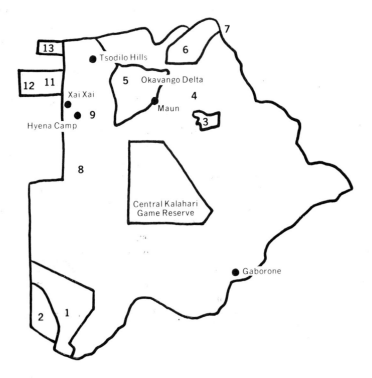

Botswana and Some Surrounding Areas

KEY LOCATIONS

in

Bush for the Bushman

(*See Maps on Opposite Page*)

1   Gemsbok National Park —B
2   Kalahari Gemsbok National Park —SA
3   Makgadikgadi Pan Game Reserve —B
4   Baines' Baobabs —B
5   Gedibe Camp —B
6   Chobe National Park —B
7   Victoria Falls —ZA/ZI
8   Ghanzi —B
9   Gcwihaba Caverns —B
10   Windhoek —N
11   Tsumkwe (place of death) —N
12   Bushmanland —N
13   Kaudom Game Reserve —N
14   West Caprivi Game Reserve —N
15   Etosha National Park —N
16   Kruger National Park —SA

COUNTRY KEY FOR ABOVE LISTING

B	Botswana
N	Namibia
SA	South Africa
ZA/ZI	Zambia/Zimbabwe

—2—
Johannesburg and Kruger

After some hair raising experiences pushing helicopters to their very limits to get over or around cloud shrouded peaks in the high Andes, the pipeline route study was completed by the beginning of August, allowing me to arrive in South Africa a few days before heading for Botswana and Dr. Jack Wheeler's Kalahari Bushman trip. I phoned my friend Rachel in Johannesburg to see if she could join me either before or after the Kalahari dates, or both.

"I can manage a few days before you go to Botswana," Rachel said, "but when you're finished, I'll be out of the country."

"Out of the country ... where?" I asked.

"Can't tell you, at least not over the phone."

"Another one of those clandestine ANC conclaves ... yes?"

"No comment," was Rachel's reply.

I had met Rachel in 1983. I was working in Saudi Arabia then, and had decided to take an R & R in South Africa. We met through mutual friends, and when two other pals and I decided to do a camp-out safari around South Africa during the Christmas to New Year's holiday, I asked Rachel if she would be our guide and companion. It wasn't really as simple as that, since at that time it was still against the law to socialize across any of the four color lines; white, colored, Asian or black. Even taking Rachel to lunch was a crime.

Rachel is an Indian, a converted Christian of Tamil ancestry. The Tamils are Hindus, some of whom are currently fighting with Buddhist Sri Lankans over control of the northern provinces of Sri Lanka, just off the Indian coast. That bloody conflict is not unlike the ongoing strife between Catholics and Protestants in Northern Ireland. Rachel is a thoroughly good person and a dyed-in-the-wool antiapartheidist, and while she and I agree on many issues, we do have our political differences. I was, as always, interested to hear her point of view on recent developments in South Africa.

Rachel's ancestors have been in South Africa for a long time, brought out from India as cheap labor and staying on. She is from a very religious family; the eldest of twelve children, her spunk has helped her mother hold the family together since her father died.

Rachel became our eyes to see 'the other side' of the South African situation as we camped out, showing us things that many white South Africans haven't bothered to see, or just don't want to know about.

During that trip Rachel told of going to an African National Congress (ANC) conclave in Zambia and meeting the American black activist, Angela Davis. Rachel and her ANC compatriots saw Davis as a valuable asset to their antiapartheid cause. We were, like Rachel, staunchly against apartheid, but had misgivings about the ANC's communist leanings.

The ANC was founded in 1912 to support the cause of South African black rights, but had been outlawed in South Africa since 1960, the year of the Sharpeville massacre when white police fired machine guns on unarmed blacks who were demonstrating against apartheid pass laws. Sixty-seven Africans, including forty-eight women and children, were killed, 186 were wounded. ANC leader Nelson Mandela had been in South African prisons since 1964 for advocating the overthrow of the white South African government by force.

It wasn't only the stories that Rachel told that brought the reality of apartheid home to us. During the '83 trip she got us hauled into a Cape Town police station by guiding us into Crossroads, an illegal shanty town where blacks without passes congregate in the hope of gaining access to economic opportunity in the city to which they were not allowed entry. The authorities do not want whites, especially whites with cameras, going into such camps. They fear the pictures will end up on America's evening news. We had some tense moments convincing the police that we were tourists without movie cameras, that our still cameras were only meant to take pictures of animals and landscapes.

That first trip with Rachel as guide further piqued my interest in the San and helped me to see more clearly the complicated history of South Africa. Rachel took us to see Bushman rock paintings at the Giant's Castle high up in the Drakensburg Mountains, then went on to Durban and made a long swing through Zululand and down the coast through Black homelands to Cape Town. We visited game parks, caves, historic sites like Zulu Dingane's Kraal along Chaka's Way, and the Blood River that looms so large in South African history. We relived the story of the Dutch Voortrekers who moved away from the Cape Province up along the west side of the Drakensburg Mountains looking for unclaimed land, to get away from an English rule they considered to be oppressive; and how, in 1838, the first party under Piet Retief crossed over to the mountains' east side into Zululand, in what is now Natal Province. The Dutch approached Dingane, the king of the Zulu nation, asking his permission to settle in Zululand. He gave them the written permission they requested, but then invited them to his Kraal and proceeded to massacre them, some seventy whites and their thirty or so colored servants. The aroused Zulu warriors then ran for endless miles across country to where the Voortrekkers' wagons and cattle were encamped and massacred some five hundred more women, children and servants.

Later, in December of that same year, Pretorius, the leader of the Dutch settlers, reentered Zululand with five hundred Voortrekker men seeking revenge. At the Buffalo River, they drew their wagons into *laager*, like the circling of wagons that our pioneers used when fighting the Plains Indians. During a one day battle the Voortrekkers killed some three thousand of the attacking Zulus. The river ran red with blood but none of it was Dutch. It was firearms against stabbing spears; not a single Voortrekker was killed. The river has been called Blood River ever since. This was considered a great victory by the Dutch settlers and they celebrate it today as the Day of the Covenant, one of their most important national holidays, a day that affirmed their belief that they had a special covenant with God to rule South Africa.

We visited both historic sites. Dingane's camp, where the Retief Party was massacred, is now an isolated, uninhabitated area in the bush. It was an eerie, spooky place to spend the night camped out under the stars. Early the next day we visited the site on the Blood River where the river flows through a broad, flat plain. The white South Africans have installed life-size replicas of the Voortrekker wagons. We walked around for an hour or so, not a soul there but us. During all that time Rachel hadn't said a word, then as we turned to leave she said with quiet passion:

"The wrong side won."

I arrived in Johannesburg again, four years later. Rachel was there waiting as I cleared customs, the first time I had seen her since she had joined my sister, niece and me traveling across Peru to Machu Picchu and through Bolivia three years earlier.

"I've got four days till I'm off to the Kalahari," I told her. "Can you join me for a run out in the bush?" Rachel said she could.

The taxi dropped Rachel by her house in the Parktown section where she was the unofficial house mother of a quasi church-sponsored anti-establishment commune, and I headed on to the Santon Sun Hotel on the northern outskirts of Johannesburg. I stashed my bags in my room and went downstairs where I rented an Avis Volkswagen combi and headed back into Johannesburg to the Safari outfitting stores I'd used in '83. Camping gear in hand, I went by and visited Rachel and her 'family'. Later on we two had dinner at an Italian restaurant and then went on to a Johannesburg black jazz night spot.

The evening was pleasant and unmarred by racial tension.

Early the next morning we were off up Highway 1, through Pretoria heading north for Kruger National Park.

"You can't know how exciting it is to be back in Africa heading for

12

the bush," I told Rachel.

Our plan was to enter the park's north gate, Punda Maria, and then travel through the full length of the park and out of one of the southern gates. But despite our daybreak start, by midday we gave up getting to the northernmost gate. I'd bitten off too much, and we'd have to cut across to the second most northerly gate. It was 4 p.m. when we arrived at the Phalaborwa gate. At the barricade I got out to check into the park.

As I walked back to the combi Rachel saw that I was upset, and asked, "What's the matter?"

"They reckon we can't reach Letaba, the nearest camp site, by the time they close everyone in for the night so they won't let us in the park," I responded.

"So what do we do now?" asked Rachel.

"Like 1983. We'll 'poach' camp, find a place in the bush tonight and be there tomorrow at daylight when they open the park gate."

Though Phalaborwa, a fair-sized community created in 1957 to support copper and other mining activities, lay just outside the park, Rachel and I did not look for lodging there. Perhaps, though restrictions had eased since 1983, we still recalled that during that earlier trip we had been obliged to camp out and only once stayed in a hotel, the Lanzerac near Cape Town, which was classed as an international hotel and so not subject to the normal 'whites only' color bar. Even there Rachel had been the only non-white, and was made uncomfortable by snide remarks and raised eyebrows.

We found a place in the bush where we wouldn't be hassled and while Rachel strummed out a few songs on her guitar, I fired up our little camping stove. A pleasant return to old times camping in the bush, with Rachel's guitar and sweet voice under the African sky.

Shortly after daylight we were through the gate into Kruger Park, and east to the park's main north-south road and then north toward Shingwedzi, Kruger's second most northern camp. Whenever possible, we chose the secondary dirt tracks over the park's main paved road. From previous Kruger trips we'd found there were more animals and fewer people on these slower, dustier roads.

Kruger has the distinction of being the first national park on the African continent. It was created by South Africa's President Kruger in 1898, not long after the world's first national park, the U.S.'s Yellowstone, was established in 1872. It covers just under 20,000 square kilometers in South Africa's northeast corner, bordered by Zimbabwe on the north and Mozambique on the east. Kruger runs over four hundred kilometers north to south, and varies in width from fifty to eighty kilometers.

From information gathered in annual aerial survey censuses, the park is estimated to have a quarter of a million of the larger mammals. The most populous is the impala at 100,000. Then, in roughly descending order: cape buffalo, zebra, elephant, wildebeest, warthog, giraffe, waterbuck, hippo, lion, kudu, sable antelope, reedbuck, leopard, tsessebe, black and white rhino, wild dog, eland, roan antelope and cheetah. There are other animals with less accurate counts such as the crocodile, hyena, nyala, bushbuck, baboon, and klipspringer. We managed to see most of these except the carnivores. We saw only one solitary lion far from the road. On this visit we saw no leopard or cheetah.

"No problem," I told Rachel, "I've got tons of good lion, leopard and cheetah pictures from Kenya and Tanzania. But, kudu, roan and sable are nearly impossible to see in the northern parks. We've gotten some good shots of them here."

We traveled steadily but slowly, covering a lot of country and patiently observing the wildlife, always looking for better photo opportunities.

The South African parks and overnight camps are well organized and run, compared to most that I'd visited in the east African countries to the north. The camp grounds are immaculately clean, and have individual rondavel thatched roof huts as well as camp-out facilities. We chose a camping spot, and I went over to the park store and bought some steak and sausage to barbecue, or *braai* as the South Africans call it, on the pit provided. Tame and friendly, glossy metallic-blue starlings with bright yellow eyes visited us, while horn bills clowned in the flat top acacia trees overhead, as the sun went down.

"Rachel, the park history says there're Bushman paintings on the walls of rock shelters here in the park. Bushmen came down from the high veld and hunted here in the winter when the mosquitos were less active."

"Yes, isn't it sad," replied Rachel wistfully. "They've left their paintings everywhere to haunt our memories, like those we hiked up to see in the Drakensburg Mountains at the Giant's Castle in '83. But we 'civilized' races had to kill them all off ..."

Our second day in the park took us back south, keeping my Hasselblads burning up film. We camped our second night in Skukuza camp, where Kruger Park's main administration center is located. On Sunday we continued south through the park then out of the Malelane gate and headed west to Johannesburg.

"Rachel, did you notice something? We were in the park for two and a half days, and aside from that one school bus with mixed colored faces, we didn't see another black face among the park visitors."

"Yes, I noticed, and don't think I didn't stop some conversations and get some cold, dirty looks from matronly Afrikaaner ladies when I pranced my dark face into the bath house in Skukuza camp last night," replied Rachel.

"It's like on our '83 safari," I said. "Traveling with you makes one more aware of the real apartheid atmosphere. If I were you I'd think about going some place else where the prejudices aren't so ingrained."

"I can't leave this place," said Rachel. "I'm South African, and I have to stay and see this whole apartheid thing through ... and I mean through and finished!"

"I feel for you," I said. "You can help fight the antiapartheid battle, but if and when it's won, you run a real risk of your black mates chuffing you aside because of your Indian ancestry. Look at what has happened to the Indians in Uganda and Tanzania. They found themselves much worse off under the black administrations after independence than they were under the British. It's like the blacks went from third string to first, from where they are now looking down on the still second string Indians. The blacks carry a lot of anger and hurt from their third string days. Look what Idi Amin did to the Indians in Uganda in the early 70s. They had to abandon everything and flee the country. They were lucky to get out alive."

"That won't happen here," Rachel said. Though I admired her faith in the inevitability of positive racial change, my years of first-hand experience in East Africa gave me doubts. Though I detest apartheid, I have private differences with Rachel over many of the practical issues surrounding how to abolish it. The lively debates that arose have always been one of the pleasures of our friendship, debates carried out across campfires on other nights similar to those in Kruger. But stronger than that was the simple pleasure of being together under the huge African sky while night settled around us, and I said as much to Rachel.

"It's great to be with you out in the bush under the stars with the animal sounds. I really like South Africa. It's a rich and beautiful place with great open spaces. We Americans, in our different ways, do hope it can get straightened out."

In Johannesburg I left the camping gear that wasn't needed on the Bushman trip at Rachel's commune. Back at the Santon Sun hotel I turned in the Avis combi with 1,986 kms on the clock, some 1200 miles for the four day Kruger Park run. Soon after I was installed in my room, the phone rang. It was Bud Gainey.

Bud was one of the party who joined Dr. Wheeler in 1986, traveling through Beijing and then overland across Tibet and Chinese Turkestan. Bud, who hails from La Verne, California, near Los Angeles, is a retired ceramics manufacturer and a good, solid character who had weathered well the duress of the Tibet trip. A little later the phone rang again.

"Big John, Jim Reed here. Joel and I just got in. We understand you've been here a few days already?"

"Yes," I said. "I just spent a few days up in Kruger, warming up my camera for those elusive Kalahari Bushmen."

"We're all hyped up, too," said Jim. "Joel and I will be down at the bar. Come join us for a drink."

I had met Jim Reed and Joel Wade on Dr. Wheeler's second trip across Tibet in the fall of 1987. Together we had traveled some two thousand miles by road, from Xining in the northeast Tibet Plateau to Lhasa, on to the base of Everest, then across the Himalayas and out through Nepal to Kathmandu.

The high altitude, cold temperatures, dysentery, and austere Chinese Army camps got to more than half of the twelve who started the trip, causing seven to bail out halfway through in Lhasa. Jim, Joel and I were among the five who stuck with Dr. Wheeler and completed the whole itinerary. Dr. Wheeler was gathering a crew of battle-tested veterans to visit the Bushman. Jim, sixty-something, an active North Carolina businessman, was to be the senior member of our group. Joel, the youngest of us, is a psychologist, at the time working on his PhD at UCLA, and, while he is modest about mentioning it, was a world class water polo player. Both are ardent adventure travelers.

We'd surely be reliving some of our Tibetan experiences around the Kalahari campfires. Our reminiscences began then and there in the lounge of the Santon Sun's atrium lobby.

"So, you went to the North Pole with Jack since our Tibet trip?" Jim said.

I related that on the North Pole trip four months earlier I'd joined communist-baiting Jack on a ride in an MI-8 Russian military helicopter for the last few miles from a Russian ice station to the North Pole, for an unforgettable experience. But they really wanted to know about my past and current African experiences. They were as excited as I was about the trip ahead of us, and they knew that I had spent many years in Africa, and they had not.

I told them about one of my most treasured African experiences—the four years living in East Africa where I could really get out in the bush to hunt, visit the parks, and exotic peoples in remote locations. And I told them about meeting Rachel and camp out traveling around South Africa for six weeks over the holidays four years earlier.

"We just spent the last four days running up to Kruger and back," I said finally. "She will be here soon to join us for dinner."

"Then Kruger is worth seeing," Jim said.

"This was my third visit," I responded. "I don't think you can beat Tanzania's Serengeti, Ngorongoro and Manyara parks, or Kenya's Tsavo, Amboselli, or Masai Mara where Dr. Wheeler is now. But Kruger is huge and has interesting terrain, lots of animals, and the Afrikaaners manage and run things better here than they are run in the emerging countries to the north. South Africa is an incredibly beautiful country to see. One of my criterion to judge countries touristically is how they affect my desire to take pictures. I really burn up film here."

I recalled driving up to the Kalahari Gemsbok National Park with Rachel, on gravel roads, mile after mile and not another vehicle. It was in January, the first days of southern hemisphere summer, blue skies, billowing white clouds, but the Kalahari rainy season. The showers had brought out a green thorny creeper on the iron red sand with abundant bright yellow blooms. They call it *dukies*. A profusion of white butterflies flitted around in the clear crisp air. It was like being in a fairy land. South Africa can be like that.

I told them about poach camping, how each evening we'd travel until dusk and then go through the ritual of looking for a place to camp off the road and out of sight where someone wouldn't find us and either molest us or throw us out. And of getting up before daylight to have our wash and breakfast, and be on the road before the sun was up, gone before we could be discovered or hassled. "We had to camp out. With Rachel and the color bar, we couldn't use the normal accommodations."

"You are a desert rat," said Joel, "leaving Saudi to take a vacation camping out in some other God forsaken desert." But Joel didn't know about the trip later in 1984 when I'd joined a campout trip across Mali and Niger, along the Niger River through Timbuktu in the very heart of the Sahara.

"The deserts of the world are one place to go and find space away from civilization." I responded. "That's why the last of the Bushmen have survived, because they learned to make it in the bone dry Kalahari that civilization avoids."

As 7 p.m. approached, I went down to the hotel's front entrance to meet Rachel. We proceeded up to the mezzanine level to rejoin Jim and Joel.

"Do you really think you'll find any Bushmen?" Rachel asked. "They were all shot out here in South Africa, and there aren't many, if any, left in the Kalahari."

"Well, we sure hope to," said Jim. "This is our first trip to Africa, and we're interested in hearing about things here. Since the news blackout imposed a couple of years back, South Africa has pretty much disappeared from our nightly news."

Rachel plunged into her view of the situation.

"It's a brutal regime. The other day the police came to our house and ransacked the place, presumably looking for ANC terrorists. They took a couple of young black South African transients away and held them several days and interrogated them—I mean, physically. Shades of Steve Biko. Those two poor kids were completely traumatized. They've moved out of the house and gone into hiding. You Americans under Reagan are not doing enough to bring down this regime. We hope Dukakis gets in since he's for stiff economic sanctions. Yes, there's some progress in dismantling apartheid, but it's not coming fast enough."

As with most South African non-whites, Rachel had little access to white visitors so she took this opportunity to tell her story. Jim and Joel listened raptly.

"You bloody Americans and your democracy," said Rachel. "It isn't doing anything for our cause. Meanwhile the communists you are so concerned about infiltrating the ANC are trying to do something to get us out from under the yoke of apartheid."

"Into their Marxist yoke," I egged Rachel on. "Communism and socialism are bankrupt systems. A fact. Although Russia has something like ten times the population of South Africa, and despite apartheid, more blacks own cars in free market South Africa than there are privately owned cars in all of communist-Marxist Russia!"

Rachel just stared away in stony silence.

"Can't you see that they're trying to take over your revolution?" I continued. "Look what happened in Mozambique and Angola when the Portuguese pulled out. The Russians get their puppets in power and the war goes on, black against black. Rachel, without realizing it, you're going down the same road. You're missing the forest for the trees."

"But what you call the regimes in Angola and Mozambique support our cause," said Rachel.

"No, they really don't support your cause of freedom," I countered. "They're Marxist in black sheep's clothing. Their Kremlin handlers want to take your revolution over for their own aims. They want to get their hands on the rich resources in South Africa and control the sea lanes around Africa. We'd be much happier to see you supporting the Zulu leader Buthelezi. He's from your Natal Province and is proposing the idea of cantons like in Switzerland, local provincial governments with black participation. He's working to improve the system from within through nonviolence, while staunchly avoiding any communist influences. His way may seem to take longer, but if you ever let the communists get the upper hand, you may learn how really long and tortuous time is. Just ask a Pole, a Latvian, a Hungarian, a Russian Jew ..."

Though Rachel and I had had debates like this before, I was getting uneasy with the heatedness of it and with the fact that our animated voices were attracting attention from people at the tables nearby. My two friends politely questioned Rachel's views, and each question lifted her passion higher.

We three had seen Communism in action in Tibet quite recently. There a freedom loving, religious culture has been crushed and practically destroyed by Communist conquest. My own anti-Communist passions were high and Rachel knew how to get me going. It was one thing to carry on a full volume debate in a bush camp, but quite another to do it in front of relative strangers in the bar of the Santon Sun.

I finally got Rachel out of there and we went off for dinner and an early evening. The departure for Botswana would come early the next morning. Better to be fresh to plunge into our Kalahari Bushman adventure.

—3—
First Encounter

The alarm brought me into Monday, day one of Dr. Wheeler's twelve day Kalahari schedule. I rechecked the itinerary. We would overnight this first night in Maun. Tuesday we would fly out into the Kalahari to camp six nights adjacent to the still nomadic wild hunter-gatherers. Next Monday we would fly north across the Kalahari to camp two nights at Tsodilo Hills, sacred to the Kung Bushman as his legendary birth place and often referred to as the Bushman's Louvre for its many rock paintings. We would then fly east into the upper Okavango swamp for two nights, staying at a fishing lodge from which we would go down river by boat into the deep Okavango in search of a solitary remaining river Bushman reported there.

Wheeler's Kalahari Bushman trip was being organized by Peter Comley and Salome Meyer of Africa Calls, headquartered in Maun. Both Peter and Salome are South Africans, Peter of English stock and Salome of Dutch. Jack had met the safari organizers in early 1986, when he took some clients along on one of his several trips into Angola. Jack does 'adventure travel' trips as a sideline, his main vocation being that of working for 'pro-freedom-anti-Marxist' think tanks. The Kalahari trip had been in the works since then, with Jack getting our group together and Peter organizing things in Africa.

Five of us, Jack, Joel, Jim, Bud and I, all Tibet veterans, met in the lobby to head for the airport to catch the early morning flight to Maun.

Turning to Jim and Joel as we waited in the lobby, I said, "Sorry my little friend got so wound up last night. After she cooled down she did ask me to apologize for her."

"What a gal," remarked Jim. "She's definitely got a strong bias against apartheid."

"Yeah, it's interesting to hear her 'other side'," added Joel. "But after what we saw in Tibet, and knowing the Communist track record around the world, I'd agree, she's on a thorny track throwing in with the Communist leaning ANC.''

Johannesburg has a modern, bustling airport by African standards. There we met up with Tom and Wally, two southern Californians who made up the rest of our group of seven. Tom Williams supports his traveling habit with a retail toy outlet near Los Angeles and has traveled extensively on the African continent, especially eastern and southern Africa. He had gone into Angola with Jack in 1986, when Peter and Jack met. Later I had urged Tom to join us on other trips, but he declined, saying, " ... but let me know anytime you're going to Africa." Wally, a retired businessman, is a frequent adventure traveler.

An Air Lesotho plane carried us north to Botswana's capital, Gaborone. There we cleared immigration and transferred to an Air Botswana flight to Maun, to arrive shortly before noon. On the rather short flight from Johannesburg to Gaborone, I was reminded of what a huge place Africa is; at over three times the size of the U.S., and though I've lived in Africa more than half my professional career, how much I had yet to see. We passed over South Africa, one of the richest countries in the world with a population of over thirty-six million, and on over southern Botswana, a less affluent country of fewer than a million and a half people, with over 80% of its territory taken up by the arid Kalahari Desert. Gaborone has a rather small, austere "county" airport compared to Johannesburg's international terminal.

On the flight from Gaborone to Maun I sat with Wally, who had also been to the North Pole, but was on his first Wheeler adventure. Wally, at 61, comes from Whittier, California. He is an ardent traveler and active senior marathon runner. "Good preparation for keeping up with the Bushman on a hunt," I noted as I asked Wally about his marathon victories. He answered in his typically wry fashion, "There are a couple of other guys in my advanced age class better then I am. If they don't show up, I win the race."

In Maun, a town of four-wheel drives and casual dress, we were met by Salome's sister, Liza. Safari organizers Peter and Salome had gone ahead into the bush to locate the Bushmen and establish our camp nearby. We would fly out to the bush camp after overnighting in Riley's Hotel.

Maun is a frontier town out in the heart of the Kalahari desert, the gateway to the Okavango, and the administrative center for Ngamiland District, in the northwest corner of Botswana, including the entire Okavango. Maun lies on the Delta's southeastern corner where the Angolan-supplied waters peter out and the lush swamp reverts to a bone dry Kalahari. Maun is also the main staging center for Okavango game viewing and Kalahari trophy hunting. Modern safari hunting was initiated here in the 1960's by a migration south of Kenyan white hunters. This paved the way for Botswana's current tourist industry, that now ranks fourth in the economy behind diamonds, copper-nickel mining, then cattle. Maun's population consists of some 10,000 blacks living mostly in mud huts. The two hundred white European residents are predominantly engaged in the tourist trade. A four-wheel drive was needed to get across town until a few years back. Now Maun has about one kilometer of pavement. Still at Riley's Hotel we found only four-wheel drive vehicles in the parking lot. A clue to what makes Maun tick, they were all specially outfitted for the bush, for hunting or game viewing. Several had high lift jacks prominently strapped to their bumpers ... an indication of what traveling in this part of the world might entail. Forget about AAA road service here!

Riley's, the only hotel in Maun, is a 'drinking hole' for the local tourist trade. The hotel is a pleasant group of one and two-story concrete structures with white stuccoed exteriors and green corrugated roofs. After checking in, to get to our clean but simple rooms, we passed through the spacious backyard where a thatched rondavel bar was situated under spreading fig trees, looking out on the Thamalkane River flowing past the lodge. Cattle, horses and their white cattle egret escorts were grazing along the river banks, with the Okavango starting on the far side. The South African writer Laurens van der Post mentions staying at Riley's when he passed through Maun on his search for Bushmen back in 1954 and '55, leading to his two earliest Bushman books, *The Lost World of the Kalahari* and *The Heart of the Hunter.*

The Thamalkane River flows south along a fault line that acts as a border between the Okavango wetlands and the arid Kalahari Desert. The river serves as an 'overflow drain', picking up the estimated two percent of water from Angola's mountain highlands that survives absorption and evaporation during a three kilometer per day, five month journey across the Okavango, to flow out the bottom end.

After lunch, Liza reappeared with the van to take us to visit some Maun sites. She was tall, slender and looked fit, as she proved to be later, hiking in the bush. Liza explained that she was joining us on the first part of the trip, having just come to Maun from South Africa to work on illustrating a book her sister Salome was preparing on local trees and plants.

In the evening, Jack took his Tibet crew, Joel, Bud, Jim and I, on a 'foot safari' — there are no taxis in Maun — across town to the Duck Inn, the other Maun 'watering hole' where hunters and safari travelers gather. Strategically located fifty meters from the small bare bones air terminal, it also serves as its unofficial 'departure lounge'. The establishment is owned and run by Bernadette, a pleasant, middle-aged Swiss woman who can serve up escargots or fondue, or as quickly bounce an unruly patron off his stool and out the doorless entry, if need be. The Duck Inn provides a view of the rustic and colorful Maun ambiance not to be missed.

In Riley's Hotel we'd seen a sign soliciting visitors to come to 'room number 5' where San (Bushman) craft articles were being sold, and the next morning we found our way there to have a look. The shop displayed hunting kits, consisting of a warthog skin shoulder bag, with a bow, tree bark quiver with arrows, spear and digging stick. There were assorted women's shoulder bags, tortoise shell compacts, and various necklaces of ostrich shell chips, porcupine quills, nuts and beads. And thumb pianos on which the people make music.

We asked Beth Oliver, the middle-aged, white lady attending the shop, where the handcrafts came from, and she answered, "From the Kung at Xai Xai and Tsodilo Hills." We would be visiting both places. (Xai Xai has a variable spelling—Cae Cae—on maps and in print and is pronounced "*kai kai*".)

Beth is an American who was formerly with the Peace Corps. Her effort is to help the dispossessed and landless Bushmen who are trying to eke out a living on the edge of the more advanced culture and economy. Beth's objective is to encourage San people living sedentarily at the cattle station wells to produce handcrafted articles that she will market. In this way a handful can sustain some independence in their struggle to exist where they have been drawn to congregate near the Kalahari's few man-made wells.

Beth showed her frustration over the Bushman's situation. She explained that Swedish government aid was willing to drill several water wells in Ngamiland at no cost to the Botswana government. There are wells at Xai Xai now, but the San people live in small family clans and traditionally don't like to be in large groups. At Xai Xai the clans, attracted by the water, are competing not only with a congregation of other dispossessed San, but also with the Herero and Tswana cattle herders. The Swedes' idea was to join in a plan to drill some wells in more remote areas where there is still game and where commercial cattle herds would be restricted, thus letting the San population spread out into family and kinship groups, but have access to their own stable water sources.

We knew enough about the Bushmen's plight to know that they cannot compete with cattle. Cattle drive the game away and tear up and overgraze the bush so there's nothing left for Bushmen to hunt or gather. "But the government has refused permission to drill the wells," complained Beth. The bureaucracy reportedly wants to keep the clans concentrated at Xai Xai so they can look after them more easily, on a bureaucratic "one stop" basis.

"Most of the people we're trying to help have lost their traditional lands and been forced to give up hunting and gathering. The government looks after them in a haphazard way. So by encouraging them to make their survival tools and implements, we are at least giving them some hope and independence, and the knowledge of how to make the implements isn't lost. They get sixty percent of the sale proceeds and we keep forty percent for our costs and overhead."

Beth drives out into the bush to pick up the goods for sale in Maun and elsewhere in Botswana and South Africa. It seemed a small thing but important to the survival of the San during a time of transition and stress on their traditional culture.

At mid-morning we proceeded to Maun's one and only airfield. We seven Americans and Liza with all our gear boarded a nine passenger dual engine high wing Islander. It was a full plane.

Xai Xai, where we would land, is 250 kms due west, very near the Namibian border. It would take just under an hour of flying, first skirting the south end of the wet Okavango Delta, then over the dry Kalahari. This is a geographic anomaly, the world's largest inland delta in the middle of the world's fourth largest desert.

After takeoff, Jack pointed out an interesting land feature. The sparse bush cover looked blue-green down below, but we could see a pattern of lighter yellow streaks stretching off to the horizon. The streaks were made up of fossilized sand dune bases several million years old. "Like the lines of Nazca in Peru which also can only be appreciated from an aerial viewpoint," Jack commented.

As we neared Xai Xai, a rock outcropping off to the north broke the horizon. "That's Aha Hills," said the pilot. This was the first interruption in the otherwise flat Okavanago and Kalahari terrain since leaving Maun. There is no airstrip at Xai Xai, but our bush pilot, Andre, showed no great concern in landing on an open, undulating pasture in the ancient, dry river course that lies in low rolling country covered with scrubby bushes and small, flat top, acacia thorn trees.

Clustered nearby our landing site and Xai Xai's wells were several thorn enclosures, circular *bomas* built by the black Bantu cattle owners to protect their cattle from predators at night. The herders' only homes, thatch roofed rondavel mud huts, were located inside the small cattle corrals. This is typical of many herder society villages one can see from the Sudan south through East Africa and Zambia where the cattle owner lives day and night with his wealth and enjoys the same protection from prowling nocturnal carnivores, while sharing the flies and barnyard smells.

A book with interesting history and details of the Ngamiland Bushmen in this area is *Land Filled with Flies—A Political Economy of the Kalahari*, by anthropologist Edwin N. Wilmsen who spent considerable time in Xai Xai. (Because we were to avoid cattle posts, we were not subsequently bothered by, or conscious of, the flies.)

After living many years in the 'not-a-blade-of-grass' barren rock-and-sand Sahara, I found this part of the Kalahari quite different and far from treeless. Deserts are usually classified as areas with less than five inches of annual rain. Here the rainfall would exceed that during a normal year, but could also be less in the all too frequent periods of drought. Still, as there are no established streams and no surface water, in the drier season the Kalahari is justly classified as a desert. But for the recent addition of a very few isolated water wells, or bore holes as they are called in this part of the world, the vast Kalahari area is a waterless, inhospitable land to the uninitiated, which is to say anyone but the Bushmen.

The small "cattle post" village, a community of approximately 250, has evolved around Xai Xai's wells; the only year-round water source in a vast area. It is at best a "mud hut" village with no running water, lights or any real commercial or community services. The majority of the population are dispossessed, tame Bushmen in tattered western clothing, then the predominantly Herero cattle owners and herders; no Europeans.

In a remote Botswana village like Xai Xai there are no vehicles and only an occasional truck or four-wheel drive vehicle passing through. The arrival of our plane was an even more rare event! Virtually everybody in the village showed up to mill around and gawk. We got out and mixed with the curious but friendly people, limbering up our cameras on the colorful gathering. They took little notice of our photographing them.

Colorfully dressed Heroro tribeswomen stood out in the crowd. They are people who came to Botswana originally from the Atlantic coast near Walvis Bay in what is now Namibia, a German domain up until the end of World War I. The wives of early German missionaries were shocked at the bare breasts of the Heroro women and proceeded to cover them with copies of their German dresses—exotically colored, high-necked, long-skirted Victorian dresses with matching bonnets. The Heroro women have persisted in this dress for over a hundred years, steadfastly refusing to give up their adopted tribal uniform though it is incongruous with the warm climate, the wild African bush setting and the more typical scant attire of other African tribes.

The Heroro first came to Botswana in the early 1900's, fleeing their tribes' war against German colonizers in which some three quarters of their numbers were killed. The Heroro took refuge in the isolated northwest corner of Botswana, grazing their cattle around the Okavango Delta. In the 1950's, an outbreak of sleeping sickness carried by the tsetse fly had driven most of them west, away from Okavango, only to have the then government of Southwest Africa, the South Africans, turn them back at the border. So some had settled here in Xai Xai, largely displacing the Kung San.

At the improvised landing strip our party was met by our Safari organizer, Peter Comley, and his white Botswanan assistant, Map. Their two Toyota pickups were the only vehicles in sight.

The pickups were rigged for game viewing with two elevated bench seats over each of the pickup beds. Liza and Jack got in the cabs while the rest of us took places on the observation seats. We left the curious crowd, and drove by Xai Xai's unimpressive 'draw-it-up-with-a-bucket' well, a hole in the ground inside a rustic post barricade. We took off east down a well-delineated but lightly traveled two-rutted track lined by a scanty, well dispersed growth of thorny trees, bushes, and sparse winter-dry grass.

We proceeded at a leisurely pace down a valley bottom under the clear blue African sky. The track snaked through rolling sandveld country with scattered tree and bush cover and more birds than one would anticipate in such a dry harsh environment. Peter pointed out some of them as we passed. They have wonderful names like kurrichane thrush and lilac breasted roller. The track was typical of many remote African "roads" where a first traveler had simply found his way through the bush, leaving a faint set of tracks. Ensuing vehicle travelers followed the same wheel marks until their tires had beaten out two ruts. Cost of road construction, zero. Maintenance, none.

About an hour and a half out of Xai Xai, we turned off the beaten track and saw the green tents of our camp. At first glance it looked slightly less elaborate but not unlike the Ker and Downey Kenya safari camps in which I'd stayed in 1965. But this camp was quite a bit more elaborate than the austere camps I had set up later, when I was hunting on my own as a resident in Tanzania and Zambia.

The whole Kalahari is a low sand-filled basin surrounded by higher country. The low point in the huge Kalahari basin is the Makgadikgadi some 250 kilometers east of Maun. The eons old shifting sand cover can be up to several hundred meters deep and the underlying rock breaks through this sand blanket only occasionally. The Aha Hills we saw in the distance north of Xai Xai are one of the isolated examples. We would be visiting two others, the Gcwihaba Hills not far east of our camp where there are caves, and then later Tsodilo Hills to see San rock paintings.

We'd been traveling along one of several ancient dry river beds running east into the Okavango basin. The next, some fifty kilometers north, is called the Qangwa, running through the Dobe area. Roughly the same distance to the south is the Eiseb Valley, A series of very modest low dunes, also oriented east-west, lie between these now dry ancient river bed valleys.

Our camp was situated in a small grove of trees called Kalahari apple leaf. Rather like a cottonwood, they afforded the most shade available from the relentless Kalahari sun. As it was winter, many Kalahari trees were leafless. A spotted hyena had also chosen this grove of trees as refuge, evidenced by several of its droppings bleached white in the sun. Porcupine quills strewn about gave a clue to one of the hyena's meals. Reading the animal sign, it seemed only natural for us to call this location Hyena Camp.

There were four two-man tents for us seven, a tent for Liza nearby, a cooking fire area, a tent for the staff, a tent for Peter and Salome some distance off, and a place where Map would sleep on the ground under the stars, near the main campfire. The simple dining facilities were two camp tables set up end to end for serving, and folding canvas chairs arranged around the campfire where we would eat from our laps.

We met the rest of the staff. Besides Salome, Peter's companion and business partner, there were three black Botswanans, Shylock, who was to be our guide and translator, and Mansu and George, who would provide camp help.

Peter is a medium built South African, sporting a ragged beard, who grew up in the Transvaal, of English ancestors. He did his national service and studied law, but wanted to get into the bush. He'd been living here in Botswana some nine years and he and Salome voiced plans to stay on, both liking the bush and the safari business, and wanting to be away from the political problems of South Africa. They find Botswana to be the most stable country in southern Africa, with the bonus of still having some wild frontiers left. One has to be a resident for ten years to take out Botswana citizenship.

Salome is a freckle faced, sandy haired, fit-looking and outdoor loving young woman of Dutch ancestry. She was born in Johannesburg but grew up in the Cape Province. She went to Port Elizabeth University, did languages, then a teaching diploma, taught several years, got into journalism and was editor for a computer magazine. In 1984 she came to Botswana on one of Peter's safaris. In 1985 Peter and Salome founded their safari outfit, Africa Calls. Salome is the marketing director and is working on a book on the flora and fauna of Botswana, between safari and other activities, but we got to know her as the hands-on cook and camp organizer.

Map is of slight to medium build, sports a scruffy beard, and on our trip was always attired in khaki shorts and shower shoes. He comes from an old British settler family in Botswana, going well back to the former days of British rule when it was still named Bechuanaland. His family owns property and raises cattle commercially. He has worked as a naturalist in the Okavango and with the Zimbabwe Wildlife Department. He breaks away occasionally to help Peter on trips like ours. Otherwise he is headquartered in Francistown.

While we had drinks and lunch, Peter explained the program. "The Bushmen are camped about a kilometer off that way," he indicated, pointing to the northeast. "We chose to camp here, a sufficient distance away so as not to intimidate them. We will go over presently and make initial contact. Though I know you are all chomping at the bit to see them, I need to warn you that these people have had no previous contact with white men. None. Thus, though Keeme, our intermediary, has prepared them for us, convinced them that we are not threatening, and to stay put so that we can visit them, we must go very slowly on this first visit. We have to take it easy and not press in too close or stay too long until they get accustomed to us, otherwise they might just pick up and vanish."

Peter's contact through Keeme was a key to this whole encounter. Keeme, whose mother was a Bushman, was our bridge to the clan and as such had risked a great deal in helping to establish the connection between our group and the clan. If we were not acceptable to the clan it would be Keeme who would be responsible in their eyes.

"There are twelve in the group," Peter continued. "It's actually a small family clan consisting of two adult brothers and their two wives.

One has four children, the other has two; three boys and three girls all together. There are also two unattached females who are in some way related to one or the other of the wives. One unattached woman is middle aged, the other a teenager. Then there's Keeme (Key-em-ay). He is related to one or the other of the two unattached females. His father was a black Bantu, a local Herero cattle owner, his mother a Kung San. He usually herds cattle, living in Xai Xai close to the wells in the dry season and ranges out from Xai Xai herding cattle in the wet season. He speaks the clan's click language as well as Tswana, or Setswana, the common African language of Botswana."

Communicating with the clan was to be an exacting task. Shylock speaks English and Tswana. He was to talk to Keeme in Tswana, who in turn talked to the people of the clan in their language, then translated back to Shylock in Tswana, who passed it on to us in English.

The Bushmen talk with very distinctive clicks which are incorporated directly into their alphabet. The clicks function as independent sounds in the making of words, rather like similar noises, signals or exclamations outside of normal speech that we use in our language when we make sound signals to a horse or admonishments to children like tsk, tsk, sounds you wouldn't find in the dictionary. To oversimplify a bit, the Kung have four distinctive clicks in their language, so their alphabet is made up of vowels, consonants and clicks, but with the clicks being quite prominent in their speech.

Buthelezi's Zulu in South Africa's Natal Province and Mandela's Zhosha also have clicks in their language. Linguists believe that these Bantu races picked the clicks up from the Bushmen and Hottentots in fairly recent times after migrating south and making contact with these click-speaking aboriginal inhabitants of southern Africa.

"It's a manipulating of the tongue followed by an inrush of air that makes the distinctive pops and clicks," said Jack. "They first fit their tongue up against the inside of their teeth and the roof of their mouth, then they draw their tongue down, causing a vacuum or rarified air between the teeth and roof of the mouth and their tongue. How or where they break the seal, letting the air rush in with a snapping noise, determines which of the four distinctive pops or clicks we hear."

We would be hearing this unusual speech for ourselves soon and I would be struck by how different is the Bushmen's language from the Swahili that I knew from my time in the East African countries of Kenya, Tanzania and Uganda. Africa is a land of great variety, and language is just one of its fascinations. In the States one might travel for great distances and still be understood by the locals of any region, but in Africa it would take a very talented linguist to master the languages of all the people. We were to be very dependent on our awkward series of translators and translations in communicating with the Bushmen.

This was the first time Peter or anyone in the local safari industry had organized a trip where the specific intent was to provide contact between white visitors and any of the very few remaining nomadic Bushmen. In the past only a very few anthropologists and scientists have attempted to search out the few pristine, still wild hunter-gatherers. Their isolation has certainly contributed to the lack of contact, as has their shyness and history of abuse at the hands of non-native people, but for the present time at least, this rarity of contact must be partly due to the fact that there are so few of them left. Whatever the reason the success of our contact with them would depend on their willingness to be around us, for if they did not want to spend time with us all they needed to do was vanish into the vast Kalahari bush and we could never hope to find them. Peter knew this better than any of us and since he was the organizer of the encounter and had accepted the responsibility, he wanted it to be a success. His was not an easy task; we were seven exuberant Americans, culturally conditioned to act in a manner quite different from the people we hoped to visit. But still, no question, we knew we were on their turf.

"Before our first contact with the Bushmen," said Peter, "I need to share a concern with you. They could just pick up and fade into the bush. Remember, these are people who have never been in close contact with whites, but have undoubtedly heard stories of whites coming into the bush and shanghaiing Bushmen as workers, serfs, or slaves, or of past acts of genocide to get their land. They are only naturally wary and suspicious." We all went quiet. "If we give them time to see our intentions are non-threatening," continued Peter, "We hope they will be put at ease, and we'll be able to observe them here in their natural setting."

Finally, with the shadows at the mid-afternoon angle, Peter asked if we were ready to go meet the wild Bushmen. To a chorus of affirmatives, we all sprang to action, gathering cameras and recording gear. With Peter, Map and Shylock in the lead, we hiked the kilometer over the sandy Kalahari terrain through sparse bush to the clan's encampment, our enthusiasm and excitement somewhat subdued by Peter's apprehensions and reluctance about turning our gung-ho group loose on the shy Kung San.

We passed over the rolling ground on soft sand, zig-zagging through the open sandy places between scattered thorn bushes and infrequent trees, mostly acacia thorn. Then in the distance we saw the small grass huts and dark scantily clad bodies moving among them.

The little clan was huddled closely together around a smoldering fire, chattering animatedly in their distinctive click language. They went quiet as we came close. Keeme came forward to meet us. The clan remained aloof, watching us with detachment and interest. The adult men were bare except for abbreviated gameskin loincloths. The adult women wore karosses made of wildebeests, gemsbok, eland or kudu skins. A Bushman woman's kaross is an untailored one-piece skin which they wear drawn in at the waist with a thong, with two legs tied over the right shoulder, leaving the left shoulder bare. The three older women wore brightly colored beadwork head bands. Their simple jewelry consisted of porcupine quill and ostrich eggshell chip necklaces and game skin arm and leg bracelets.

As we cast our eyes around, we were struck by what little there was in the camp. The grass thatched conical huts, four in number, were in a semi-circle with their open sides facing the central fire area, each hut with its individual family hearth or cooking fire immediately in front of it. The clan was gathered at the communal fire, out in the open space delineated by the half circle of huts. There was no evidence of any cooking utensils or anything else to speak of either inside the open huts or in the camp area outside the huts. Everything was stone age simple and austere.

"All their activities take place here in the center of the camp near their campfires," whispered Map. "Except if they had game skins staked out, those would be outside the encampment in case they attract carnivores."

One anthropologist has dubbed these 'the 90 second people'. In their traditional nomadic life-style, they have retained a basic survival culture with so few material encumbrances that they can always pick up and leave a campsite like this in 90 seconds or less.

There was one small child in the breast-feeding stage, probably less than a year old. Everyone in the group took a turn entertaining and caring for the little boy, naked except for a small ostrich egg chip necklace. The rest of the children were older, ranging from probably five years to the largest boy who looked to be about ten. The group acted and interacted closely, several talking at once in the click speech that sounded so very distinctive to our ears. Their talk was punctuated with frequent laughter, indicating a closely knit, congenial and happy interdependent group.

Most of us had cameras, either still or video, and some had both. We took a few pictures as unobtrusively as possible. The clan seemed to take no particular notice. All indications were that they had never been introduced to the concept of photography. We were inclined to linger on a bit, but soon Peter indicated it would be well for us to push off, not to overwhelm them on this first encounter. As we turned to leave, one of the brothers inquired through Keeme and Shylock, "Who are you people and where do you come from?"

Dr. Wheeler had trouble responding to the question. These cloistered people can only think in terms of what they have seen in their limited Kalahari range and can't be expected to understand the concept of a Europe or of an America. To the Bushman depicted in *The Gods Must Be Crazy*, the end of the world was the Zambezi River Valley below Victoria Falls where the hero went to throw away the evil Coke bottle. So we all shared Jack's loss to explain where we were from and what we were doing here. Peter asked them if we could come and visit them again the next day, a request to which they agreed.

We turned back to our camp feeling that this first encounter had been satisfactory and looking forward to the next one, but then Map voiced his fears. "Let's just hope we don't find an abandoned encampment tomorrow."

The camp crew was busy preparing for the evening meal when we returned. In the lengthening afternoon shadows we gathered in our circle of canvas chairs around the fire, Lion beers in hand. Peter related some of what he knew of the clan.

"These people have been camped here only a few days. They move around frequently. Since we are entering the driest season and all the standing water is gone, nomadic people will tend to gravitate towards Xai Xai and its permanent man-made water wells. They're living now without any water, surviving only on the moisture from melons they can gather and underground bulbs, tubers and roots they can dig up. If the melons don't dry up, and they can continue to endure without going in and camping near the wells, they will. Their preference is to avoid the cattle post village of Xai Xai.

"They may well be drawn into Xai Xai for a month or two, but they will move back away from Xai Xai as soon as the rains provide water again in the dry pans out in the bush or there is a new succulent crop of melons and the like. Both game and the Bushmen avoid the cattle that tend to stay close to the wells. So it's only when there is not enough moisture in the veld food and the stress on the clan reaches a critical point that you'd expect the clan to be drawn into Xai Xai and its wells, to confront and compete with the cattle and with civilization."

We wondered about the Kalahari seasons and weather cycles and how they affected the clan's movements. Peter explained that there are five more or less distinct seasons around which the nomadic Bushman's life revolves. "Remember we're in the southern hemisphere and the seasons here are reversed. We're now in the last of their winter, a cold, dry season from the end of May through August that could bring some freezing at night, especially further south in the Central Kalahari. It never, never rains in the Kalahari in August, so this can be a difficult time for them."

The next season is a dry spring from about late August through to October when the first rains are most likely to come. It is the driest and most difficult period for nomadic Bushmen and the period that could force a clan into Xai Xai. Spring rains in October or November, if they come, trigger plant growth and animal reproduction.

The main summer rains come in December through March. Relatively speaking this is the season of plenty, the all too frequent Kalahari droughts notwithstanding. Then, if the rains are ample, some wetland game from the Okavango could migrate west into drier areas, like where we were camped.

There is a brief autumn in April or May when it gets colder. At that time the Bushmen harvest nuts, melons and berries until the supply is gone. "That's their year, and we are just coming into the driest part,

The Wheeler group poses in front of the Islander in Maun (l. to r.): Joel, Jack, Wally, Jim, John, Bud, and Tom. —BG

Most of the Kalahari trees are in their leafless winter attire. Hyena Camp finds shade in a grove of Kalahari apple leaf. —JW

Clan's youngest plays with tasama melon. —JP

The clan's youngest observes his first white stranger. —JP

the season that the nomadic Bushman dread most," continued Peter.

Even during normal weather cycles the San don't store food, so a drought makes it tougher on them. More of their young and old will perish during drought.

We recalled together an account of van der Post. After spending some time filming and studying some Bushmen in what is now Botswana's Central Kalahari Reserve, van der Post was cutting across country to get back out of the desert. There was a severe drought on. Late one afternoon a band of traveling Bushmen stumbled into his overnight camp. The clan was in dire shape, moving across the desert, desperately searching for any source of water or food, near death from thirst and starvation. Van der Post gave them food and water. Revived, some of the clan backtracked and brought in an old couple who hadn't been able to keep up or continue on, whom the clan had been forced to leave to die. Such occurrences are not rare in the harsh, unforgiving Kalahari.

In fact, during a long stretch of Kalahari drought from 1982 through 1987, the Botswana government estimated that eighty to ninety percent of the Rural Area Dwellers (RAD—a euphemism for Bushmen) were dependent on Government programs of drought relief feeding. Up to a third of Botswana's cattle herds have died out in such prolonged periods of drought.

Average annual rainfall in the Xai Xai area, where the Kung Bushmen are, is twelve to fourteen inches. To the South in the Central Kalahari and Ghanzi areas, it is more like ten to twelve inches. In Kalahari drought years, rainfall can go as low as two inches or might reach eighteen inches in good years. This is a great difference from the forty to fifty inches I was used to in my boyhood home in the redwoods of Northern California, where lush growth and running streams were taken for granted.

The Kalahari is a landlocked plateau a thousand meters high. The predominant Kalahari winds blow dry from the north to northwest, but in the summer rainy season winds shift to come out of the northeast bringing with them cloud masses that have passed over the lowland bordering the Indian Ocean, and these clouds dump rain on the higher Kalahari plateau. A study of forty-six years of rainfall data for Maun, 1922 through 1968, shows that there are drought conditions on average two out of five years. A severe drought occurs on average one year in four.

In one sense, the Kalahari being an inhospitable thirstland is a blessing in disguise for the surviving San. Bushmen in lusher areas like South Africa have long since succumbed—dispossessed early, as their land was more desirable, and was taken from them by more advanced and purposeful people like the Dutch and Zulu. The harsh cruel Kalahari protected the Bushmen until much later, since others couldn't survive, where these special people so uniquely adapted to their forbidding environment have survived for eons.

We next inquired how they build the simple shelters which are little more than a sun shade and wind break. Map explained that the men gather a few one-inch diameter poles for the dome. They dig one end six inches into the sand, tie the branches together at the peak, leaving an opening on one side. The women gather the grass to give it a quick thatch and that's it. The huts are used only as occasional shelter from the sun or rain. The clan sleeps on the ground around the individual family fires, rather than in the huts. There is no furniture. The huts are quickly made in the matter of an afternoon and more quickly abandoned when these 90 second people move on.

"You noted four huts," added Map. "That's one for each of the brothers and his immediate family. One for the two unattached women. The half-finished one is probably Keeme's. But they live around their individual fires, not in the diminutive huts."

Peter and Salome had brought along a fairly well-stocked field library, including several books giving some background on the San peoples, as well as animal and bird identification guides. Van der Post's two earliest books, *The Lost World of the Kalahari* and *The Heart of the Hunter* published in 1958 and 1961 respectively, were included, as was a copy of van der Post's later *Testament to the Bushmen* (1984) with photographs by Jane Taylor. Also included was *The Bushmen* (1979) with text by Alf Wannenburg and photographs by Peter Johnson and Anthony Bannister, a large coffee table book heavy on photography. But in its narrative, it has a rich synopsis of the findings of anthropologists and, specifically, the Marshall family who spent considerable time with Kung Bushmen during the 50s and early 60s in Namibia just across the border from where we were located. Another book, *The Bushmen* (1978), by Tobias, had contributions by several anthropologists, much of the research centering in the Dobe area just north of Xai Xai. *When Animals Were People*, (1984), by Bern Woodhouse deals with the San's creation legends and rock paintings.

The van der Post books, his BBC film presentations and the works of the American Marshall family, in books and National Geographic films, through the 50s and early 60s drew people's attention to the Bushmen and reminded the public of these special people who, surprisingly, still survived, if in only very limited numbers in the waterless and unwanted wastes of the Kalahari.

At UC Berkeley in the 50s and 60s, Washburn and Clark encouraged these efforts and were of the opinion that the study of hunting and gathering people like the Kalahari Bushmen, before they disappeared, might shed light on the evolution of human behavior and ecology. They reasoned that a study of campsite behavior would be an aid in the interpretation of prehistoric living sites then being studied by Leakey and other scientists in East Africa.

Map called our attention to something we might have overlooked. "Back in the mid 50s when van der Post decided to try to search out and make contact with some traditional wild Bushmen, he spent several months roaming around Botswana before he found any. Your first encounter may have seemed easy for you all, but it's a truly unique experience in this day and age."

The Marshall family also had a chore finding still wild nomadic hunter-gatherers. From 1950 through 1961 they made annual trips looking for wild hunter-gatherers in Botswana and Namibia and even Angola. Like van der Post, they visited the Central Kalahari, but found the most unacculturated Bushmen in Nyae Nyae, across the border in Namibia, only a relatively short distance from where we were camped. From 1960 on, the South Africans made an effort to civilize Namibia's primitive Kung Bushmen people after the Marshalls had found and studied them for some ten years. John Marshall's 1973 video for *National Geographic* titled "Bushmen of the Kalahari," records the results. By then, John's old acquaintances showed up in felt hats and ragged European clothes, none in the traditional game skin clothing the clan we had just met were still sporting.

Dr. Wheeler did his undergraduate work at UCLA in anthropology. Pursuing an active lifelong interest in the area of surviving primitive stone-age cultures around the world, he knew that we were seeing here probably the oldest living remnants of a people and culture on the family tree of man from which we all evolved. Recent DNA testing of the genetic markings of primitive cultures has tended to confirm that conclusion. He had previously been with groups that were credited with first contacts with aboriginal cultures. In the Amazon drainage in eastern Ecuador near the Peruvian border on the Tivacuna River in 1972, Jack's group first cataloged the Aushiri, primarily a hunting and gathering tribe who also slash and burn limited forest to plant yucca. In 1977, in Papua New Guinea, Jack was with a group who first discovered the tree house dwelling, 'Wali-Ali-Fo', in an area in the central highlands above the April River. His interest in and knowledge of primitive cultures was invaluable to us in our campfire Bushman. seminar.

"Anthropology has made great strides even though it is a relatively new branch of science," said Jack. "When I was young there were only about forty active anthropologists in the United States. Today the U.S. alone is turning out 400 doctorates in anthropology in any one year. With that tremendous increase of scientific talent there has been a parallel, even exponential advance in interest in and knowledge about primitive peoples."

Darwin's, *On The Origin Of Species*, in the mid 1800's speculated that the cradle of man would be shown to be through evolution in Africa. This horrified the scientific and religious communities at the time, and it wasn't until a century later that archaeologists and paleontologists like Leakey and others have pretty convincingly proved Darwin right.

It started with Leakey's Olduvai Gorge discoveries in Tanzania's Rift Valley, of an upright walking humanoid dating back nearly two million years. Leakey's son later made other important discoveries at Lake Turkana in northern Kenya dating back nearly two million years. Then the discovery in Tanzania of the Laetoli tracks of three upright walking humanoids, left in volcanic ash which later hardened, dating three and three quarter million years ago, was in important link. With the discovery of what anthropologists named Lucy and her companions in Ethiopian lakeside deposits dating back about three million years, the pieces of the puzzle have come together. Lucy proved almost conclusively that the human branch off the ape family tree first evolved to walking upright, developed a larger brain and lost their canine teeth. This evolution all took place in Africa. These discoveries have all been fairly recent, Olduvai Gorge was in 1959, the others since that date.

But about 20 years ago, Wilson and Sarich, two biochemists from Berkeley, approached the question from an entirely different angle, not by studying bones but by studying blood proteins. Their approach has two premises: first, that over millions of years the genetic material, DNA or deoxyribonucleic acid of different species, has gone through random changes. The second important premise: that these changes occur at a more or less consistent rate. These two assumptions have been fairly well proved in experiments. Scientists take blood from an ape and blood from modern man, establish the difference in DNA, divide by the rate of change, and they have the fork in the road back in time to when they split. It is now believed that this genetic divergence occurred roughly five million years ago. But what is five million years? It's a lot closer than the anthropologists had first thought. To give some time scale, dinosaurs appeared on earth two hundred twenty-five million years ago, and disappeared some sixty-five million years ago. Five million years is like yesterday in the overall scheme of evolutionary development on earth leading to today's humans.

In the past five million years, there were other offshoots of the after-ape branch that have since become extinct. The survivors, our ancestors, developed slowly—to us, but rapidly in a relative sense—to a fairly well-developed, upright, large-brained creature, with their arms free, eventually learning the use of tools, and then fire, and learning verbal communications. Probably by one million years ago he was in transition from a scavenger-gatherer to a hunter-gatherer and was on the verge of starting a slow first migration out of Africa north into Europe and Asia. Eventually the more advanced surviving humans migrated from Africa through Asia, then through Indonesia to Australia and from Asia across the Bering Straits to North America and then into Central and South America.

It is generally conceded that homo erectus who evolved onto the scene some 1.6 million years back was the first to use fire and the first to leave Africa, so fire as a tool has only been in use during the last million and a half years or less. The use of fire was an enormous advance. Animals are afraid of fire, but humans have harnessed it.

The one million year date back into time when man had pretty much made the four million year transition from an ape is a bit fuzzy, but for arguments sake, let's accept it. In the last one million years, man, in Africa or wherever he migrated to, was a hunter-gatherer. It was not until roughly 10,000 years ago that the first man became a cultivator of plants or domesticator of animals, which permitted him to give up his nomadic roaming and settle down in villages. That is when one of the single most important milestones in man's evolution started; the agricultural revolution. This momentous advance probably first took place in the Middle East, but then independently at several other locations. Scientists believe it occurred first in the 'fertile crescent' including the Tigris and Euphrates Rivers in today's Iraq and Syria and in a strip along the Mediterranean, today's Lebanon and Israel. Today, roughly 10,000 years later, less than one person in 100,000, is a true full-time nomadic hunter-gatherer. Of the world's population of five billion, there are less than 50,000 true hunter-gatherers left in scattered remote pockets on earth.

Let's try to visualize that transition. A million years could be 100 squares of 10,000 years each. In your mind's eye, draw a long narrow strip, dividing it into 100 sections, stretching from today back in time one million years. Color green every square where mankind still consists of all hunter-gatherers. Color yellow those squares representing time since the start of the agricultural revolution when mankind is making the change from pure nomadic hunter-gatherers to a more sedentary mixed economy with some cultivation or animal domestication, with diminished to no foraging. Color red the squares where all the traditional nomadic hunter-gatherers are gone, extinct as a culture. Now, stretching back a million years, we've colored ninety-nine of the one hundred squares green. Only the one we are now in is yellow. In the next five to twenty years, authorities say we will most probably see the start of the red square, indicating no hunter-gatherers left anywhere on the globe!

This indicates that 99% of our advanced evolutionary time as humans was spent living just like the people of this small clan are still living today. Only in the most recent one percent of time has man made the transition into cultivating and herding. Then followed rapidly the bronze age, the iron age, the industrial age, the atomic age and today's information age. "But these very Bushmen," Jack pointed off toward the clan's encampment, "are a living reflection of 99% of our evolution. I mean it's really spooky, and they're about to disappear. With all our current knowledge and resources, like visiting the moon, you'd think we could figure out a way to give them a chance to continue their culture."

We were seated around a traditional Bushman style fire, made of three small logs laid out, meeting at the middle like spokes of a wheel, and pushed in periodically as they burn. It made for efficient use of wood, but a rather small fire. Running the camp seemed to be Salome's bailiwick while interfacing with the Bushman was Peter's. So Salome,

Mansu and George were keeping the diminutive fire going, demanding less wood be scrounged and hauled in from the bush, but it wasn't the big robust cheerful campfire we Americans were used to. And the Kalahari winter nights are chilly.

As the sun set Peter announced that the shower was on and dinner would be ready in an hour. The only water we had was the thousand liters that Peter had brought in two small one axle tank trailers he was pulling behind the Toyotas. A canvas bag with a shower spout that Peter placed in a tree held only about three gallons, and we were to try to get two or more showers out of it. The 'one-gallon-shower' trick is to turn the water on and quickly get wet, shut the water off and lather up, then quickly rinse the soap off, remembering as each precious drop touches your body that there is no water source closer than Xai Xai's wells. One of our lads got up to initiate the bush shower as the campfire discussions went on.

"Peter, what do you think of what Beth Oliver, the woman selling Bushman-made handicraft in Riley's Hotel, is doing for them?" Jack Wheeler asked.

"I have mixed emotions about it," answered Peter. "She's not doing anything to help these people stay nomadic in the wild if they so choose. But still it encourages those that have given up on a nomadic life to survive on their own as it augments what the government is — or more correctly isn't — doing for the tame Bushman, so her heart is in the right place."

Peter and Map had made clear to us that these wild Bushmen out here were happy, healthy, bright, in stark contrast to the ones at Bantu cattle post villages and wells like Xai Xai and Tsodilo Hills, who have lost their land and been forced to give up their traditional nomadic life. They are suffering cultural shock and depression, squatted around a well, unemployed or at best working for barter or minimal wages by herding for the Tswana speaking or Heroro cattle owners. Our hearts went out to the few wild ones who are still hanging on, like the little clan we were visiting. It was clear from what Peter said that this clan faces the same fate. Once this habitat can no longer support their traditional foraging, even these Bushmen will be drawn to the water at the cattle post wells where they will avoid death by thirst, only to face death by starvation or "death by dispossession" as John Marshall calls it.

Map briefed us on the history of the San people in southern Africa. The Bushmen in South Africa have essentially all perished. A few years back, there was one last small group at Lake Chrissie in the Transvaal, and there are a few that drift into South African's Kalahari Gemsbok Park out of Botswana, but otherwise South Africa's once significant Bushmen population have perished. Some of their genes and those of their Hottentot cousins are spread around, making up some portion of the Cape colored population, but as a distinct culture of people, the South African Bushmen are extinct.

The Dutch first landed to establish a settlement in Cape Town in 1652. The Dutch brought cattle. Their objective initially was not to populate the country but rather only to establish a way station to provide Dutch ships sailing around South Africa from Europe to India and the Dutch Indies and back with beef and water. It was some fifteen years later that the first Dutch altercation with the San was recorded. The Bushmen pulled back. But the Dutch continued pushing out from the Cape and hunted in what the Bushmen considered their areas. Before the Dutch showed up it had been their sole domain. The Dutch killed the wild animals that the San considered theirs.

In their lore and myth, the Bushmen were created by the great God, who then created animals for them. Then in a series of what might be called 'evolutionary myths,' animals were created from people until animals and people all have human qualities and personalities that are intertwined. To the San, the animals are more than theirs; they are all part of the same fabric.

So if the Dutch were going to kill his animals, then the San hunter would retaliate by killing the Dutch animals; their cattle. This naturally provoked the Dutch Boers, who wouldn't allow such action by mere savages to go unpunished. The battle lines were drawn. The ensuing hostilities continued and escalated and by 1715 the Dutch had organized regular mounted commandos to hunt down and kill any and all Bushmen, men, women and children. Records from around 1760 indicate that the Dutch, for the first time, were keeping some women and children as prisoners rather than killing them all. One of many tactics the Dutch used was to kill hippos as bait to lure the Bushmen out into the open for the meat. The Dutch then reappeared from ambush and massacred them.

Bantu tribes like the Zulu migrating south in Africa, with their wealth in expanding cattle herds, also encroaching on traditional Bushman territory and, wanting more land, simultaneously made war on the San. The Bushman's last stand in what is now South Africa was in the late 1870's when they were hunted out of their last caves and retreats high in the Drakensburg Mountains. It is reckoned there were anywhere from 150,000 to 300,000 San (Bushmen) in Southern Africa from the Congo and Zambezi watersheds south, before they got caught in the pincer between the Dutch and Bantus. The Bushmen were tough. They wouldn't give up despite having only their puny little arrows to use against horses and guns. Furthermore, the European firearms were rapidly improving, increasing in accuracy and range, until toward the end the Dutch could knock off the Bushman from well out of their poisoned arrow range. It became less of a battle and more of a massacre. Still the San stood and died for their land, and for their animals.

Both the white settlers and Bantu were agriculturalists and pastoralists. In their materialistic expansionism, they needed the land and took it, the same land the San also needed for hunting and foraging. The game was steadily destroyed. Van der Post has been quoted as saying, "We other races went through Africa like locusts, devouring and stripping the land of what we could get out of it. The Bushman was there simply because he belonged to the land."

Many parallels can be made with the American Plains Indians. Settlers took their land and killed their game. With the gold rush in 1848, Europeans came in ever larger numbers and killed the Indians and annihilated their buffalo. For the Indians, the confrontation was about protecting their land and traditional hunting rights against agropastoralists, farmers and ranchers, wanting their land to farm or run domestic animals. Custer's last stand was in 1876, and Wounded Knee in 1890, about the time of the end of South Africa's Bushmen. The American Indians saw the inevitable. Before complete annihilation they gave up and a few survived, but sadly without lands to roam free. Very little, but ceremonial vestiges of their rich and varied cultures, has survived. The big question as relates to the San seems to be: Do we learn from the sad history of San slaughter in South Africa, that of America's Plains Indians, and of Australia's Aboriginies, or must we repeat it with the last of the Bushman in the Kalahari?

The San people in South Africa stood, fought and all died. Anthropologists generally believe that those in the Kalahari are not a few survivors who fled north from South Africa. The rock paintings at Tsodilo indicate that Bushmen were there well before the Dutch came. San tend to be very territorial and stay and defend locations where their fathers are buried. Scientists have worked out that the click language falls into three main groups: southern, central and northern, with subdialects which are now mutually unintelligible. Anthropologists tell us this indicates that though the people were nomadic, they did not migrate or move over distance, and thus did not keep the language universally updated or understandable.

The San's story is all so similar to that classic one of Tasmanian man. He was basically the same Aborigine that we still find in Australia, nomadic hunter-gatherers living in small family bands and prolific rock painters. Some of these same Aborigines migrated as far south as Tasmania. Then some ten thousand years back at the end of the most recent ice age, the water came up in what is now the Bass Strait and made Tasmania an island cut off from the rest of Australia.

When permanent white settlers first came onto Tasmania in about 1800, they found about two thousand of these Aboriginal hunter-gatherers spread out in small family bands of twenty to thirty. The European settlers to Tasmania wanted the land and started shooting. Then following an outcry, the government stepped in and, finally, by 1835 with only about two hundred left, the killing was stopped. The surviving Tasmanian Aborigines were herded onto Flinders Island out in the Bass Strait of Tasmania. With the disruption of their culture and forced dislocation which did not allow them to continue living off the land as free ranging nomadic hunter-gatherers, they died out from despair, starvation and disease. First contact with whites to total extinction in fifty years or less.

There is a striking parallel between Tasmanian man and the Bushmen in South Africa, both now extinct. Meanwhile the Aborigines on the Australian mainland are struggling on, as is a last small remnant of the Bushman culture in the Botswanan and Namibian Kalahari. Unless something is done, the Kalahari Bushman will be the next to go.

We were feeling a bit overwhelmed by this sad tale of "civilized man's" inhumanity. Between Dr. Wheeler and Map, we had a pretty clear picture of the history of this dry corner of the globe and the people who have inhabited it. The more we learned, the more we wanted to know.

There was a lull in the conversation. I got up and pushed the logs of the fire together, enjoying the clear starlit night and small but cheerful fire. Jack was pointing out the southern cross to Joel and Wally. There was a rattling in the ice chest as more beer was drawn out.

"Are there any lions around here?" asked Bud, lifting his Lion beer can high.

"It's possible but not probable," answered Peter. "Lions suffer from the same dispossession. As cattle and civilization move in, game has been driven out or died out. Remember the hunter-gatherer can and does survive on gathering only without a lot of meat. The lion is a hunter only. He eats meat or dies. The sparse game here is slim pickings for the lions." However, Peter proceeded to relate a tale he had heard from Keeme in which Keeme and three other Xai Xai residents had set out on a recent hunt into the bush in the general direction of our Hyena Camp. They had four donkeys with them. When they camped for the night they left the donkeys tethered nearby. They were awakened in the middle of the night to find a pride of nine lions attacking the donkeys. All four were killed. Keeme and his companions left on foot for Xai Xai at sunrise, spooked and vowing not to hunt in the area again.

"There are lion in the Nyae Nyae area just west of here in Namibia," added Map. "Now that the Bushmen are leaving Tsumkwe and returning to the bush with their small subsistence herds of cattle, they complain that lions are decimating their herds, and they appeal to authorities to control them or give them the guns they'd need to protect their livestock themselves." But the Kung in Bushmanland complain that the South African government will not give the Kung guns to protect their cattle, while they allow foreigners to come into the area and shoot lions for sport. The paradox is not lost on them.

All the talk of death in the bush caused us to wonder about the burial practices of the Bushman and Jack had the answer. "According to authorities, when someone in a Kung clan dies, they are buried in a sitting position facing the Great God in the eastern sky. Personal effects are broken and sprinkled over the grave to warn others to stay clear of the spirits of the dead. The nomadic clan then leaves the area, carefully avoiding passing downwind of the grave, since the spirits of the dead travel on the wind. They will not revisit the site again for generations. They especially fear the spirits of younger persons, as their spirits are more restless than the more satisfied spirit of someone who lived a long life."

The talk went on. Those of us who had hunted in Africa told stories of the hunt, of adventures on safari among the people and animals of Africa. Not so long ago—before books, radio and then TV—people from around the world once passed their legends, their history and their very culture from generation to generation through storytelling. For centuries small clans like the one we had just met have spent much of their time around campfires in just this fashion. And from all around us came the sounds of African night, birds and insects in the scrub surrounding the camp. And overhead the stars passed. The Bushman would be sitting around their fire too, telling stories to ease the dread of the night that is common to all people the world over. Almost certainly they were talking about the white giants that had visited their camp that day.

Then there were flashes of thunder in the night sky and a few drops of rain fell.

"But it never rains in the Kalahari in August," we scolded Peter and Map. It was only a light sprinkle, but backed by the thunder and lightning and the lateness of the hour, it put an abrupt stop to the talk. We headed for our first night under canvas.

—4—
Gathering We'll Go

Our first morning in the bush began with birds announcing daylight with their song. We were amazed that despite the harsh waterless nature of the Xai Xai region, there is a relatively abundant bird population. Laughing dove, Cape turtle dove and Namaqua dove live here as well as finches and shrikes, a variety of bee eaters, lark and babblers and many others. First up, I stoked the few smoldering embers left from our previous night's fire. There was a cool chill to the Kalahari winter morning, but our previous day's experience told us it would get hot during the day. The harlequin quail would be seeking shade.

Our camp's sanitary facility was a wash basin and a GI shovel and a toilet roll in front of each tent. As I walked out of camp to improvise a latrine, I spotted a large fallen tree snag which I dragged back to camp. Not seeing an axe, I laid this large log over the depression of what was left of the previous night's diminutive fire to let the snag burn in two.

Salome spied the big log and exclaimed, "Who brought this great whacking tree in? It will burn us out of the camp!"

I sheepishly confessed to being the culprit and received a frosty look from Salome for treading in her bailiwick and for changing from an energy efficient Bushman fire to a big blazing European one. Thus I inherited the ongoing chore of supplying the wood to keep our cheerful campfire going. Salome and her lads henceforth concerned themselves only with the smaller cooking fire.

"You're like Laurens van der Post," Map said as he appeared in his shorts and shower shoes to warm his hands over the rejuvenated fire. "He admitted to liking a large, cheerful Kalahari campfire. The Bushman traditionally build a small fire to conserve their energy expenditure in wood gathering and prolonging the wood supply close to their encampment. When van der Post was with them he built a small fire like the one Salome and her lads prepare. However, van der Post confessed to looking forward to building a rousing bonfire when he was away by himself."

Then, as Dr. Jack joined us, we fell into a discussion about the small clan nearby.

"Here in Botswana, first in the Setswana language and carrying over into English, the San or Bushman are now most commonly referred to as *Basarwa* in the local press," added Map. So we could call these people Bushman or San or, here in Botswana, the Basarwa.

Just as our American Indians are delineated into geographical and tribal groups such as Sioux, Hopi, and Apache, so too the San are grouped by distinct geographical distribution and variations in their click language and customs: the Kung that we were visiting; the Auen to the south; the Naharo who live near Ghanzi; the Xo south of Ghanzi; and the Gwis and Ghana, east of Ghanzi in the Central Kalahari Reserve.

In one of the earliest written historical reference by J. Wintervogel in 1655, the early Dutch described these people as " ... a certain tribe very low in stature and very lean, entirely savage, without any huts, cattle or anything in this world, clad in little skins" ... who the Dutch called Bosjesmans, anglicized to Bushmen for "people who reside in the bush without dwellings." The Bushmen were related to the only other small-stature, click-speaking people the Dutch encountered who were called the Hottentot. The Hottentot were pastoralists or cattle herders and called themselves the Khoi Khoi. The Bushman didn't have a name in their own language for themselves, but were called the San by the Hottentot, meaning "aboriginal hunting people" in the Hottentot language. The combined click language group is now called Khoisan, or that of the Khoi Khoi and San together.

Jack informed us that in recent years the scholars have decided that to call the Bushman by that name is disparaging. Scientists have adopted the term San in place of Bushman, in much the same way that the former term 'Eskimo' is going out of favor and being replaced by 'Inuit' in North America. Thus, while the general public may still often use the timeworn 'Bushman' and 'Eskimo' for these two hunter-gatherer cultures, officials and academics and the more enlightened public now tend to refer to them as San and Inuit.

The Inuit got tagged with the name 'Eskimo' when early European explorers, working north, heard the more southern Canadian tribes refer to their Arctic dwelling neighbors as 'people who eat raw meat' or 'Eskimo' in the southern language. It is not a term that exists in the Inuits' own language, or one that they appreciate.

Earlier writers, like van der Post, referred to those Bushmen as "wild" who were still traditional nomadic hunter-gatherers, and as "tame" for those that had been dispossessed of their land and largely given up their traditional culture to follow more modern pursuits, as hired cattle herders or in other paid employment. More recently the academics have taken to using the terms "unacculturated" for what were earlier called wild, and "acculturated" for tame. These last terms seem unmanageable to me, and so I will, on occasion, use van der Post's terms, wild and tame. And while Basarwa seems convenient and specific, it too has problems. Basarwa is only correct when used to refer to people in Botswana and becomes inappropriate in referring to genetically related peoples in nearby Namibia, Angola or other countries. Our group and our guides referred to them as Bushmen and that term seems most comfortable to me, but I will also use the term San.

It was about 9 a.m. when, with breakfast and discussions over, we were off again, looking forward to a more substantial visit with our neighbors. Would they have silently vanished as Map had suggested was possible?

Keeme had provided the names of the two men, Qui (Gwee) the older and smaller of stature, and Noishay (No-wa-say) the younger and slightly larger. Qui and Noishay are brothers. When we arrived at the little encampment of four shelters, we found only Noishay's wife sitting on the ground next to her cooking fire, caring for the clan's youngest member. Without Keeme, Shylock couldn't communicate with the woman, but presently we heard voices off to the northeast, and moved off in that direction to find the rest of the clan engaged in a spirited and vocal food-gathering effort. They had fanned out through the semi-sparse bush, picking up, or in most cases digging up, food. It had the appearance of an Easter egg hunt. We tagged along as they collected melons, tubers, roots and bulbs.

Map pointed out the tasama melon which has markings similar to the green and yellow striping of our watermelons but is much smaller, more the size of our cantaloupe.

"That is their main source of liquid."

Later, we watched as one of the mature women dug up a big brown tuber of a coconut's size and outside texture. She sat on the ground and started scraping across its surface, exposing the succulent white interior. After scraping off several thin layers, she scooped the dripping material up in her hand and proceeded to squeeze moisture out of it which she used like a wet sponge to wash her arms and face. Then she squeezed another handful of the white scrapings and liquid literally ran from her hand. We were all amazed that such wetness could come from this harsh, otherwise bone dry environment.

"That particular tuber is called *bi*," Map explained. "It's a good source of moisture, but generally too bitter to drink, so she's washing with it. By mixing or blending its juice with other bulbs or roots, they can drink it if extreme conditions force them to."

"These people have no source of drinking water at present," Peter reminded us. "They get all their moisture from tasama melons or underground tubers and roots like you see them doing here."

Both the men and the women, and even the five children were all actively searching and digging. The women were depositing the treasures in the draped backs of their karosses above the thong belt.

"Usually the men do the hunting," Map added, "the women the food gathering. It's a bit unusual for Qui and Noishay to be taking such an active part. Still, when they're out on a hunt the men gather enough to sustain themselves, living off the land as they go."

Observers have noted that when the women gather, they know where the productive areas are and when specific food plants ripen, and they plan their lives and annual nomadic movements accordingly. They are more apt to move to a new area for the plants available than for the game. But then they don't aggressively exploit the environment. They take only what they need, always leaving plenty for seed or future crops. The San develop a visual memory of plant locations and can go long distances to gather plants they've seen in years past. They take children along, first carrying them and then as toddlers so they will learn early to be observant and knowledgeable about the plants that are a key to their survival. The women do go long distances gathering, but more usually harvest near camp until it is picked over or depleted, then move their encampment.

The women's main tool is their digging stick, a stout limb or branch three or four feet long and about an inch in diameter, cut diagonally to form a point and frequently resharpened. We noted that the women usually sit on the ground to dig rather than bend over and be off balance. This puts them down where they could go armpit deep for the hidden treasures, spending up to twenty minutes digging at a single location. Qui and Noishay used their spear shafts, spear point in the air, as a digging stick in the sandy soil.

As we watched, Noishay was down on his knees digging deeper and deeper in the sand until his head was on the surface and his arm stretched full length in his excavation. Finally, he pulled out yet another tuber to add to several he had dug up. The tubers looked like sweet potatoes. When he got up, his upper body covered with sand, he placed his several tubers in the drapes of karosses of the women and female children. The kaross styles were universally the same, with two legs of the animal's untailored skin twist-tied to form the single right shoulder strap. The left shoulder is bare or strapless. One day the animal's tail hangs down from the hem like a designer's trademark. The next day, the same tail points skyward from the shoulder drape, indicating there's no up or down to the skin that becomes the day's kaross, or leather dress. The younger the child, the more tattered or 'hand-me-down' their kaross. The Bushmen women have no carrying devices—no bags, sacks or baskets. The harvest was stored and carried by reaching under their left arm and into the back drape and depositing it against their body. Babies carried on gathering expeditions are placed in this same drape. For underwear, mature women wear small leather aprons front and back under their kaross, the front one often decorated with beads.

In the heat of the day, when the kaross drape was not in use as a pouch, the women would often undo the right shoulder strap and fold their kaross down over the belt line, baring them to the waist except for their ostrich egg shell chip necklaces. At one point the whole clan gathered in the rather fragile shade of a cluster of trees to nourish themselves. They cut the tops out of some of the tasama melons they had gathered using a metal bladed knife that one of the women produced, cutting the melon like we cut the top out of a pumpkin to make a Jack-o-lantern. They then pulped the inside with the rind acting as the bowl, the women using their digging sticks, the men the shaft of their spears. Then they hand scooped the pulped melon into their mouths. This provided a sustaining food, a bland but moist snack, their equivalent of a drink.

"In the more barren Central Kalahari where the tasama melon is the main food and water source, anthropologists reckon the Bushman consume up to five kilograms of tasama a day," Map added.

Then, in the same shady spot, Qui and Noishay took out their fire-making equipment to light up a smoke. The men twist a fire using a flat base stick with a hole through it and a round twist stick. Some shredded bark is put under the horizonal base stick for tinder. The round twist stick is held vertically and rapidly rolled between the palms of the hands until smoke rises.

"Only men make fire using fire sticks," Map explained. "The vertical twist stick is hard wood and is called male and the larger softer horizontal stick that receives the twist stick is called female."

Qui and Noishay alternated palming the twist, or male, stick. As one pair of hands descended with a downward pressure to create the friction, it made room at the top for the other pair of descending palms on the twist stick, then back to the first. In about a minute, smoke was rising. The hot wood dust was then used to coax the tinder into flame to light the tobacco in the metal tobacco holder. They were not actually using tobacco, but rather foliage from a local bush called silver leaf. This process of fire-making and smoking was accompanied by a great deal of animated giggling, back slapping and chattering from the women and children seated nearby. Soon Qui, then Noishay were exhaling great clouds of smoke as the crescendo of playful chatter and laughter from the women and children rose.

"A silver leaf high," quipped Jack Wheeler.

On this occasion the women didn't smoke, but on later occasions we saw them smoking around the campfires.

"You notice they don't have an ignitable cigarette," Peter pointed out. "They smoke their leaves inside that metal cylinder, something they've traded for, like the metal knife with which they cut out the tasama top. The metal tobacco holder, or cigarette, is often a brass rifle cartridge with the detonator end removed."

We stayed with the clan for three or four hours while they foraged through the bush collecting food. There was a continual animated clicking chatter as they roamed, laughed, dug, picked, shared, ate and smoked. Eventually the clan was loaded up with melons, roots and tubers. The drapes in the back of the karosses of the mature women and female children were bulging. Anthropologists note that the women can carry up to forty pounds of harvest in their karosses, walking all day to harvest several kilometers from their encampment. The draped pouch leaves the women's hands free to gather or to handle a child.

"These people should be called gatherer-hunters," Map said. "They survive mainly on gathering rather than hunting." Studies have shown that even when game was abundant, meat only made up at most forty percent of their diet. In recent years with dwindling game fairly scarce, probably eighty to ninety percent of their food and moisture comes from plants. Anthropologists who have studied these people have found that the men and especially the women, have an intimate knowledge of up to some hundred and fifty plants and trees from which they harvest some food at some time in the seasonal cycle. The food might be in the form of berries, fruits, beans, nuts, root, tubers, cucumbers and melons and are found over large areas.

Anthropologist Richard Lee of the Kalahari Research Group, in studying the Kung San from 1963 onwards, was able to compare them to fifty-eight still known or surviving hunter-gatherer cultures around the world. He found that plant food predominated over meat, or that half the societies survived predominantly on gathering plant food, about one third on fishing, and the remaining one sixth predominantly on hunting. Still, with rare exceptions, all hunter-gatherer societies derive at least twenty percent of their nutrition from hunting animals, so though hunting is rarely the primary source of food, it is important.

Fascinated by the gathering expedition, our group was busy filming. The clan seemed to take no notice, carrying on in a natural, unselfconscious way. "These people are a dream to photograph," Tom observed. They did not 'stiff-pose', as many Africans do, once they have got onto cameras, frustrating attempts at natural photography.

This clan fit the physical descriptions of which we had read. The individuals are relatively small, delicate and graceful with light movements. Their skin is lighter than the black Bantu like Shylock, tending to be more yellow-brown. Their hair is the short, peppercorn type. They have broad noses, high cheekbones, somewhat Mongoloid or slant eyes, and small ears. Average male weight and height are 100 to 110 pounds on a 5 foot 3 inch stature; for women, 85 to 95 pounds and 4 foot 11 inches.

Back in camp Noishay and the women provided Noishay's wife with some of the food the clan had gathered, to make up for the meal she had missed by remaining in camp to babysit the clan's youngest member. Authorities have noted that when men have meat, it is shared throughout the clan, but with daily gathering, each woman gathers for her immediate family only.

"Can we visit you in the evening?" Peter asked through Shylock and

Keeme. After the usual translation delay, we heard a "yes."

Back at our camp we settled in the circle of folding canvas chairs around the campfire to discuss our unfolding exposure to the Bushmen. A Kalahari robin worked the ground nearby and a Sabota lark sang from one of the trees surrounding our camp. Map added to the knowledge we had gathered firsthand.

"These are what are called Kung San. They are up here in this remote, dry corner of Botswana, the last to be dispossessed of their land and the last of their kind to hang onto the traditional hunter-gatherer culture. That's why people like the Marshalls chose the Kung just across the border west of here to study in the 1950's to 1960's, and most of the later studies by anthropologist authors like Tobias and Lee concentrated about fifty kilometers north of Xai Xai in the Dobe area."

The British made what is now Botswana the Bechuanaland Protectorate in 1884. This was to keep the Germans in what is now Namibia from encroaching, and to keep the Dutch Boers from entering from the south, and also as a stepping stone to gaining control of Northern and Southern Rhodesia, now Zambia and Zimbabwe. The early British administrators took a rather passive role, largely leaving rule in the hands of the black Bantu tribes who had by then entered what is now Botswana from the east to overrun and often enslave the sparsely dispersed population of leaderless and nomadic San. The San, who were in Botswana first and had it to themselves until the early 1600's, were not considered tribes. They lived then, as they do today, in small, nomadic, family clans without headmen, not permanently installed and not sedentarily in tribal areas or villages with tribal chiefs and ruling methods like the Bantu. The Bantus were so organized as to have armies to fight for land for their ever expanding cattle herds.

When the British took control of the area they found eight principal Tswana speaking Bantu tribes, the Batswana who spoke the Tswana language; the same eight major tribes that exist in Botswana today. The most dominant of these tribes is the Bamangwato, making up a quarter of the country's population. Seretse Khama, the heir to that tribe's chieftainship, was Botswana's first president. Khama's tribe is in the east. Their tribal capital was Serowe.

The next two largest tribes are the Bakwena and the Bangwaketse, who lived in the southwest near Gaborone. Smaller tribes are the Bakgatla, Bamalete and the Batlokwa in the southeast and the Baralong who extend over into South Africa. The eighth tribe is the Batawana who are found up in Botswana's northwest corner in the Ngamiland District, where the Kung Bushmen are and where our Hyena Camp was located. The Herero are more recent arrivals from German Southwest Africa, now Namibia, and are not counted in the original eight tribes that divided Botswana up some one hundred years before the Hereros' arrival.

The whole issue is land. Until fairly recently, the San had it all; now they have none. In Botswana, the Bantu say, "everything revolves around cattle, land and rain." Without land the others don't matter, so that the Bantu majority with their cattle ended up with most of the land.

There are three types of land ownership in Botswana: tribal land, freehold, and former British crown lands. A large percentage of the tribal land was left by the British for the eight established tribes to administer as they chose. Freehold land is that with individual title given or sold, like the Ghanzi farm block, European towns, land for industry, ranching, railroad and mines. The British crown land is now Botswana government land and mainly is in the parks and game reserves like the Central Kalahari, Chobe, Gemsbok, Nxai Pans and the like. The one group that did not get land in this scheme of things was the nomadic San. Because they were considered a savage people, drifting around in the bush or working as slaves for the Bantu tribes, they were not even considered for land in the tribal hand-out. They obviously wouldn't be given freehold land, since that was choice land given to someone to use to contribute to the gross national product. The San people's only chance at land was Crown land in the parks and game reserves where their animals live. That makes sense until the game conservationists suggested that anyone in the parks was a poacher or a threat to the animals' survival. So we find the San, who were here first, displaced and dispossessed of their land.

Botswana has a population of something like 1.2 million, spread over 570,000 square kilometers, an area slightly smaller than Texas. It has two people per square kilometer (five people per square mile), similar to Wyoming, America's second most sparsely populated state. Our least populated state, Alaska, has less than one person per square mile.

Botswana's population, which is only about one percent white or non-black or non-native, is concentrated in the railroad corridor from South Africa to Zimbabwe. The railroad cuts across the southeast corner of Botswana, passing through Mafeking, the old headquarters of the Bechuanaland Protectorate, then runs northeast through Lobatse where slaughter houses support the country's beef industry, through the modern sprawl of the capital Gaborone and on up to Francistown. It then passes out of Botswana into Zimbabwe, through Bulawayo to Victoria Falls and across the Zambezi into Zambia.

Eighty percent of the population is concentrated along the less arid railroad corridor that comprises less than twenty percent of the country's area. Everything else in Botswana west and north of the corridor is the sparsely populated Kalahari. It's there that the San have held out until recently.

"There are indications of Bushmen being dominated to the point of enslavement by the cattle raising Bantu, before the British came," said Map. "Probably more in the east where seven of the eight Bantu tribes live. These tribes have had longer contact with Bushmen and have, to a degree, assimilated them."

In fact, in 1926 the British High Commissioner found it appropriate to read a statement in the village of Serowe's *kgotla*, the traditional open air meeting place or administrative center in Bantu villages, in use up to today, that the government would not allow any tribe to demand compulsory service from another, and that Bushmen who wished to leave their masters were at liberty to do so. A later British proclamation in 1936 showed continued concern over the issue and stated that slavery in any form was unlawful.

"A common practice today is *sejara*," continued Map, "in which tame Bushmen will hire out for a year at a time to herd cattle for the pay of one cow. Under this system, Bushman often graze cattle deep into the bush away from permanent water holes, or they might bring them back to the corral daily. The Bantu practice has been to pay the Bushman with a male calf—not a female with which he could start his own herd—and thus keep him in a perpetual state of serfdom."

Anthropologists have noted that Bantus often refer to a San who does get a cow or two as an "uppity Bushman," not unlike how a white southerner might have disparaged a black who tried to improve his life a generation ago in America.

The livestock industry has become heavily dependent on the San as a labor source. Unfortunately, the top politicians and government officials are Bantu herd owners and have an ulterior motive to keep the San in their current deplorable state—simply not to lose their cheap labor source. So, as the San lose their land, they are incorporated into a system of exploitation they can't escape.

Looking forward to our evening visit with the neighboring clan, Tom asked Peter if it would be all right to take some Polaroid pictures to give to them. We'd been taking stills and videos with the Bushmen taking no apparent notice or objection, so there seemed to be no problem in taking their pictures per se. We had decided among ourselves that we wouldn't give them anything alien to their culture—nothing plastic, no food, no cans or bottles—remembering the disorienting results wrought by the infamous evil Coke bottle depicted in *The Gods Must Be Crazy*. Could giving them Polaroid photos of themselves contaminate or corrupt their natural existence? After some considerable discussion weighing the pros and cons, Peter voiced his reservations with, "We'll give it a try and according to what happens continue or back off."

Jim was not convinced that it was a good idea to take this risk of corrupting them. We knew, too, that many Africans who have been exposed to cameras don't like having their pictures taken, thinking that the person who takes the picture has a replica of them or has captured their spirit, which might be used in voodoo to cast an evil spell over them.

So, as the afternoon shadows were getting long, we again trod the kilometer through the sparse acacia thorn bush to find the clan around the communal fire. They were grouped closely together chattering and playing with the baby, interacting and enjoying their congenial family

Above: Noishay stretches down an arm's length for a tuber. With no surface water, the wild game also gets moisture from melons and tubers—but can't harvest to the depths a Bushman can.
—BG

Right: Noishay transfers tubers to females' karosses for carrying. —JP

Noishay digging tubers with a digging stick. —JP

Part of the barren Kalahari's reward for a day of foraging. —WT

Tasama melon gives the clan their daily sustenance— both food and drink. —BG (left), JP (above)

Right: Qui and Noishay "twisting" a fire for a smoke during a break from foraging. —JP

Below: The small girl in the foreground wears a typically tattered "hand-me-down" kaross. —JP

Above: A bi peeks out of the young unattached woman's kaross. —JW

Right: Noishay's wife pulping a tasama melon. —JP

Clan's older, unattached woman transferring harvest to her kaross. Women wear a breechcloth (has green spots in this case) under the kaross. —BG

Older unattached woman washes in the bitter juice of succulent bi tuber. —JP

Bushman awed at their first exposure to photography, explained by Keeme and Shylock (far left). —WT

... Polaroids spark a spontaneous celebration. —WT

unit. Shylock explained through Keeme that, if they agreed, we would give them Polaroid pictures we would take of them.

Thus, though the clan showed no objection when told that they were to be photographed with Polaroid, it is only fair to assume they couldn't possibly understand what it all meant, which proved to be the case. The amazement they showed when the pictures started coming out of the Polaroid camera was something to behold. They stared at us and at one another in amazement and disbelief.

Tom worked quickly through the clan so that after a short time there were pictures of everyone. Tom showed them the trick of waiting for the picture to develop. They stared, giggled, studied, compared, and to our relief, exhibited general elation over seeing pictures of themselves, especially the children and women. Our gamble had turned into a very animated, cheerful, gratifying session for us as well. Here was something that we could give these people that interested them. Having had their pictures taken at least once, the women grouped themselves around the communal fire and began a spontaneous clapping, accompanied by song; their way of showing their happiness and appreciation.

The elder of the clan, dour old Qui, held two Polaroid pictures of other clan members in his hand, looking at his clan members, then at the pictures, then at them with a look of utter amazement in his eyes.

Then Qui tied rattles, belts of cocoons filled with ostrich eggshell chips, around his ankles, took a wildebeest tail fly whisk in his hand and started a stamping dance to the accompaniment of the women's singing and clapping.

"We're seeing a little preview of their healing dance," observed Peter.

Jack summed up our feelings, "These people in their wild state are a priceless treasure. Peter, Map, what can be done for them to insure their cultural survival?"

"Something should be done," Peter responded. "You see how happy, healthy and active these people are. When we go through Xai Xai again, and on to Tsodilo Hills, you'll see the struggling tame Bushmen who have lost their land and given up their foraging culture. They seem starkly different. They look and act like people in a prison, their freedom and liberty taken away."

"But how many pure hunter-gatherers are there still out in the bush like this?" we wondered.

There are not very many, a few hundred at best. Back in the 1950's, van der Post and the Marshalls had a hard time finding any. With the rapid changes in the years since, there are certainly fewer now, and the forces of civilization and nature have them in a pincer. They are being forced out of their traditional places, game is dwindling and if a bore hole is put in, cattle herders move in and push them out.

Anthropologists believe that at most there are 40,000 San surviving in Botswana today, another 30,000 in Namibia with some fewer numbers in Angola. Further, that at the turn of the century, as many as sixty percent were still full-time hunter-gatherers, but by about 1975 the estimate was under five percent and dropping rapidly.

While Qui was dancing, Noishay picked out a tune on his thumb piano, a six-inch square piece of wood with metal keys that were probably made of wire off the border fence pounded flat on one end. This was one of the few possessions we saw beyond the clothing and jewelry on their bodies and their hunting and gathering tools. Music is important to them.

"Part of every leisure day," writes Lorna Marshall from her extended visits with the Kung in Namibia, "in a San encampment someone makes music." It could be tapping quiet tunes on a bow, or playing on the *gwashi*, a basic four or five stringed instrument like a guitar, made from a gourd, or the thumb piano. They have no drums, being ninety-second-travel-light people, whatever they possess must be carried in their small shoulder bags. And the voice has to be considered as an important but unencumbering musical instrument. The bow they must have, and with the bow they make music. Some say it was the original stringed instrument. In bow playing, the string is loosened from hunting taut, and the head end of the bow is placed in the mouth, which serves as a resonator for the music. Players strike the string with a small stick, or pluck the string with fingers. Sometimes a gourd resonator is used, leaving the mouth available to be a voice instrument. So, they improvise to make music in unencumbering ways.

Peter broke off our late afternoon visit by asking them when they were planning to hunt, and indicating that we'd like to tag along. Could we? There was an involved discussion with glances of skepticism cast in our direction. They hunt in small, quietly moving parties of two or three. We obviously looked a soft and fat crowd to these lean hunters. Eventually they said "yes." Yes, they were about to go hunting, and yes, we could plan to go with them the next day. We left for our camp in high spirits. The Polaroid picture gamble had worked out, and now they were going to let us join their hunt.

Back in our camp we gathered in our campfire circle of folding chairs and got into the Lion beer.

"Big John," Jack asked me, "in all your years in Africa have you ever seen anything like that?"

"These people's reactions to their first exposure to Polaroids was something to see," I responded. I recalled a somewhat similar experience when I was in the isolated Masai Steppes in Tanzania, an area as remote and unvisited by civilization as this. In that area in those days the Masai people were shy and had virtually no exposure to whites. Not the cheeky money-grabbing Masai that often line the road frequented by tourists in Kenya. They would come up and crowd around and be entranced to see themselves in the Landrover's side view mirror. They resisted being photographed. They feared the camera as an instrument of voodoo. But when given a Polaroid picture of themselves, they became completely engrossed in it. They went from fear, reluctance and apprehension to amazement and joy, and begged to have their pictures taken until film supplies were exhausted. The Polaroid broke the ice. While they were engrossed in Polaroid pictures, leisurely, unposed photographs with still and movie cameras were possible. Tom had obviously used his Polaroid as a come-on, much as the early explorers used colored beads.

The huge log I'd dragged in the previous morning had finally burned in two. I pulled the two logs together to fuel the fire. We could see a Wahlberg's eagle casting in the distance.

I knew I had been extremely lucky to have spent considerable time in the African bush, and with people like these. Part of the reward, whenever I get out in the bush, is I can really relax and I feel layers and layers of the tension that accumulate in a more hectic civilized life peel off. I mean really relax.

"But then you ask yourself," said Tom, "would you want to give up all you have and be like them?"

"No, you can't uninvent the wheel, but why ask them to give up their happy existence to join our materialistic rat race?" responded Jack. "We should want them to continue to be like they are, *if they want to.* Let them have a choice. Give them some land and leave them alone. Even the parks, where the last concentrations of their game are protected and where they can get some protection inside the park boundaries from civilized predators, the cattle barons, mining interests, whomever."

"They are caught in the crush of civilization," answered Peter. "It has gone on for over three hundred years, since the Dutch landed at Cape Town, and the Bantu cattle herders invaded from the east. There are very few that still hunt and gather, but as we've seen, those like Qui and his clan who have stuck to their traditional ways are a lot better off than those who have given up and squatted at a permanent water site like Xai Xai or Tsodilo Hills."

"That's the history, but what's the solution?" said Jack.

"The key is land," said Map. "They have been pushed off their traditional bush. Hunter-gatherers need a lot of territory. This clan is better off than the ones van der Post visited in the dryer and more barren Central Kalahari. It's more hostile there. But anthropologists and others that have studied these people think that it takes between ten and fifty square kilometers a person to support full time nomadic hunter-gatherers, to provide enough space to satisfy the requirements of the seasonally nomadic nature of both the San and their wild animals. Say twenty-five square kilometers as an average."

"That is a lot!" said Jack. "That's like ten square miles. The first population census in the United States back in 1800 showed that there were already five people per square mile!"

"What could we do for them? Lease some land as a sanctuary for them?" Joel wondered—a good-hearted if impractical idea.

The competition for land goes on. The Central Kalahari Reserve in Botswana was originally created for the Basarwa in the early 1960's. Van der Post books and lobbying activities deserve some credit for that. Anthropologist Silberbauer, who authored a chapter in Tobias', *The Bushmen*, in our field library made recommendations to the Bechuanaland government on the question and pushed for the Central Kalahari as a Bushman reserve. But now, under the banner of game conservation, some people want the San to be kicked out of the only Botswana reserve created for them. The European Community has given out sweetheart contracts to buy Botswanan beef at above open market prices. It is rumored that animal conservation organizations have put pressure on the EC, who have in turn pushed Botswana to eject the Bushmen from the reserve or lose their advantageous beef market.

Whether it is under this environmental-conservationist pressure or whatever, the government actually made the decision to evict the San in 1986, but there has been flack. The MP from the Ghanzi district, the administrative area within which the Central Kalahari Reserve falls, said he would leave the government if they evicted the Basarwa. They haven't moved, and have voiced a desire not to. It's still being debated. Survival International, a group headquartered in London, who champion the cause of aboriginal cultures worldwide, has mounted a letter-writing campaign against the eviction. They report some success in meeting with the Botswana government on behalf of the beleaguered Bushmen. The situation could conceivably be reversed. One problem is that Botswana hasn't found a suitable place in which to relocate the Bushmen outside the Central Kalahari.

"Isn't that where the Owens spent several years studying the lions and brown hyena and wrote *Cry of the Kalahari*?" Jim asked.

"Yes, that's the place," Map replied. "It's a huge area, twenty percent larger than Switzerland. The peoples inside the Central Kalahari Reserve are resisting the eviction. Third parties have lined up on both sides of the issue. It is rumored the cattle interests would like to get at the grazing, and the mining interests have prospected in the Reserve and supposedly they've found diamonds there. Hunter-gatherers face some strong, well-financed and politically savvy, antagonistic lobbies."

There's a saying in Botswana, "Beef is our currency." Among the Bantu, bride prices are usually negotiated in cattle, not the local currency. A large portion of the Bantu population owns cattle, but still half of all the cattle are in the hands of five percent of the owners, and, it has been pointed out, many of the top government officials in Gaborone are among those substantial cattle owners.

"The very people who have historically dispossessed and enslaved the Bushmen," said Jack. "The Central Kalahari sounds like the Black Hills of South Dakota. We gave the Indians some worthless land. Then when gold was discovered there, out with the Indians. How about getting some land elsewhere and making a people reserve, a bit like Bushmanland in Namibia?"

"But the South African government running Namibia is carving away at Bushmanland and other areas formerly occupied by Bushmen," said Peter. "Namibian game parks, like the recently created West Caprivi, Kaudom and the earlier Etosha are all traditional areas occupied until recently by the Bushmen, but when the parks were created they were evicted. As for creating a Bushmanland in Botswana, where? The Central Kalahari is the logical Bushmanland, and they are being kicked out."

"Jack, the real nut to crack is to get the conservationists to make an exception and accept Bushmen in the parks and reserves," I threw in. "They have been treated as worse than fauna, shot like wild dogs, overlooking their 10,000 year track record as practical conservationists. Now with a flip-flop of sorts, they are being lumped with the rest of us civilized, materialistic, poaching humans and excluded from the parks."

"Why can't an exception be made?" said Jack. "These people are uniquely valuable human beings. They are the quintessential foragers left on earth. People have called them living Paleolithic, or pre-agricultural revolution stone-age men. How much more exceptional could they be?"

"Yes. It was the rest of us—whites and Bantu—with our greed and firearms, who put the qagga into extinction," said Peter. "The qagga proliferated alongside the Bushmen for thousands of years before we came along."

The qagga was basically a variety of zebra, but striped only on the front quarter and brown on the back half. There used to be thousands of them in South Africa and Botswana. When Livingstone walked up through Botswana in the mid 1800's he reported great herds. They were shot into extinction by the early settlers during the last part of the 1800's.

"Just like the alarming rate the black rhino is disappearing all over Africa now," Jack added.

Game Conservation International, a hunting and conservation group headquartered in San Antonio, which I support, keeps abreast of the black rhino situation. They report poaching is worst north of the Zambezi River. In Zaire, Zambia, Tanzania, Kenya, Uganda and the Central African Republic it's especially bad for rhino but also for elephants. South of the Zambezi, in Botswana, South Africa, Namibia and Zimbabwe with most of its white game departments still in place, the situation is less grave. Authorities reckon that when Teddy Roosevelt, and as late as when Hemingway hunted in Africa, there were a half million black rhino. Ten to fifteen years ago they were down to 70,000. Today two, or at most three thousand are left. In Uganda, not one rhino has survived the proliferation of firearms in all the political and tribal turbulence that began with Idi Amin. And only a few hundred remain in the other east African countries, which is where the bulk of them originally were. There is a black market price tag of up to $25,000 on each of them for their horn, but the African poacher who actually kills them is led to do so for the payment of only a few hundred dollars. The bottom line is bleak.

"The black rhino is about to join the qagga as only a mount in a museum or a picture in a book," Jack said. "Like the endangered wild Bushmen who ironically couldn't care less about rhino horn or ivory."

Flashes of lightning and claps of thunder drew our attention. A thunder storm was blowing up. Our evening discussions were curtailed, then brought to an abrupt halt as rain drops began to fall. For the second night in a row we chided Peter with, "Hey, it never rains in the Kalahari in August, does it, Peter?" We headed for our tents. And did it come down!

—5—
Gcwihaba Caverns

I was on my knees in the predawn chill, rekindling the rain-doused campfire when Jack's voice came from his tent, "So, it never rains in the Kalahari in August, hey Peter?"

We were stirring early. It was just 5 a.m. We had arranged to be at the Bushmen's encampment to depart on the hunt at first light around six. We would have a full moon in a couple of days, and now the luminous moon hung in the western sky, making everything in camp softly visible despite the early hour.

It was clear and chilly after the rain. As I got the fire going, Map strolled over in his everyday uniform, short pants and shower shoes, to warm his hands.

"How was your bed under the stars," I asked.

"Not to worry," Map replied. "I took refuge in the pickup cab till the storm passed."

Soon Salome, Mansu and George were scurrying around preparing breakfast which we ate as we organized our gear for the long walk. "The day of the big hunt!" Joel exclaimed as he ran his belt through a loop in a liter water bottle on his hip. The level of excitement and anticipation was high, as, led by Peter and Shylock, we trooped off over the now familiar kilometer to the Bushmen's encampment. The white luminous moon was still hanging in the sky to our left, as the sun rose on our right.

We found the clan huddled in the morning chill around their diminutive, fuel-efficient family fires, in front of each flimsy shelter. Shylock and Keeme and the two hunters engaged in a rather long and involved conversation with animated gesturing and pointing, to a rapid fire staccato of clicks. Shylock turned to us with disappointing news. "Because of the heavy rains of last night, Qui and Noishay think that all the tracks will have been wiped out. They proposed to let game move about and establish new tracks and reschedule the hunt for tomorrow morning.''

Despite the jolt to our enthusiasm, Peter could only agree on our behalf to the postponement. We turned tail and retraced our steps.

"No problem. We'll visit Gcwihaba Caverns," said Peter as we proceeded back over the sand veld to our camp. "It is about twelve miles further down the road, away from Xai Xai to the east. Its really quite a cavern which only became known to Europeans when a Ghanzi farmer named Drotsky was taken there by Bushmen in the 1930's.''

Eleven of us set out in the two Toyotas. We paused several times as Peter, an ardent ornithologist, focused his binoculars on birds. There were guinea fowl and red billed francolin, a goshawk Peter identified as a pale chanting, several sabota lark as well as red capped lark and a lilac breasted roller.

Eventually we began to catch glimpses over the flat top trees of a large rock outcropping, a singular distinctive feature dominating the horizon ahead. Except for the rock formation at Aha Hill, this was the only prominent landmark or break in the rolling terrain we had seen since leaving Maun. There was a fork in the track as we approached Gcwihaba Hills. The left-hand track continued east around the south edge of the Okavango into Maun. We took the right branch up a slope leaving the ancient river bed and on to where the towering shiprock rose out of otherwise sandy terrain.

We stopped and climbed down, greeted immediately by a sharp, harsh barking sound. A male baboon was silhouetted on top of the rocky ridge a couple hundred feet above us.

"He is warning his clan, hidden from us on the backside of the hill, of the approach of humans," Peter said. The baboon persisted in barking and glowering down at us, then, turning and showing his red backside, disappeared over the hill out of sight and earshot.

"There's a Bushman fable concerning the baboon," Peter said. "Women won't go out food gathering alone for fear of meeting up with a legendary lusty baboon who is out to waylay any solitary woman.''

Armed with flashlights, we went to the north entrance of the cave. "This is a near virgin cavern," Peter had briefed us. "Because of its remoteness, it's seldom if ever visited by tourists. Someone has, however, strung a cord so we can find our way through the maze of cavernous rooms and passageways, but the cord is covered up with dust and sand in many places.''

"Sounds like something from Tom Sawyer and Huck Finn's cave exploring tales," said Bud.

Barn owls flew out as we entered the cavern's north entrance, and further in we encountered flying bats. Casting our lights around we saw more bats hanging from the stalactites decorating the ceilings. We all experienced a heavy foreboding when everyone turned off their flashlights for a few moments. The stale, musty air was laced with the scent of bat dung.

After going through a series of narrow passages into large chambers and then through even narrower passages then again into cavernous rooms, we came to an apparent end of the cave. A hemp rope hung down from a ledge on the cave wall. To proceed on from here we would have to use the rope to scale a vertical wall of some twenty-five feet to continue in a natural tunnel on a higher level that swung back in the direction we had come.

Map was the first up the rope, then Joel, Peter, Liza and Shylock struggled up the sheer wall.

"It's pretty tight here just after the rope climb," said Map. "Big John will have a time getting through. I suggest you go back out and walk around to the south entrance and come in there and meet us coming out."

As the five rope scalers continued through the maze of passages and chambers, we six others retraced our steps out into the bright daylight and along the flat, sandy terrain to the south entrance where we had to climb down a steep rubble slope through thick bush to reach the cavern's entrance level. Again we encountered barn owls that flew out past us as we descended to the cave mouth, and inside, bats took flight, retreating further back into the cavern's darkness. We followed the cord over the undulating, sand-covered floor, weaving through narrow passageways which then opened out into cavernous rooms between stalagmite columns and stalactite chandeliers.

We heard the muffled noise of the wall-scaling party approaching. "It was spooky," said Joel. "The string is gone or covered with dust or bat dung in places, and the way out is not obvious."

After clambering up the rubble incline out of the south entrance, we gathered around a sign board near the entrance bearing information about the cavern.

****

GCWIHABA CAVERNS

Protected under the National Monuments Act

These caverns have been formed during the last 50,000 years in dolomite marble of Damara age, mainly during periods when rainfall was probably four times heavier than it is today. Acidulated water flowing underground dissolved out the caverns. Later a river forming nearby lowered the water table emptying them. Rainwater, highly charged with bicarbonates, percolating through the upper rock, and dripping into the caverns, lost its carbon dioxide and formed fantastic stalactites and stalagmites.

Once on two levels, the intervening floor has collapsed in places leaving ridges on cavern walls to mark its original position.

Reflooding, evacuation and further dripping have resulted in deposits of different ages forming one upon another.

Earthquakes were probably responsible for the breaks in some stalactites.

Presently the caverns are refilling with wind blown sand.

There are two entrances. Visitors can pass from one entrance to the other through the whole series of caverns and passages by crawling and climbing, although great care should be taken.

In 1934 Martinus Drotsky, a Ghanzi farmer was taken to the cave by Qung San and publicized their existence. They remain today as he found them, unspoiled. PLEASE RESPECT THEIR BEAUTY, our natural heritage, and leave them undamaged for future generations to enjoy.

****

"How about the same concern for maintaining the wild Bushman and his culture unspoiled for future generations," groused Jim.

The cave exploring over, we gathered at the two Toyotas to head back to camp. The more avid exercise enthusiasts, Wally, our regular runner, Tom, a daily nervous walker, and Shylock and Liza decided to walk the twelve miles back to our camp.

Shortly after we rejoined the main track to head back for Hyena Camp, Bud pointed out a male ostrich in his black and white plumage making his high stepping exit, paralleling us on the ridge, his wings and tail feathers flopping.

Except for small birds this was our first game sighting aside from the baboon, and I found myself wondering how much game there is out here to hold the interest of the San. The country is fairly open, but still there is enough tree and bush cover to effectively camouflage the presence of any animals. But the real question was 'How could any animals survive in such dry country?'

Gemsbok, eland, wildebeest, kudu, ostrich and small game like duiker and steenbok can survive without surface water. They are found in this part of the Kalahari single and in small groups, but not in great numbers. They exist on the moisture in what they eat, which includes tasama melons and digging up underground tubers and bulbs. Animals which require more water, like buffalo, elephant and zebra, are not found here.

When the hikers got back in earshot of camp we heard Tom booming out, "Liza just about killed us." Wally and Shylock joined in grousing about the fast pace that Liza had set on the return hike from the cave.

"That was to get you in shape to keep up with the Bushmen, who are legendary walkers," was Liza's light-hearted rejoinder.

We gathered around our campfire to discuss the morrow's hunt. "Women don't go on the hunt," informed Liza. "That's taboo."

Observers have found that the men consider it bad luck to let women touch any of their hunting equipment, as it could weaken their 'hunter's heart' and detract from their hunting luck and skill. Women's power is creative and procreative, not killing power. Men also avoid contact with women just before they go out on a hunt.

Nor do women touch the oracle discs, usually a set of six, that the men throw and interpret as to which direction they should go and as to what will be the results of the hunt. The discs are two to three inches in diameter, made of a thick animal hide like eland to which the diviner or thrower gives different designations. There is always one called the brown hyena, a death thing to the hunters as it eats carrion, which we might call the joker in the deck. After throwing the discs they interpret them according to how they fall and which side of the different discs is up, in what might be considered the Bushman's version of a combination of tarot cards, dice, and heads and tails.

"Map, tell the lads about the Ghanzi farm block where Drotsky, who discovered the caverns, came from," Jack said.

"Well, first, Ghanzi is about as far south of us as Maun is east. Remember, most all of the towns and population in Botswana are in the narrow railroad corridor east of the Kalahari. Besides Maun, out in central and western Botswana there are no towns with Europeans except Ghanzi, the only other Kalahari community of any size with two to three hundred Europeans. The predominent population in the Ghanzi area is San."

In the 1890's, Cecil Rhodes got the British to settle some fifty Afrikaaner families in what is now called the Ghanzi farm block as a buffer to counter German expansion out of Southwest Africa, now Namibia. At that time the area was mainly occupied by San and a sprinkling from other tribes. The eighth Bantu tribe, the Batawana, who were concentrated to the north in Ngamiland where we were, claimed the area but the British ruled that the Bantu only hunted there, did not occupy it and thus, could not claim it. The Bushmen seemed to get along fairly well with the early Dutch Afrikaaners, who were poor and who often picked up the San languages. They employed some Bushmen as cattle herders and others for chores, and treated them paternalistically.

Ghanzi is also where the three main San languages meet geographically. Anthropologists and linguists have worked out that the Bushman click languages can be classified as Southern, Central and Northern. The now extinct South African Bushmen belonged to the Southern 'language group', a variation of which is still spoken in the southwest corner of Botswana by the Xo. The main Bushman population in Ghanzi are Nharo, who speak Central Bushman, along with the Gwi and Gana Bushmen of the Central Kalahari. The Auen Bushmen, who range northward from Ghanzi, are of the Northern language group, as are the Kung in the northwest corner of Botswana. This language group extends across into Namibia's Bushmanland, and on to the north into Angola.

Up until the mid-30's the area was still largely unfenced, with plenty of open veld between the Afrikaaners' cattle outposts. Game ranged through the area, and San continued to hunt and gather. But after World War II, especially in the 50's when the British government increased by fourfold the number of ranches, the mode of ranching was changing to fenced, less labor intensive, mechanized, efficient cattle raising. The game was cut off and driven away by the increasing and concentrated cattle herds, and the San were less needed as labor and herders.

This new breed of English rancher had no sentimental ties to the Bushmen, and, in fact, found them to be pests. The Bushmen became dispossessed squatters on land which had traditionally been their own, with wild game having dwindled or completely disappeared. The Bushmen, for whom stealing is unknown in their own culture, were now forced as a matter of survival into cattle thieving. One of the Bushmen would get a job, and his whole clan would move in to try to subsist on his meager income. If he then got fired, the clan would be run off the ranch, and no longer able to survive by hunting and gathering, would tend to squat around the water source. The Bushman was caught in a void between his vanishing culture and the encroachments of modern society.

The women, important contributors and providers in the foraging society, now had nothing to do; they had lost their identity and purpose, and tended toward prostitution and, like the men, drifted into alcoholism. The 10,000-year-old kinship family structure fell apart. The Ghanzi San are in an unhappy state, in conflict with Europeans and Bantu alike and unable to compete economically due to years of economic exploitation and low social status. Their culture, which was tied to the land and nature, has been destroyed. The Bushmen struggle to survive on the edge of the dominant culture, at or below the lowest rung of the social and economic hierarchy. They have been dispossessed of their land and culture, in exchange for what? The white man's diseases and vices?

The Ghanzi land board chairman has recently said that by establishing settlements in the area, the government wanted to encourage the Basarwa to abandon their hunter-gatherer ways and nomadic lifestyle. "It was easier for the government to provide social and other facilities in permanent settlements," Map concluded.

"There they go again," said Jack. "Change the Bushmen from happy nomads to despondent, sedentary types so government bureaucrats can administer them on a one-stop basis."

Ghanzi is the center of one of the largest concentrations of San in southern Africa. At Botswana's independence, two thirds of the 16,000 to 17,000 population were San, one quarter of all Botswana's Basarwa, a majority without work and, when employed, working for wages one third to one half that paid to Bantu. Its water wells have made it a concentration point for nomadic people from other areas during the frequent droughts. In the past there have been proposals to solve the

Bushman 'problem' by relocating them from Ghanzi to the Central Kalahari. Now, with the 1986 decision to evict the Bushman from their only Botswana reserve, the Central Kalahari, the very real Bushman problem is further exacerbated. Recent surveys by anthropologists in the Ghanzi district indicated that seventy-five percent of the San were intensely dissatisfied with their status as unwanted squatters on their own traditional land.

"So," Map said, "Ghanzi is a bigger and worse example of Bushman despair than you'll see at Xai Xai or Tsodilo Hills."

"Tell us a bit more about this area," said Jack. "We've been here two days, haven't seen another vehicle, or, outside of Qui and his band, another soul from Xai Xai to the caves."

"Bushmen had all of the Kalahari, in fact, all of Botswana, to themselves, until about 1770 when the first significant numbers of Tswana-speaking black Bantu herders came in from the east, from what is now Zimbabwe," Map said. "Bantu herders did not appear on the scene up here in Botswana's northwest corner, Ngamiland west of the Okavango, until the 1880's, when they first visited seasonally in the summer rainy season to graze their cattle herds. They had an annual trading session with the Bushmen, which was the first time the Bushmen were exposed to metal for arrow and spear points. It was not until around 1925 that the Bantu started to take up year round residence.

"No whites have ever lived up here. The first small trading post was not opened until 1967 in Qangwa, a village north of Xai Xai of about a hundred people, and then the first school opened in 1973 to serve a scattered population of about a thousand, two thirds of whom were Bushmen."

In 1950 the Marshall family decided that the best examples of wild Bushman were in Nyae Nyae, just west of the present camp of Qui and his clan. They spent considerable time over the next ten year period with the Ju/wa Kung, whom they found isolated, without contact with whites or civilization except for fleeting glances. One old Bushman recounted having seen the Germans pursuing the Herero through the area in the 1905-1906 wars. The Bushmen reported a solitary German had escaped British imprisonment at the end of World War I by fleeing into their remote bush area.

The border between what are now Namibia and Botswana was surveyed in 1933, bringing white surveyors briefly into the area. In the days before the four wheel drive, the Kung reported twice seeing Southwest African police come on camel patrols to expel Herero who were grazing across from Botswana. The Bushmen reported having seen one white diamond prospector prior to the Marshalls' arrival. That was the extent of their exposure to the outside world until 1950!

It had taken the Marshalls eight days to cross the remote, trackless Kalahari into Nyae Nyae from the west in 1951. A few months later white farmers followed the Marshalls' track into the previously virgin bush and shanghaied Kung as unwilling workers, people who were never seen again by their nomadic kin. There was a 1957 police visit in a four wheel vehicle, to persuade Botswana Herero to take their herds back across the border.

"The long and short," said Jack, "Up here in Ngamiland, the northwest corner of Botswana, is one of the most desolate, remote, sparsely inhabited areas in Botswana, if not the globe."

It was late in the afternoon. Peter suggested we make a short visit to Qui's camp to tie down the particulars of the next day's rescheduled hunt. As we left our camp, Jack and Joel were lagging a bit behind. We had already arrived at the Bushman encampment, and started our discussions when Jack and Joel showed up.

"I just came within an inch of stepping on a snake!" exclaimed Jack. "Joel skip-jumped over it and warned me. I stepped right up against it, not on it, but right against it." Jack described the snake to Peter and Map.

"From your description, it was most probably a puff adder," Peter said. "They're the most common poisonous snake." Puff adders are lethargic and tend not to move, but strike when stepped on, and account for more snake bite incidents than all the other more potent and feared species together. They inject a cytotoxic poison which attacks the flesh and turns it rotting and gangrenous. Little did we know we were in for more puff adder encounters later.

The Bushman clan was closely grouped around one of the family fires inside the circle of shelters. The baby was getting its usual attention, being held by some of the children in the clan until he wanted to nurse and was passed to his mother's arms. Then as we watched, he amused himself by crawling after and rolling a tasama melon around in the sand.

The Kung children have a close mother infant bond of long duration. They nurse longer than western children, often suckling until they are three years old or older, since this is often the only source of liquid nourishment in their usually waterless environment. Children receive close exposure to other children and adults in the extended family. Mothers and the whole clan practice full-time bonding for eighteen months to two years after the child starts walking, which studies show they do early, relative to western children. Perhaps if western mothers walked everywhere they went, western children would walk earlier than they do.

"Bonding is all the rage in the psychiatry field right now, " noted Joel. "With more mothers working, they often don't nurse or have a lot of holding contact— bonding—with their infants, and it's now blamed for much of the neurotic, emotionally disturbed behavior in later life."

"Yes," added Jack. "We've lost it. They still have it, in spades."

Bushmen women have no means of birth control or abortion and so are occasionally forced by the harsh survival conditions into practicing infanticide. Children nurse for three or four years and are usually

Noishay's wife—a
Bushman profile.
—JP

Noishay's wife
quietly observes
the intruders. —JP

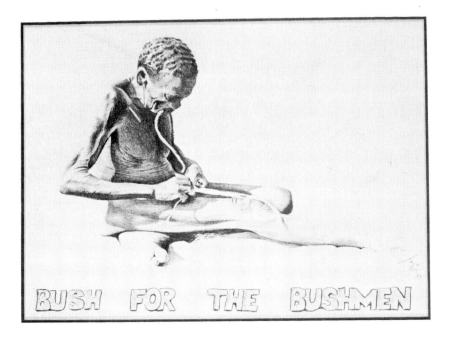

BUSH FOR THE BUSHMEN

A QUAIL IN OFFICE IS WORTH 2 FOR BUSH!

Liza's sketches inspired by the Wheeler group's passionate save-the-Bushman campfire discussions. —IP

74

spaced this many years apart because mothers can't carry or nurse two babies at a time. Should a woman become pregnant too early with a second child she might 'throw down' her newborn, rather than risk neither child surviving the 'on-the-edge-of-survival' nomadic life. Other circumstances leading to infanticide are an obvious birth defect, twins, or a mother being too old to provide the required milk.

A Kung woman goes into the bush near camp to give birth. She is usually alone but might be accompanied by her mother if she is young and inexperienced. If it is decided not to keep the baby, no crime or moral sin has been committed. The incidence of infanticide is quite low—one study showed six cases in five hundred live births—due to naturally low fertility and high natural infant mortality from other causes.

The planning for the next day's hunt had precipitated an involved discussion. Much pointing off in different directions took place, while we listened to the staccato of clicks. Finally the plan for the hunt was decided. Had they thrown the oracle discs to help them decide what the hunt's direction would be?

"Tomorrow we will hunt in this direction," Shylock informed us, pointing off to the south east. "They want to visit a bush some miles out that way where they get the grubs that they use to poison their arrows." They were to come down the vehicle track to our camp, and we were to leave from there. We could expect them about seven in the morning.

Back in camp we gravitated around our campfire. "Shower is on," announced Peter, starting the evening parade through our bush shower as the sun went down in the western sky.

As darkness fell, the Kalahari's evening winter chill set in. As we enjoyed the warmth of our fire, Map began to tell us more about the Bushman. "The importance of the fire to the Bushman cannot be overemphasized. We have houses with a stove or fire. The Bushman has his fire close to his meager shelter, but the shelter is largely symbolic. He lives around the fire."

Authorities have pointed out that in their simple existence the hunter-gatherers have three necessities: food, water and fire. The fire is for comfort and protection and, in the case of the Bushman, to a much lesser degree for cooking. But Bushmen live by and sleep by their fire, not in the diminutive shelter.

One of the Bushmen stories sung to the strumming of the gwashi, is the stump song. It is about a man lost in the bushveld. As he wanders around, it is getting dusk. He is anxious about a night in the bush alone with no fire. Anyone ever lost in the woods would know his feelings. Then he sees another man in the distance. Happy, he imagines company, two at a fire, companionship. He waves to the man in the distance, runs towards him, but on approaching he is disappointed to see that it's only a stump. He faces a sad night alone in the bush with no fire.

In San custom, there's a male and female side of the fire. As one faces the shelter, looking over the fire, the men sit on and sleep on the right, the women on the left. It is taboo for the women to sit on the men's side and vice versa.

The fire also has spiritual significance. If the Bushmen are dogged by misfortune at an encampment they will move sooner rather than later. They look to a new fire at a different location for a fresh start, leaving any past misfortune behind. Their ceremonial dance fire is set apart, out in the center of the encampment, not at one of the family hearths. This fire is always started new by twisting a fire, not by coals from one of the individual family hearths burning nearby.

The Bushmen shout out "Fire" each time they pitch the oracle discs, since fire is so crucial to their fortunes. The Bushmen, as the Aborigines often do, burn off the dry grass at the end of the dry season, to clear the way for the new growth the rains bring. Our own fire was settling into embers and the surrounding darkness was softened by a moon growing full.

"Map gave us a campfire thumbnail of the Bushmen's history since the Dutch landed at Cape Town in 1652," said Jack. "There's an amazing parallel in Australia since the first Australian settlers landed in Botany Bay, near today's Sydney, in 1788."

The Europeans had come to Australia for land, and they took it, like the Dutch had in South Africa and the Americans did from the Plains Indians. Up to the 1880's the official Australian policy was "pacification by force," which meant that if the Aborigines resisted the taking of their land, they were dealt with severely, and this led to some appalling massacres.

In 1988 the Australian Telcom Company handed over to the traditional Aborigines a telegraph station in Barrow Creek in the Northern Territories where a massacre of 90 Aborigines took place in 1874, during the construction of the overland telegraph. It had been a drought year. The local Aborigines were searching for food and water, and the white linemen refused to share their rations. In the altercation that ensued, two whites were speared by the Aborigines. In retaliation the authorities sent out a force and killed 90 Aborigines, most of the Aborigine clan. As late as the 1920's there was another infamous Aborigine massacre at Coniston. These were but two of many.

By the early 1900's it was thought that the remaining Aborigines would just conveniently die out. The Australians had an unstated policy towards the Aborigines, somewhere between planned extinction and extermination. Those in metropolitan areas were to become coloreds, then whites, through mixed marriages. Those in rural areas were to quietly die out of disease and drunkenness, dispossessed of their traditional land, and thus their culture. In the 1920's and 1930's Aboriginal reserves were created, and Aboriginal people were herded onto them to be looked after by the government in a bureaucratic, paternalistic way. In many cases their children were taken from them, to be educated 'not to be savages.' Adults were trained to do menial work, house servants for the women, livestock station hands for the men. Traditional and ceremonial life and culture were discouraged, continued only under cover and out of sight.

The rough and ready land hungry settlers had no appreciation for a culture that had existed, in tune with nature, with more than 40,000 years recorded in rock paintings; a culture and economy that had provided for centuries a living standard in terms of food and shelter that was up until 100 years ago higher than that of Europe's middle class!

When the Aborigines appealed the taking of their land in the courts, the white man's system, they were confronted with a doctrine that maintained that if an indigenous people had not risen above the state of nature, i.e. occupying the land with permanent buildings, fences, tilling, planting, improving the land where they resided, then the territory that made up their nomadic range could be classified by the discoverers as *terra nullius*, or empty land. The newly arrived white settlers could gain permanent legal title to those lands by discovery and effective occupation, or by dispossessing the nomadic aboriginal people, who were considered to be on a level little better than wild animals.

The genocide, the dispossession, first by force and then by law suffered by the Aborigines led two Aborigine leaders of the day, Ferguson and Patten, to call Australia Day in 1938, commemorating 150 years of white occupation, as a day of mourning with their proclamation:

****

The Old Australians

You are the new Australians, but we are the old Australians. We have in our arteries the blood of the Original Australians, who have lived in this land for many thousands of years. You came here only recently, and you took our land away from us by force. You have almost exterminated our people, but there are enough of us remaining to expose the humbug of your claim as white Australians to be a civilized, progressive, kindly and humane nation. By your cruelty and callousness towards the Aboriginies you stand condemned in the eyes of the civilized world.

****

Aboriginal people were pushed off 'their country.' Earlier on there were the massacres, and there were 'white men's diseases,' but a lot of aboriginal people simply died because they could not carry out their responsibility to 'their country.' They were put under too much stress, being arbitrarily moved to strange places and forced to adapt to a strange 'civilized culture', at odds with their concept of living with nature, an undisturbed nature. Aboriginal people still die today because of the extreme cultural shock of rapidly changing from near stone age hunter-gatherers to moving into our atomic age.

The Aborigines' notion of the relationship with the land is a very complex one. In one of its meanings the 'dreaming' was the formative or creative period at the dawn of time when the mythic ancestral beings shaped or created the land, establishing human life and culture, and brought various animal species into life. The early ancestors left their marks on the land, and disappeared into it at various points which are of extreme significance to Aborigines. Aboriginal people 'know' where they come from and their genealogy starts from those original people. That's one level of the spiritual tie to their land.

"But finally in the 1960's and 1970's," said Jack, "There were watershed changes, and the Aborigines got some of their land back."

Two things happened in the 1960's that got the whole Aboriginal question into the political arena. First, thirteen clans of Aborigines living in and around the Yirrkala mission on the Cove Peninsula on the east tip of Arnhemland in the Northern Territories were confronted with the federal government offering some of their land to a consortium which was going to mine bauxite. The Aborigines tried but failed in the high courts to stop this giveaway of their land. The Aborigines went as far as painting their title to the land on a 'bark petition' and taking it to Canberra, Australia's capital, where it is still on display in Parliament House.

Secondly, in 1966 the Gurindju, an Aboriginal clan, walked off a cattle post owned by a wealthy European white where they had been assigned, to protest poor living and employment conditions. They camped at the nearby Wave Hill welfare center, and petitioned to lease some 600 to 700 square miles of what they considered their land. In line with the policies then in vogue, the Governor General of the Northern Territory turned them down. These events got press coverage, leading to increased public outcry to do something for the Aborigines, to give them more land and equal treatment.

"It was all part of a strong ground swell movement," said Jack. A 1967 referendum was a turning point. It gave the Commonwealth in Canberra the power to count Aborigines in the census for the first time, and took steps to treat Aborigine people as full citizens, rather than paternalistically as incapable and inferior wards of the government. For the first time, this new policy allowed and encouraged assimilation of the Aborigines into the mainstream, with self determination, but with their culture intact, instead of the earlier forced integration with destruction of their culture.

The ground swell led on to the 1972 election of the Labor government, espousing Aborigine rights, helped by the international embarrassment of months of the tent 'Aboriginal Embassy' in

Canberra. Labor's election led to the Northern Territory Land Rights Act of 1976. By the late 1980's, under the Aboriginal Land Rights Act, 36% of the land in Northern Territory has been granted to the Aborigines! There was another 12% in the courts under Aborigine claim. The way land claims have gone over the past few years, it is likely that out of that 12% the original Aboriginal owners will probably get about half back. So the Aborigines may end up with something like 42% of the Northern Territory.

Under the 1976 Act, it is now on the Aborigines' say-so that mining goes ahead or not on their land, and if there's mining they get their fair share of the rewards. Since the land reform of 1976 the Aborigines are the official owners of the Northern Territory's national parks, like Kakadu and Uluru, which is where world famous Ayer's Rock is. The Aborigines lease the park land back to the Australian national parks, but the Aborigines retain the power to throw out people who desecrate their ancestral sites, or the parks in general.

What caused the ground swell? By 1967 the Australians were 180 years down the track of Aboriginal dispossession, genocide, massacres, persecution and neglect, then more recently continuing unjust laws against the Aborigines. Too many Aborigines were dying in police custody. The Aborigines continued to be held back at low economic levels by the vicious cycle of poverty, ignorance, disease and infant mortality, which in Australia runs five times higher for Aborigines than for whites.

The Aborigines themselves and their non-Aborigine protagonists were getting more of these issues into the press and on television. These were the days of the civil rights movement in America. It was the international mood of the day. The movement aroused a latent guilt movement in the white electorate. The Aborigines were in a sad state, and the 'winds of change' were blowing. Anti-colonial sentiment since World War II had spread internationally, and Australia's citizenry was sensitive to the intense and unprecedented criticism of its treatment or mistreatment of the minority Aborigines with uncomfortable and telling parallels being drawn with South Africa under headline banners like "Australian Apartheid".

Then an 'Aboriginal Embassy' sprung up in a tent in Canberra during the 1972 elections, which further captured the imagination and attention of the media in Australia and around the world for the Aborigines' cause.

Until recent changes, the Aborigines did not have a vote, weren't counted in the census, couldn't buy or drink alcoholic beverages, were treated as sub-civilized human wards of the government, and were denied title to their own land. Down through the years, whenever the Aborigines got in the courts claiming land in disputes with whites, they always lost under the umbrella of 'terra nullius.' So in 1972 the Aborigines finally said, "We are foreigners in our own country! Foreigners have an embassy to look after their interests." So some

Aborigines set up a tent embassy in Canberra. For months this proved to be an international embarrassment to the Australian government.

With the 'Aboriginal Embassy' and changing public sentiment, Labor won the 1972 election. Labor was in power for the first time in 26 years and initiated drastic changes benefiting the Aborigines, not the least of which was the Northern Territory Land Rights Act of 1976.

In the Northern Territory, land councils were created to help Aboriginal communities cope with the complexities of 'white man's law' involved in the Act.

Aborigines have been quoted as comparing white man's laws to the Aborigines' saying, "The Aborigine law is straight like an arrow, as it has been for centuries. White man's law is crooked like a snake!" The Aborigines are reacting to their frustration with our myriad of complicated laws to which we are continually adding new ones, changing or repealing the old ones, and changing interpretations in the courts. Then we have our frequent elections, bringing in new regimes that have a different emphasis, who treat the Aborigines differently, or subjectively. In the Aborigines' view our bureaucracy, and its laws, are 'crooked like a snake.'

The Australians have, however, made some accommodations for the conflicts between the Aborigines' strong culture and simple but strict laws, and 'modern' law. Aboriginal culture and laws include 'payback,' wherein injustices are dealt with directly by Aboriginal individuals in an 'eye for an eye, tooth for a tooth' justice without the intervention of courts, police or third parties. There have been several recent examples of what we would term murders between Aboriginal individuals. The white authorities have come up with an accommodation in both systems. First, on the report of an Aboriginal killing, the authorities approach the Aboriginal elders. If the case is deemed to be a case of 'payback' condoned by the Aboriginal elders in Aboriginal law, the police close their books on the case. Only if they are informed it is not a 'traditional Aboriginal' killing do they pursue the case further under white man's justice.

"That there was such a turnaround," observed Jack, "Even if only in the Northern Territory, in giving the Aborigines land and control over it and their lives in the 70s and since, is a concrete example that might be emulated or give direction for something similar for the Bushmen in Botswana and Namibia."

There was some comfort in the knowledge that their Aboriginal cousins' recent experience could provide a light in the tunnel for the Bushmen. Could this be the avenue, the answer the San need for land and cultural self determination?

"The real point is," said Jack, "How to achieve the 'not yet' parallel of reacquiring for the aboriginal land owner in Botswana and Namibia, the San, similar secure land and self determination. Being positive the Aboriginal precedent in Australia is in place. Parallel or similar treatment for the Kalahari Bushmen coming up!"

On this optimistic note we departed the glowing campfire for our tents.

We did not know it then, but a similiar land deal was brewing in Canada, to be announced late in 1991—giving the Inuits the Arctic frontier, approximately 20% of Canada's significant land mass.

—6—
The Hunt

It was getting light. Another magnificently clear and winter-crisp day was unfolding on the Kalahari. The sun had yet to peep over the horizon and a large luminous white moon still hung in the western sky. I was pulling logs together, livening up the fire. "The big day of the hunt ... again," whispered Joel with an air of excitement as he came out of our tent. Soon our group were gathering around the fire, drawn by its welcome warmth.

"These men usually hunt solo or in pairs," Map briefed us. "It is very unusual for them to agree to have such a troop as you along on the hunt. If they get on a good track, you'll have to lay back and let them go ahead and shoot or you could spook the animal before they get close enough. With their light bows and flimsy arrows they need to get to within thirty meters. If the animal is hit they'll take off cross country, following its track at a trot. You'll have a time keeping up with them."

The San use a small bow only three feet long with an animal sinew bowstring. Their tree bark and hide arrow quiver is about two feet long, holding arrows twenty inches long. The arrow has a four part construction: the tip, formerly made of bone, now usually made from pounded fence wire, the shaft, and a two-part connection between arrow and shaft designed to encourage the shaft to drop off so the animal cannot, in running, remove the poison arrow point. Similar four part arrows dating back 5,000 years have been found by archaeologists leading them to speculate that the present day arrow design and use of poison have been known for a considerable time.

Map was not to accompany us on the hunt; he was preparing to go ahead and set up our next camp at Tsodilo Hills, taking one of the two Toyotas. We would temporarily miss his wealth of information.

While having breakfast, we gathered canteens of water and cameras and other gadgets, some of the latest from Eddie Bauer or Banana

Republic, and attached them to our clothing, around our necks and on our belts. We had been impressed with the tales of the way the San cover country, so we expected a fast and strenuous walk over a considerable expanse of terrain, but how long we would be out or how far we would go, no one knew. Despite our effort to travel light, we were to find we were still too loaded down. We waited anxiously for the hunters to arrive.

Jim, the senior member of our group, decided not to participate in the toilsome day, but rather to stay in camp to read from our camp reference library. We remaining six, plus Peter and Shylock, would shadow the hunters.

Qui, Noishay and Keeme put in their appearance, gliding swiftly and silently down the vehicle track at about 7:30, stopping well outside our camp area.

"They would never think of barging into a European camp like we do into theirs," Salome commented.

We joined them as they headed off smartly into the bush at an easy, fluid pace. We were going south. Our backs were to the track leading east toward Maun and west toward Xai Xai and the direction of the Namibian border. The two hunters and Keeme were leading at their brisk pace, and as we had expected, we were pushed from the outset to keep them in sight. At times we were all in single file. At other times the two hunters and Keeme would fan out and parallel each other ten to twenty meters apart, allowing them to cut more territory in their lookout for tracks or any other signs indicating game.

And what a contrast between us and the Bushmen! The hunters were bare of foot and body except for their brief gameskin loin cloths. Their breechcloths feature two tabs at the back, shaped like butterfly wings placed at exactly the right place to protect their otherwise exposed buttocks when they sit down. Qui had on a green and white beaded headband. Qui and Noishay each carried diminutive shoulder sacks made of warthog skin containing quiver, arrows and spears. During the course of the hunt, they would produce out of their shoulder bags tobacco, metallic tobacco holders and fire-making sticks.

Keeme, taking a short leave from his herding, was not armed, indicating that he was along primarily as the translator.

Shortly after we got into the Bushmen's pace, we were sweating profusely. Despite it being the dead of winter here in the southern hemisphere, we were already feeling the effects of the day's rising heat and lack of any significant breeze.

The hunters came to an abrupt halt about an hour out, spying a single distinct track crossing our path and leading off to the right.

The hunters entered into a low-voiced, animated, clicking conversation. Keeme briefed Shylock, who then turned to us, pointing to the tracks and where the bark had just recently been rubbed off a small bush. There was excitement in the air!

"It's a gemsbok. It passed here just about daylight."

We could see clearly where this large antelope had stopped momentarily and scraped at the bark with his long, straight horns. In the soft Kalahari sand the gemsbok's deep tracks had broken through the sundried surface to wet sand underneath, where the heavy rain of two nights before had penetrated. Even to our untrained eyes, the tracks were still moist and fresh.

The San are renowned trackers, able to deduce a wealth of information from a set of tracks, from leaves or bent grass. They have been observed tracking a wounded animal into a herd and, when the wounded animal later split out, never losing the track of the wounded animal, despite the jumble of similar tracks. To San hunters an individual hoof track is as personal as a fingerprint.

Our level of anxious anticipation rose. What luck to be on such a good, hot track so early. The hunters set off swiftly, following the track. Then after a few hundred meters they stopped. After some rapid clicking discussion and gesturing, they abruptly turned around and walked back through our puzzled group.

Dr. Wheeler, with a bit of consternation asked Shylock what they were saying.

"It's a good fresh track," was Shylock's response. "But the wind is at our backs. They've worked out that if we follow the gemsbok and get close, our scent will be carried ahead to it on the wind and he'll run. They reckon it's no use."

We were left standing around, a bit confused and frustrated. Would they reconsider? This was a really good track, too good to pass up in an area which as far as we could tell was sparsely populated with game. But the Bushmen were rapidly back-tracking to pick up the point where we had encountered the gemsbok track. They then resumed their original course at a swift pace. It was their hunt. We were just excess baggage and observers. Off we went at a fast pace to catch up or risk being left lost in this vast monotonous bush, devoid of any landmarks or clues to direction.

When you pit man against animal, it is man's advanced knowledge, communication abilities and planning versus the animal's physical advantages. The animal's most significant advantage is a much better sense of smell. The hunter must approach the animal from downwind so that the animal does not get the hunter's scent and bolt and run. Here we were seeing an example of man the hunter using knowledge and acute observation to overcome the animal's sensory advantage. Wind direction is everything to the hunter.

So, too, is silence. How these hunters must be annoyed by this gaggle of eight noisy strangers! Despite our efforts to be quiet, we sounded like a small army moving through the dry bush rattling leaves and breaking twigs. I thought back to when I was hunting seriously in East Africa. If a bunch like ours had shown up and wanted to tag along on my walking and stalking hunts, I'd have said, 'No way!'

We proceeded another half an hour, when a steenbok jumped up just off to our right and darted and dashed off through the low scrub and bushes and disappeared some twenty meters away. The hunters in the lead had already passed, thus had not seen the small buck flush. Shylock, bringing up the rear, called ahead to Keeme, who told the two armed hunters. They doubled back and pulled their bows and poisoned arrows out of their shoulder bags and armed their bow strings. They seemed a bit disinterested in this rather small animal that reaches a maximum of only thirty pounds, while the gemsbok they had just passed up might be as big as 450 pounds and well worth the chase. Without much delay or effort at tracking, they soon pushed on again.

The country was without much grade, just gentle up and down rises of sandy ground. Still, walking was difficult, the sand giving away under our feet. While we slogged along trying to keep up, the San hunters seemed to glide over the surface. The area we were passing through was covered by sparse stalks of dry winter grass, with only a few thorny bushes and well-dispersed small stunted trees, providing only a minimum of shade.

Then about mid-morning the hunters again abruptly interrupted their progress, tracking out to their left where a large animal had crossed us. They tracked it for about 150 meters, stopped and had a brief clicking discussion. Then they gave it up, came back past us to resume their original direction, always towards that one bush that would provide the grubs and poison for their arrows.

"They say it was a blue wildebeest," said Shylock, "But from the leaves and condition of the tracks, it must have passed through here about three in the afternoon yesterday. It will be too far away by now to be worthwhile to track."

The gnu or blue wildebeest can weigh up to 350 pounds. It is one of the more common large game animals in the dry Kalahari environs, surviving on moisture off leaves, by eating melons and gemsbok cucumbers and digging up some of the shallower bulbs and tubers with its hooves. In *Cry of the Kalahari* the authors, the Owens, reported that in recent years in the northeast corner of the Kalahari Game Reserve, wildebeest died by the thousands up against hoof and mouth control fences, which kept them from migrating to water sources outside the reserve during a prolonged drought.

Another welcome rest period came when we passed a clump of tall reeds, and the hunters stopped to gather some of the stalks.

"Those reeds are what they use for shafts for their arrows," Peter informed us. "They seem quite light and fragile, but keep in mind, the shaft only has to deliver the poisoned head into the animal's flesh and can then drop off."

It is the powerful poison that eventually kills the game, not the physical wound made by the arrow point and shaft. The poison is not put on the arrow tip, for fear of the hunter accidently sustaining a cut, but rather is placed just behind the arrow tip where the poison will come in contact with the open wound.

A little later we were back moving rapidly through the bush, fanned out in three parallel lines. I was in the middle file following Qui, Noishay was off to the left while to the right was Keeme. Suddenly our attention was drawn to Keeme who took a sudden jump step, went a couple of steps, and turned. Joel who was just behind Keeme was staring intently at the ground. Everybody had stopped to see what had occurred.

"He just about stepped on another snake," Joel said in hushed tones.

We all gathered around for a look. It was an eighteen inch puff adder lying directly across Keeme's line of march. We were meandering and zig-zagging along in the light scrub, keeping to the naturally open avenues between the bushes and small trees. There were no trails, per se, since there was neither enough game nor any people to make distinct trails. The fat, lethargic snake had not moved. Keeme's foot print was right up against the snake. By pure chance he had not stepped on it, but only up against it.

Keeme's not having seen the snake until he was almost on it was understandable. We had to peer intently to see the well-camouflaged mottled grey-brown-black colored snake, lying in multi-colored dried leaves and twigs. It was a very close call. Keeme was well within striking range of the motionless snake, but fortunately no damage had been done.

Without disturbing the snake, the hunters pushed on and we were back to playing catch up. At one point they stopped and dug up some tubers to give them a bit of food and moisture.

"They travel light, no food or water," Peter said, "picking up what they come across." Meanwhile we were using our limited water supply much too fast. I had two one-liter plastic bottles and was already well into one of them. I admonished myself to go slowly on the water, as we would not find more and had no idea how far this hunt might take us.

"How are you faring, Big John?" Jack asked during one of our welcome pauses.

"Like a greenhorn. I know better, but I'm drinking my water too fast," I admitted. "On daylight to dusk elephant tracking walks in my Tanzania hunting days, my Masai Steppes Ndorobo tracker counseled me not to drink at all before noon, and then to drink sparingly, rather than drinking early and having to endure the heat of the day and the long afternoon painfully dry." I had been out of the bush for too long.

Then we were off again. Wally, the fit runner, and youthful Joel were doing better than the rest of us keeping on the hunters' tail. Eventually, toward mid-day, Qui and Noishay stopped at a particular bush they recognized and started digging. Shylock informed us that it was here that they expected to find the grubs that they use to poison their arrows.

Dr. Wheeler, who had been lagging a bit behind, was the last to arrive and started to collapse to catch his wind in the meager shade of a bush slightly apart from the digging operation.

"Jack! Look out," Tom cried.

Jack bolted up and away, then whirled around to look. All eyes turned to where Tom was pointing. There, under the bush, was a hole, and framed in freshly disturbed sand was the protruding head of yet another puff adder. We stood transfixed, watching the motionless snake. Then it slowly came slithering up out of the hole and moved in under the bush through the mat of twigs and dead leaves, exposing the three-foot length of its fat and grotesque body.

"Look at the size of that bastard," exclaimed Jack. "And I almost sat down next to it ... this place is crawling with snakes."

Meanwhile, the two hunters, attracted by the disturbance, gave the snake a quick, disinterested look and then returned to their digging. After about fifteen minutes, having excavated two feet below ground and sifting the sandy soil through their fingers, they came up with two brown cocoons the size of large beans. They showed obvious disappointment at not finding more.

"They need about eight of these grubs to poison one arrow," Shylock informed us. It was becoming clearer why the hunters were so careful in their search of prey. Not only was game scarce but the things they needed for killing an animal were scarce as well.

"These cocoons and larvae come from a beetle with the Latin name *Diampaidium*," Peter said.

The beetle responsible for the buried larva first lays its eggs on the leaves of the host plant, often the marula tree. The larva hatches and crawls down under the bark to the base of the tree and into the ground, where it encloses itself in the cocoon to pass through the metamorphic change from larva to beetle. It is only the larva in this cocoon stage that is poisonous, not the beetle itself. The San can find the larva in the cocoon stage only seasonally. Scientists have puzzled over how they ever discovered the poisonous qualities of the beetle's larva, which is so essential to their hunting culture. When questioned, they have been quoted as saying, "The Great God gave only us the knowledge of poison, while he gave the Bantu the knowledge of planting and domesticating animals."

After this welcome break in the fast pace, we were on with the hunt. Having reached their grub location, which until then had determined the direction of the hunt, the hunters did not turn back north toward camp as I was secretly hoping they would, but they did shift their course perceptibly to a more easterly, or even northeasterly direction.

As the day progressed and got hotter, we continued to get strung out after each pause and were having more trouble keeping up with the sizzling pace.

Then the hunters stopped abruptly, having cut some new tracks. After the usual animated discussions Shylock reported, "A pair of eland."

Eland! The eland, biggest of the antelope, can weigh up to 1500 pounds. They are the subject most frequently featured in the San rock paintings. In the Bushmen lore and mythology, the eland was the first animal created by the great God, to accompany them on earth. There is an oft repeated tale of a judge many years back having some Bushmen before him for breaking some white man's law which they little understood. The judge was curious about these strange savages and their beliefs and asked them, "Where is your God?" The men responded, "We can't tell you, but the eland know."

After following the eland tracks for a reasonable distance, the hunters deduced that the tracks were too old. It was their opinion that the two eland were too far ahead for serious tracking. So we set off again. Then, as we topped a slight rise, we started to see for the first time a rock outcropping breaking the skyline over the flat top trees off to our right. Peter passed the word along the line, "That's Gcwibaba Hills, the site of the caverns where we were yesterday." But, where's the road we traveled from the camp to the cave, I wondered? Shouldn't we have crossed it?

On we went at our fast pace, which in my case entailed walking as fast as I could and resorting occasionally to a forced jog to pick up lost ground. Our next welcome break came when the hunters paused to pick up several tasama melons. It was about an hour after first sighting the rocky hills, with the Kalahari's winter sun wilting us and both my water bottles dry, that we came upon two ruts. This had to be the sand track from our camp to Maun and the caverns which we'd traveled the day before.

We now knew the way to our camp, but it was still several long miles away. The hunters crossed over the vehicle tracks and continued up a slight rise to where there was a small cluster of trees affording some meager shade. They sat down under the trees to have a snack of the tasama melons.

We were all glad for this break. The drift of the click conversation was that we now would be heading back to camp along the road.

Fortunately there had been unscheduled stops every hour or so. Each time the hunters went off to check a cross track, found something to dig up or a melon to gather, or stopped to dig for grubs or make a smoke, we were given a breather. As the day wore on, some of us had continued to straggle out well behind. Dr. Wheeler was loaded down with a video camera, still camera, a back pack and canteens. He was also carrying a supply of energy foods some of his La Jolla friends wanted him to field test. Shylock had acted as the rear guard, keeping stragglers from getting left behind or lost in this trackless bush.

"I'll walk to camp and come back to meet you with a Toyota," Peter volunteered. Utterly exhausted, we welcomed Peter's offer, and soon he took off walking down the track.

The hunters were cutting the tops out of the tasamas and sloshing the inside with their spear shafts, the rinds acting as a bowl. Their hands were the spoon for scooping into their mouths the white pulp which provided an essential combination of food and moisture. When

Right: Disappointed Qui with a harvest of only two grubs—it takes approximately 8 to poison an arrow. —WT

Below: Well camouflaged puff adder Keeme almost stepped on. —JW

Left: Qui on the hunt. Every plant and feature of the terrain provides for the Bushman's needs. —BG

Below: A flushing steenbok prompts the hunters to arm their bows. Head to foot, a male Bushman wears only a scanty loincloth. —WT

During the hunt, Qui pauses to gather reeds for arrow shafts. —JP

A pause to gather refreshment during a long hunt. —JP

Right: Qui enjoying a traditional wild Bushman's vice—smoking silver leaf. Bushman do trade for metal and tobacco. —JP

Below: Tame "half-Bushman" Keeme uses his knife to remove a thorn from wild Bushman Noishay's foot. —JP

they offered, we tried some, having been out of water for some time. The succulent, if rather bland, tasama slush was refreshing and we were thankful for it.

Having had their tasama refresher, the hunters next brought out their fire-making gear to twist a fire and have a smoke. They were having a light-hearted clicking conversation, which Shylock translated.

"They're taking a bit of the mickey out of you at not being able to keep up with them despite your robust statures and having carried a supply of water and all your other aids and gadgets."

"I've got news for them," Dr. Wheeler said. "If they really took off at their pace and maintained it, there's no way we'd keep up."

These people are certainly better adapted to surviving in this land of heat, thirst and thorn than we are. There has been a great deal of speculation about where the San originated. One theory has them migrating from North Africa, where the early Egyptians had Asiatic features. This would explain their yellow skin color and Asiatic eye folds. Others propose that they are an offshoot of the central African Bantu, who developed independently in southern Africa, only to be rejoined by the Bantu in their recent migrations south. DNA blood comparisons indicate this latter is more probable. Why then are they so dwarfed in stature, and why the pedemorphy, or what laymen call infantile facial features? One theory is that man has evolved and adapted to changing hunting cultures. First, to kill with a bludgeon or club, he had to be a strong brutish sort. Then, with the development of a spear, a slender individual who could run was in favor, but fairly big and strong in the shoulders to throw the spear with effect, which fits the Aborigine. With the development of the bow and arrow and stalking, a smaller person, husky in the shoulders would do. Then, with the advent of poison, one didn't kill with the arrow's firepower, the arrow had only to wound enough to get the poison in the bloodstream. The Mbuti pygmies of the Congo and the Kalahari San are both small, and both use poisoned arrows. So the theory is that natural selection over long periods adapted the anatomy to the weapon which was successful, and that is how the hunter survived.

It might be, too, that the body has simultaneously evolved and adapted to survive in the arid environment. On the hunt we saw how little moisture or nourishment the small statured San needed to sustain them during the long, strenuous day, while our own large bodies bogged down, demanding water and food that was not to be found in this environment.

Steatopygia, the tendency to build up fat on the buttocks, and to a lesser degree on the thighs, while remaining thin waisted and without fat elsewhere on the body, is another idiosyncrasy of the San people. It is less common, but still somewhat evident in black Africans in general. One theory is that it is too hot in the desert to have fat all over like we Caucasians tend to have. Steatopygia is postulated as another adaptation to the hunter-gatherer's culture and droughts, storing up fat on his buttocks and hips like the camel stores fat on his hump to make a long desert crossing. The women often have pronounced steatopygia, some say to get them through pregnancy and lactation.

After their leisurely smoke, the three moved off down the road at a rapid but easy pace, tracking Peter toward camp. We lingered on, giving Peter more time to get to camp and head back with the pickup to shorten our remaining walk. We were bone weary. Eventually, after an hour's rest, we were revived enough to move off down the road, and after another hour of walking, finally saw Peter's white Toyota pickup ahead. We piled on, and Peter U-turned back toward camp. Much farther down the road and fairly near our camp we came around a bend in the track to see the two hunters and Keeme gliding along at their effortless pace. Peter stopped the Toyota. With a motion, Shylock invited them to get up in the pickup bed. First Keeme got in, then with clicking encouragement, got Qui and Noishay to climb over the tailgate, to stand stiffly and ill at ease in the small space between the tailgate and the back seat, hanging their arms over the seatback. Later Shylock quoted Keeme as stating that this was the first time his wild bush kin had ever been in a vehicle.

As we pulled up adjacent to our camp, Peter stopped the truck and we dropped off. Peter was staying on the track to take the Bushmen further on up the road adjacent to their camp. The usually very serious Qui at this moment pointed his spear at us in a mock menacing manner.

Jack Wheeler threw his hands in the air. "I give up," he said to a chorus of laughter from everyone. We took this joking on their part as a sign of friendly acceptance.

Joking is a very structured and involved part of Kung culture. Among themselves, in their clans, there are specific people who have an intimate or joking relationship with one another, while others according to their rules are treated with respect, or a certain aloofness, even fear or avoidance—those you don't joke around with. It is very unusual for them to have a casual or joking relationship with strangers.

Like all of us, the Kung adhere to their behavioral rules. Among the Kung you can joke or tell sexually tinged stories about or in the company of only those with whom you have a joking relationship, like Qui would have with Noishay. Keeme being from outside the clan most probably did not have the 'you-can-joke-with-him' relationship. Brothers joke, sisters joke, but because of their ribald stories, brothers and sisters don't have the joking relationship with one another. Some anthropologists see this as an outgrowth of their strong incest taboo. The Australian Aborigines have similar features in their everyday culture. Thus, if Qui and Noishay had a sister in the clan they wouldn't joke with her, nor would they, by their customs, with her husband. But they can joke with their sisters-in-law, under joking customs, because they can joke with one another.

The Kung have what could be described as a generation skipping in their joking relationship. Qui and Noishay would not joke with their parents or their children, but grandparents joke with grandchildren and vice versa. It is much the same as in our culture; parents are often stern with their children and command respect from them, while grandparents are more likely to spoil them.

A related issue comes out of the practice of bride service where the groom initially goes and lives with the bride's clan, and is obliged to hunt and provide for his bride's parents. But one of the strict avoidance customs is that not only can he not joke with his wife's parents, he can't talk to them at all. Imagine her parents' flimsy grass shelter and cooking hearth only a few meters from his and his wife's, as close as Qui and Noishay's shelters are. Well, the sly Bushman have worked this out. The groom's in-laws simply talk across to their daughter with something like, "Why doesn't that lazy husband of yours get his backside away from the fire and go out and hunt something for us?" which he, of course, will overhear, but because of the speaking avoidance cannot respond to. Thus no arguments with his in-laws ever ensue.

The Marshalls report that in their first encounter with wild Bushmen who had no prior close contact with whites, Toma, one of the clan leaders, observed them closely for three days before he decided their intentions were not threatening. Only then did he open up to the Marshalls. Ten years of close contact followed, first with Toma's band and then others in that area. This was our third day? Had we broken the ice of Qui's reserve and suspicion of strangers?

Back in the comfort of the camp, after the long dry walk, we had a beer—that tasted as good as a beer can! We nursed our new blisters—and walking on the soft ground had produced a few.

Around the campfire, the conversation turned to our two close encounters with puff adders. I had spent five years in remote locations in East Africa with only two snake incidents. In Kenya, a seven foot cobra sunning itself in an elephant path had struck out at and barely missed the legs of our black tracker. In Tanzania, a black mamba had fallen out of a tree I was camped under into the middle of our camp, causing pandemonium. Yes, our three puff adder encounters in less than a week seemed unusual to me.

"Van der Post relates an interesting parallel," Peter said. "On a day of hunting with Bushmen in the Central Kalahari, the hunters were on a fast track after a wounded eland. Van der Post was following along filming and then he paused momentarily to photograph a large mamba he happened to see. As he moved off to catch up he saw the lead hunter jump over a striking cobra he had disturbed. Snake encounters are like that—they happen when they happen."

"What happens when someone gets bitten like Keeme almost did today?" Tom asked.

The Marshalls reported an incident like that. They had made contact and spent some time with the Kung in Namibia, near Nyae Nyae. On a subsequent trip to Nyae Nyae they learned that Little Qui, one of the more renowned and productive hunters, had been bitten in the leg by a puff adder. In a situation similar to what we had just experienced, the hunter was walking along and stepped on a motionless puff adder, which then struck and bit him just below the knee. By the time the Marshalls found out about it several months had passed. When they finally caught up with Little Qui the cytotoxic poison had turned his leg into a horrible oozing gangrenous mess, exuding a foul odor. Part of his calf had dropped off, and grayed bones were showing. Some of their party transported the hunter into Windhoek for his traumatic first encounter with 'civilization.' There doctors amputated his lower leg, saving the upper portion of his calf and fitting him with a peg below the knee.

When they returned to Nyae Nyae a year or so later, Little Qui was out hunting again and walked some hundred miles to visit the Marshalls on his peg leg.

The Marshalls reported two other snake incidents. In one, a young boy had been bitten by a mamba and died the next day from the potent and fast-acting neurotoxic venom. In the other a girl was drowned when a python at a water hole dragged her into the water. They also made note of a song sung on the Bushmen's stringed instrument, the gwasha, about a man out spring hare hunting who probed down a burrow with his pole and brought out not a hare but a puff adder. He was bitten on the hand, and his hand was permanently deformed. The song lamented that he could no longer "twist a fire".

When not helping Salome with camp chores, Liza often sat in on our running campfire discussion. She had heard most of our discussions and evolving ideas in search of a salvation for the threatened San and their fragile culture. We noted she was quietly working on some sketches, but we didn't pay that much attention to her drawing, since we knew she was in Botswana to help illustrate Salome's book. We were to discover later that the idea of her current sketches was tied directly to our ongoing discussions of what to do to help the Bushmen and how they needed a highly placed person to lobby for them, and for a return to them of some of their Kalahari bush, our 'Bush for the Bushman' theme.

During the course of our discussions of the plight of the Bushman, we each drew on our own experiences, finding parallels, remembering things we had learned in other contexts. I recalled for the group that I had grown up in northern California where my father was a cattle rancher. He owned a finite amount of land and economics pushed him to run as many productive animals as possible. In his case he was a pragmatic 'game conservationist' of cattle. A direct comparison might seem odd in that cattle are not a naturally-occurring species in the Pacific northwest, but I think the analogy is useful and relevant.

My father watched over his herd and the feed conditions carefully. To stay in business he needed to get full use out of his land over the long term, while guarding against overstocking or overgrazing the ranch.

All animals produce an equal number of male and female offspring, but one bull can cover up to thirty-five cows. If there are too many bulls left in the herd they will fight, tear up the ground, break the fences and eat the grass—taking it away from producing cows bearing young. So my father sold all the males except the small number he needed for breeding and kept only enough females to replace each year those breed cows that get too old to be reproductive. It was a form of herd cropping.

The impala is an example of how male redundancy works in nature. On my first hunt in Africa I regularly saw herds of thirty slick-headed female impalas surrounding one antlered male. This was a breeding herd. Over a hill or two was the bachelor herd of some thirty, all antlered males. If something happens to the male of the breeding herd, he is immediately replaced by the next strongest male out of the bachelor herd. Looking at it practically, if a percentage of the bachelor herd were to be cropped, there would be more feed available for the breed herd, the females and their young, and more of the species could survive within the fixed area available inside the now-fixed boundaries of parks and reserves. And why shouldn't some still nomadic Bushmen be the ones to do the cropping? They are a natural part of the ecosystem and have been for thousands of years. It certainly is not the San who have brought various species to the brink of extinction. That has been modern white man's doing, with his firearms and those he gave to the Bantu.

Most of the African parks eventually must resort to some form of wild game cropping. In Kruger Park the managers regularly cull certain species in certain zones in order to keep the number of animals within the carrying capacity of the range. To protect the game for the long term they deem it necessary to keep their numbers within the available, if arbitrary, supportable limits of the reserve.

"The nut to crack is to get the conservationists, politicians and others to accept the Bushman as a special exception inside the parks," I said. Unfortunately the conservationists pit the animals against the Bushman. But a case can be made for dual Bushman and wild game use of the reserves being a win-win situation. The Bushman would serve as owner croppers, not unlike my father did on his ranch, and they would be there to help assure the survival of the animals and as a deterrent to poachers who have no regard for the animals' long term survival. The Bushman are going to practice good game husbandry. They want 'their' herd to go on.

"It will take some help from the outside for a government like Botswana or newly independent Namibia to sort out their priorities," said Jack Wheeler. "Only some earnest international lobbying will move the Bushman from the bottom of the priority ladder to nearer the top and do it before they're gone." We theorized on whom we might convince to go to bat for the Bushman. It had to be someone with global clout and the power to influence world opinion, someone who could offer trade or aid incentives to the young democracy in Botswana.

But perhaps all that meant was first arousing the public.

"Today you wore out my tent mate, Wally," said Jim, "and now hearing your account and all of this impassioned talk has worn me out. I'm off to our canvas abode. 'Bush for the Bushman,' I say. May Bush or someone step forward and get these people some of their bush back. And sleep well."

The rest of us remained staring into the glowing fire. The bright moon cast soft shadows in camp. This evening's discussion was over, but surely there would be more talk tomorrow. Our African adventure seemed to be turning into a cause.

—7—
Day of the Dances

The moon paled from yellow to white as the sun lightened the eastern sky over the cool, clear Kalahari. I scrounged a new supply of dry snags near the camp and revived the smoldering fire into life. No one else was yet moving in camp.

After the gathering and hunting expeditions, we had no further specific rendezvous with the Bushman clan. Peter was playing it as we went, trying to give us as much exposure to the Bushmen as possible, without overwhelming them. Reining in our genuinely enthusiastic, even sometimes over-zealous interest was a legitimate concern.

Our camp began to stir and soon we were in our ring of canvas chairs around the fire having breakfast.

"Have you heard of the Bushman's legend of the argument between the moon and the hare?" Peter asked, gesturing toward the luminous moon hanging prominently in the sky.

One of their many creation, or how-things-came-to-be, myths, it deals with man's mortality. In those early creation days the moon put forth that people would die, but would be reborn as the moon is repeatedly reborn. The hare, who was mourning his mother's death, said "No, she's dead and won't return." They argued, the hare insisting, "Once dead—always dead!" The moon said "But see how I go through cycles of death and rebirth." But the hare refused to watch or listen and an altercation ensued. The moon struck the hare and split his lip, which we can see to this day. The hare scratched the moon's face leaving the permanent scars we see. So the irritated moon said, "Very well, I withdraw the offer of immortality to man. Henceforth he will die and not return." Venting his wrath further, Moon said, "And you, Hare, are no longer a human, but an animal to be hunted and eaten by wild dogs and other carnivores.

"Their myths are very similar to the dreamtime stories of the

Australian Aborigines which serve to explain why things are," Jack added. "It is interesting how all the hunter-gather cultures have similar stories and myths; they seem very like our Plains Indians and like the Inuits in that regard." Then, turning to Peter, Jack asked about the day's program.

"I have nothing specific in mind," Peter replied, "but we left the clan in good spirits after the hunt yesterday. We'll go along and visit with them mid-morning." By now we were less apprehensive about the clan picking up and vanishing into the bush.

We were all feeling our muscles from the previous day's walk, so to relax around the fire and read from the camp library was in order.

At mid-morning Peter said, "Well, let's go look in on our mates."

When we arrived at the encampment the three mature women were gathered together around the campfire in front of Qui's shelter, the baby getting its usual tactile attention—bonding. Qui and Noishay were missing, but Keeme was there to tell us that the men had gone hunting. Our attention was drawn by clapping and singing down the slope slightly below the cleared encampment. The unattached teenage girl and two of the other young female children were engaged in an animated dance. "That is called the melon dance," Shylock informed us. "This is a traditional dance done only by girls."

The girls were in a loose line dancing to the accompaniment of their own singing and hand clapping. Their animated movements were like a form of hop-scotch to music. As we watched, the girl at the front of the line would run forward five or six steps in rhythm to the singing, turn side to side, take a long step backwards, a little hop, a long step forward, and at a proper point in the melody, blindly toss the melon underhanded, backwards and upwards to be caught by the next girl in line. The girl catching the melon became the head of the line as the first girl circled back to the end. Each girl in her turn imitated the distinct movements of a particular animal, a wildebeest, a kudu, gemsbok or eland, accompanied by clicking lyrics about that animal.

The vigorous, rhythmic movements accompanied by their animated singing and laughter made a striking sight. The tightly-hemmed, ankle-length karosses of the smaller girls flipped smartly as they moved through their routine, clapping and darting to catch the tasama melon while it was still airborne.

"Lovely, happy people," Jim observed, voicing all our sentiments. They appeared truly happy, and we felt a warm glow, just observing them.

"Qui and Noishay were especially excited over the eland tracks they saw yesterday," Peter told us after an exchange between Keeme and Shylock. "They've gone to see if they are still in the area."

No question, the eland is their favorite animal. It has a close spiritual connection to them; is the most frequent subject portrayed in the Bushman rock paintings at Tsodilo and all over southern Africa. Some observers have reported that when a hunter gets any other animal he brings the meat back to camp, but in reverence to the eland's high status in the San's mythology and legend, they pick up their camp and go to the eland. However, others have pointed out a practical aspect to this could be the size of the eland. At some 1000 to 1500 pounds, there is a lot of weight to lug miles and miles when the nomadic San can more easily just pick up and move to it.

"Notice that Keeme has remained in camp with the women," Peter observed. "That indicates that he went along on yesterday's hunt as our translator rather than a hunter."

The Bushmen are noted as solitary and stealthful hunters, getting up very close to their quarry with their fragile, featherless arrows. So today they were off on a real hunt, just the two hunters moving fast, looking for tracks and ready to stalk game.

It had been a real concession to let our thundering mob accompany them on the previous day's hunt. Besides wind, silence is an important element of the success of a hunt. When they get up close to their quarry Bushmen move as quietly but as rapidly as possible to minimize their exposure time. To lessen the likelihood of alerting the game with sound, they lay down shoulder bag, quiver and their spear, carrying only their bow and a handful of arrows. They use hand signals, not voice communication, as whispering in clicks is not practical. Then the hunters lean over to resemble the silhouette of an animal. They stalk while the animal has its head down grazing, and freeze when its head is up. Once close enough, thirty meters or less, they let fly with their arrows as rapidly as they can. Only one poisoned arrow has to wound the animal and they are in business. There is no way we could have conformed to their stalk rules.

After conversations with Keeme, Shylock informed us that when the men came back in the evening they planned to perform their healing dance, to which we were invited.

"This is something they do only when the mood hits them," Peter explained. "It's not something they do just to be doing it. We're lucky that the mood should hit them while we are about."

"The fact that the moon is full tonight may well have something to do with their choice of timing," added Jack.

Back in our own camp we were gathered around the campfire as the sun dropped in the sky. When it became time for us to go to the clan's camp, Peter suggested, "In line with the Bushman's customs of gift-giving, it would be a nice gesture to give the clan something, but we have to be careful not to corrupt or contaminate them with our civilization."

"The Kung see us whites as people with unlimited wealth, who do not freely share our possessions as they do in their society," Jack said. "They bargain with non-Bushmen who want something from them. They expect something in return, a trade. Now we've been treated to the hunt, so a gift of appreciation is in order."

Observers of the San culture have noted their custom of gift-giving, and that, despite what little they have—traveling light as they do—they are continually giving. Ostrich eggshell chip jewelry, bows, arrows, spears, thumb pianos, metallic cigarette or tobacco holders, make a slow but steady circuit from one owner to the next to maintain the good will and future help of others. The more gifts given, the more future help and assistance can be expected. This is a form of 'bush' insurance in their perilous lives, since they survive constantly on the edge, never knowing what natural or personal calamity may befall them.

Gift-giving is not trading. Bushmen steadfastly refuse to trade among themselves. They do, however, trade with other cultures—with the Bantus for tobacco, beads, or metal tools, for instance. Among themselves, when given a gift one is obliged to return the favor, but only after a reasonable time elapses, as an immediate reciprocal gift would smack of trading.

Meat sharing is a related example of this. The lucky hunter whose arrow is determined to have gotten the animal owns all the meat. This is not necessarily the hunter who fired the arrow, who may have borrowed it for the hunt. The arrow 'owner' is obliged by custom to share the meat among the other hunters, their immediate clan and other kin, and other Bushmen present at or near his encampment. But he looks for the same in return when someone else is the lucky hunter. Thus all the meat is eaten while it is fresh, and the custom avoids hunger-driven jealousy. The meat-sharing process helps ensure the survival of a whole band, not just the most successful hunters.

Sharing leads to problems when San try to become agropastoralists, planters and herders for whom the main goal is to conserve and build up a herd. Other San who are still nomadic hunter-gatherers will come and visit their now sedentary cousins and think the animal owner stingy for not killing and sharing his precious breedstock. To be 'stingy' is a stigma to be avoided in traditional culture. This paradox created by the meeting of two very different cultures has led many Bushmen to give up trying to become owners of cattle. Instead, many have stoically remained in serfdom as hired herders or tried going back to foraging, hunting and gathering.

Peter's suggestion to give the clan something led to a lively discussion. We didn't want to give them anything plastic or shiny—no evil Coke bottles. None of our food was appropriate for them. Eventually, Peter said, "What will draw them into the Xai Xai cattle post village and conflict with civilization is the lack of water. The safest and best thing we can do is give them some drinking water."

The issue decided, Peter drew a five-gallon plastic jerry can of water from the remaining tank trailer. Map had departed for Tsodilo Hills with one Toyota and the second water trailer. We carried our gift of water along on our late afternoon visit.

The hunters were back. The whole clan was in a close group out in the center of their encampment, around the ceremonial fire they had

Only women perform the melon dance. —BG (above), WT (right)

Left: The kaross has no up or down. Tail of the young unattached's skin here is down. Her kaross on back cover of book has tail up. —JP

Below: Clan's women at shelter. Traditionally, they sit to the left of the fire-to-shelter line; men to the right. —JP

prepared for the healing dance. They launched into an animated report of the hunt, pointing, gesturing, frowning or laughing hilariously, all in their rapid-fire popping and clicking speech. Shylock gave us a brief report.

"Yes, they saw more tracks, but they didn't get up on anything to shoot."

From the number of tracks we'd encountered the day before and now with this report we were encouraged to know there was some game about. Still, even with determined hunting, bringing home some meat was obviously not a cinch.

Observers like the Marshalls who have lived with the San for extended periods—even before game had diminished or been driven away by cattle—have noted how few large antelope each hunter kills. Studies show an average of six or less a year per hunter. This is more reason to consider letting the few still nomadic San continue a traditional hunting life inside the parks and reserves.

Specific hunts reported by the Marshalls in the early 1950's will serve to illustrate. On one occasion, the clan they were studying killed a giraffe, a species since protected by law, which the San now cooperate in not hunting. The band hunted each day for eight days, staying out some nights, until they shot an arrow into a giraffe. They then tracked it for five days, during which time the giraffe traveled thirty miles. Thirteen days of hard work before there was meat to share. This is a high ratio of energy expended to reward. The reward for energy ratio is much higher for the women in gathering, thus it is the real mainstay of their survival.

On another occasion, after several days tracking, the Bushmen finally came on their wounded quarry, a kudu, only to find a lion there first, having polished it off and leaving only the bare bones. On yet another occasion the hunters were out eight days in exhausting heat before they encountered an eland which they were able to stalk and shoot. They then tracked it for three days, and it took two days to carry the meat back to their encampment around a water hole. This had been a thirteen-day effort. Some of the meat went bad, transporting it so far under the unrelenting Kalahari sun. An aside on gift-giving, the particular arrow that got the eland, and determined who decided the meat sharing, had been given from one person to another in the clan five times.

Qui's clan showed genuine appreciation for our group's gesture of making them a gift of water. But where to put it? Their only containers were a few empty tasama melon rinds, which they used to provide drinks to all the clan members. Their immediate thirst satisfied, they stored as much of the water as the half-dozen available tasama rinds would hold. We had to leave the still half-full jerry can with them to be returned to us later.

As it got dark they started their healing dance. The women sat on the ground, clapping and singing near the clan's communal fire. Qui,

Noishay and Keeme started dancing in a fifteen foot circle around the outside of the fire with the women seated inside the circle, close to the fire, cuddling the baby. The two younger males observed from off to the side outside the dance path. The three mature men had twisted the strings of cocoons filled with bits of ostrich eggshells around their slender ankles and then tied them. These cocoon strings gave off a soft but distinctive rattle as the men did their stiff-legged, foot-pounding dance.

Eventually there was a deep rut worn in the sand as the men slowly circled around and around the communal fire. This typical rut in the sand has led to the Bushmen's explanation of the ring around the moon, which they see as being caused by the spirits of the dead dancing. The moon is their ceremonial fire and the moon ring is the circle made by their dancing feet. Throughout the dance, the females seated inside the circle continued to sing and clap.

This first part of the dance went on nonstop for about an hour. There was a soft light from the full moon hanging in the sky. The flickering fire cast shadows of the moving bodies of the freely sweating men dancing and the women clapping and chanting. The blending of the women's sharp clapping and high pitched singing, and the men's more muffled foot stamping and the rattle given off by the cocoons on their ankles blended into a pleasant and hypnotic pattern of sound that made chills run up one's spine.

There was a slowing of the tempo, and the dancing stopped for a short time. When the dance resumed the tempo built up slowly to a crescendo and Noishay became what the San call *kai*. He staggered out of the beaten dance path and toppled to the ground, face down. After a slight pause, Qui went over and put his hand on Noishay's shoulder as the singing and clapping went on. After several minutes Noishay slowly revived, got up on all fours and eventually stood up and resumed dancing as if nothing had transpired. There was a trace of fine dust on his forehead and shoulders, sticking to his sweaty body where it had touched the sandy ground. Twenty minutes later the tempo dropped off and the dance was over.

Peter commented on what we'd seen.

"When Noishay went into that deep trance, if Qui hadn't gone and put a hand on him to bring him back out of it, it could have been fatal."

The Kung and most other San believe in an afterlife in which their spirits depart their mortal bodies and go live with the great God and creator. There is an interaction between the spirits of the dead acting as messengers between God and the living. The spirits of the dead bring ailments, bad luck and misfortune in the form of invisible arrows. The healing dance is a form of battle or contest that removes these arrows from living bodies and sends them back to the spirits of the dead.

The Kung have explained that 'kai', the state of trance, is achieved when the dancing causes an intangible energy or vapor-like warmth to build up in the pit of the stomach and with the rising dance tempo, travel up the spine to the base of the skull, causing conscious thought to temporarily cease and the body to tingle all over as the energy flows throughout the body. In this trance state they believe the spirit can temporarily leave their body to successfully do battle with and repulse the arrows of the spirits of the dead. During a healing dance, healers will be seen to place their hand on others, drawing the arrows into the medicine man's own body, who then, with shouts and curses, hurtles them back at the spirits of the dead lurking in the darkness beyond the fire. Not all male dancers can achieve trance, but observers have reported that as many as sixty percent can. Women dance too, and a smaller percentage go into trance. This special curing ability is one aspect of the culture admired by the Bantu, who often come to the San for cures. In the recent past, it has been reported that large groups have held marathon-like healing dances that have gone on all through the night. Qui's small clan was danced out much earlier.

All during our contact with the clan, we'd been bursting with questions, but with the rather involved translation process and everything else that was going on, many of our questions had not been asked, much less answered. Besides, Peter had cautioned us that some specific questions or too many questions were inappropriate. With the dance over, a straightforward non-controversial question we asked was, whether the clan did any snaring of small game to supplement the bigger game that was proving so difficult to hunt.

"Yes, they do snaring," Shylock passed their response, "and if we want to come tomorrow morning, they will gather some of the plants from which they make fiber and show us how they set snares."

Our next day's plan tied down, we proceeded back to our camp under the bright stars and full moon. Those with flashlights scanned the ground as we kept a wary watch out for puff adders. As most of the Kalahari snakes avoid the blazing sun and are nocturnal hunters, walking around the bush at night raises the odds of a snake encounter. The San conduct their affairs in daylight hours, and stay close by their fires at night.

Back in our camp, we gathered in our circle of chairs, stoked our fire and resumed our ongoing discussions. We searched for ideas on how to assist the San in their struggle to survive in a world sometimes hostile and often indifferent to their existence.

"The Aboriginal connection has merit," said Jack, "but don't forget, Australia has a white government, and 'white' guilt was a large part of the groundswell to do something for the Aborigine and give him back some of his land."

In Botswana there is a fairly recently installed black government where there is not the same long term guilt feeling for what happened to the Bushmen. It is a more recently inherited problem. There is a parallel between the Kalahari and the Northern Territory, where there is 'still a chance,' and the rest of Australia and southern Africa where it's 'graveyard history' as far as the survival of the aboriginal cultures is concerned. But in Africa, as compared to Australia, it was and is more complicated. The Bushmen were caught between two 'invaders', the whites from the south and the Bantu blacks from the north. The Bushmen were caught and chewed up in the white versus Bantu, as well as the Bantu versus Bantu history. For example during the Zulu campaigns, tribes were fighting for territory and being displaced, and they were driven to encroach on the Bushmen's last remaining Kalahari territory. Then the cattle herding Herero tribe was driven out of German Southwest Africa, now Namibia, into Bushmen areas. But with the white government in Bechuanaland, now Botswana, being fairly recently replaced by a new black government, and that in Namibia in the process, most of the past guilt has been lost or dissipated.

"A more complex history could lead to more complex solutions. There is no easy solution, no panacea," said Jack.

It was about this time on our Kalahari visit, maybe this night, that one of our number said, "Somebody should write a book."

—8—
Snaring

At breakfast, we pressed Peter to use our final 'snare setting' rendezvous with the clan to ask more of the questions we were all bursting to have answered. He was reluctant, on the one hand, to bore in too close on the lives of these shy people, but on the other wanted us to gain as much knowledge as we could in our abbreviated contact.

"Let's go learn to set snares," Peter said when breakfast was over. "Maybe an opportunity will present itself."

By now we had beaten a visible trail in the leaf and twig strewn terrain on our visits between our two encampments. This was to be our last visit, as this was the sixth and last day we were scheduled to have contact with Qui and his clan.

We were nine: Peter, Shylock, and seven Americans. Map and Mansu were by now well on their way to install our next camp at Tsodilo Hills, some 150 kilometers to the north.

When we arrived at the encampment, Qui and Noishay were down on the ground, busily processing the long green cactus-like plants they had gathered to produce snaring cords.

"The plant they're using is sansevieria," Peter informed us. "Local Europeans call it mother-in-law's tongue because of its long, pointed leaves and sharp barbs." This got a side glance of some disbelief out of Tom, and a chuckle out of the others.

The plant looked like a wild version of the cultivated sisal one sees in Tanzania where it is grown as the source of most of the world's hemp rope supply, now largely replaced by plastic or nylon.

To process the wild hemp into snare cords, Noishay was sitting on his left foot, his right knee up, his right foot holding down his thumb piano. He was pulling the green shoots under the point of a digging stick and over the wood base of the thumb piano to shred out the white inner fiber.

"His thumb piano is his improvised work bench," Peter pointed out.

Qui was seated on the ground nearby with his legs extended straight out, rolling the fibers on his thigh to produce strands which he then braided into a tough string.

"They can make any size cord or rope by braiding more strands," Peter explained. "In emergencies out in the bush we've had rope made of this plant which was strong enough to tow a vehicle."

There is an oft-repeated Bushman legend, in many variations, about this rope. Long ago the San and Bantu were one people, one nation. The great creator commanded them to have a tug-of-war, giving them a rope; the San half was made of wild sisal, the Bantu half of cow hide thongs plaited into rope. The two were knotted together in the middle. During the tug-of-war the rope broke in the sisal section. Because they had won, the Bantu got the best things, cattle and goats and milk to drink and manufactured clothes. San got the leftovers. They were told to use their sisal to make snares to survive as best they could on the meat they could get in this way. One Bushman said in his frustration, "Next time we'll choose the cow hide end of the rope."

By now our group was completely enchanted with these gentle people. Who wouldn't be? Despite the general belief that in this day and age the wild Bushmen were all gone, here we were seeing them happy and healthy, doing quite naturally what we'd only seen in picture books or heard through the writings of visits of years ago by van der Post, the Marshalls and other anthropologists.

One of our pressing questions, which went with our concern about their threatened culture and basic survival, was "But how many others like Qui and his clan still exist?" Not the tame Bushmen that have been enticed or forced into the small miserable communities or villages near a well, but the wild nomadic people who were still in skins, hunting with poisoned arrows, living essentially as they had hundreds and thousands of years ago?

Qui responded while continuing to work industriously on making snare cords. Keeme and Shylock translated.

"Last October Qui's clan saw another family clan, and they will probably see that clan again this November or December when it rains and they all can move around more freely."

"How big is that other group?" asked Jack.

"It is a bigger group than those here," came the answer. "But that clan should possibly be getting even bigger. They had more bigger people and a couple or three of them were pregnant by the time the two clans left each other, so they should have small babies at the moment. This means they will not be traveling long distances each day. Once they've had an opportunity to find a place where there will be water, they will hang onto that place until the water all dries up, or until the rains start. It is then they can start moving all about, knowing water will be plentiful all over."

"About how many people in the group, more or less?" asked Jack.

After querying Qui further, Shylock replied, "Something like twenty."

Studies of earlier days, before the crush of humanity had disrupted the Bushmen's traditional nomadic culture, indicate that the optimum clan size is thirty individuals. This is a number large enough to lend mutual support, but small enough not to over-tax the surrounding environment before the clan moves on. This optimum number is consistent with other nomadic hunter-gatherer cultures; the Australian Aborigines, the Mbuti Pygmies of the Congo, and the Arctic Inuits. A clan as small as Qui and Noishay's is more vulnerable to natural or individual catastrophe.

Again Qui was queried.

"How will Qui and Noishay's children meet other people and marry?"

Eventually Shylock reported, "This other clan which they possibly will be meeting again, they are the kind of people who would inter-marry with Qui's clan."

Qui elaborates and Shylock continues on translating: "That other clan's people are not related to these young girls here," Shylock turned and indicated the innocent-looking girls in their oversized and tattered karosses grouped around one of the clan's cooking fires. "When these young girls grow up, they will marry with boys from the other clan and these boys here with the girls from the other clan."

The San, like most hunter-gatherer cultures, notably the Australian Aborigine, have strict rules against incest or marrying closer than second or third cousins. They practice, by custom, exogamy, or marriage outside their own group or clan.

"Does the girl go with the man to his clan, or does the man go to the girl's clan?" asked Tom.

Eventually after the round-robin translation, Shylock pointed to the elder boy of Qui's clan, "Right, he is Qui's son. So if he marries a girl in another group, he brings his wife here where his father is."

"So, if one of these girls should marry a man from another group, she goes to that clan?" Tom queried.

"Yes," Shylock replied.

Most anthropologists have reported that among Bushmen the groom first goes and stays with the bride's family, to perform his bride service obligation in which he is expected to hunt for and provide for his bride's parents, often until the young couple has had three children, after which time he is free to return to his own clan. In this manner the San groom can contribute to the bride's family since, unlike the Bantu, they have no cattle or other material wealth to give for a bride price. A boy begins hunting at age twelve to fifteen and cannot marry until he has proven himself as a hunter by killing a larger animal, such as a wildebeest, kudu, or eland. Qui's brief explanation would indicate that there may be some diversity in customs among different clans or different regions. More probably Qui was just simplifying to avoid complicated translation and referring to the fact that his son would eventually rejoin his father's clan, but only after bride service has been completed.

Qui and a parent from another clan could arrange a marriage, and it could well be with a girl who is only eight or ten years old. Qui's son would probably go to live with the other clan, hunt with them, have his own shelter and hearth with his adolescent bride, waiting for her to mature. On that basis it would be several years before she reached menarche and could have children. Qui's son would eventually have done his bride service and then could come back and rejoin the clan. Qui's clan has daughters, so in the meantime some of the other clan's sons would be hunting with Qui and Noishay and helping provide for them if anything happened to Qui or Noishay.

The wedding itself starts with a simple ritual of shelter construction undertaken by the couple's young peers. A fire would be made from brands from the fires of each set of parents, with the groom's clan visiting the bride's clan encampment. The bride's sisters and girlfriends carry her to the new home and the groom is brought there by his brothers and friends. The adults stay fairly uninvolved. The next morning the bride's mother will rub her with animal fat—especially eland fat, if they have it—and mark her face with red ochre.

"And divorce?" asked Tom.

"Divorce, too, is a simple affair," said Jack. "Nothing legal. They have no judges, no paper work."

Divorce custom sheds light on their culture. The San have no property, except their limited personal tools and what they can pick up and carry. All possessions belong to individuals, not mutually to man and wife. The only thing they can claim, and it is not ownership per se, is the right to hunt and gather and get drinking water in an area which they inherit from their ancestors. On divorce, children remain with the mother, but a boy could be expected to rejoin his father when it is time to learn to hunt. "But divorce for an adult is simply leaving the hearth," Jack added. "When a man and woman decide to pack it in, each takes whatever very few belongings they have, and one of them just leaves."

"And what about extramarital fooling around ... adultery with the Bushmen?" asked Bud.

"It happens ... but it's a definite no-no, and a few poisoned arrows have flown over it," said Peter.

"It has been pointed out, the Bushmen are basically non-belligerent. They don't fight over land, or for tribal dominance, only over 'personal issues', and adultery would be one of them. The Bushmen live in such close quarters, have so little privacy, and are such good trackers, that the odds aren't good. Unfortunately, as their nomadic culture breaks down, so does their practice of moral taboos."

Then, for the first time Noishay, who had remained silent while busily shredding the wild sisal, burst into the conversation. Noishay was not answering our questions. In a determined, even irritated

112

manner, he was asking one of his own.

"Noishay has just asked where you all come from," announced Shylock.

Shylock took it upon himself to explain that we had come from far away, a phrase which the San without any training in geography could not be expected to understand. Maun, America, Machu Picchu or Mars—they are all far away!

Noishay's next question, as Shylock translated it to us: "It's a long way! Then why the hell did you choose to come here and trouble us with all these questions? What do you actually do back home, other than coming here and asking us all these shit questions?"

The actual choice of words was probably Shylock's, not Noishay's. As the ideas moved through a three language multi-level translation, some words were substituted or changed to fit the vernacular of the next to hear.

This brought an immediate reaction in guilty Peter-told-us-so side glances, and a burst of nervous laughter from Peter and our group. Peter *had* warned us about too many questions.

"Well, that's what he said," added Shylock.

We tried to explain through Shylock and Keeme.

"You are very special people known around the world. We've come a long way just to see you and learn about you."

Noishay continued his determined popping and clicking query which Keeme and Shylock passed on to us.

"All these questions that you ask us and we give you answers back ... other than just being able to see us, is there any way else you benefit ... and how do we benefit from you asking all these questions?"

We were all talking at once, trying to put forth good reasons for our visit and our questions, reasons that would make some 'Bushmen' sense.

Most of our answers were in the vein of, "To know each other better ... to promote world understanding and peace ..." We all wanted to help Shylock form a reply, to tell them somehow that we were in awe of them, that we understood how threatened they were by forces they could not control or even understand, but that we might better understand controlling those forces and wanted to help them. But our responses were too nebulous and intangible to mean much. Shylock was visibly perplexed. He was unable to give them any specific answers. And, truthfully, unless we could do something for them, what good did our gawking at them really do?

Over our several voices trying to give Shylock ammunition to formulate a reply to Noishay's queries, my shouted response to Shylock ... trying to articulate our admiration for these 'wild' Bushmen, as they are in their scant game skins, and knowing the threat of civilization boring in on them ... "We'd like to give them a bore hole for water, the one Beth Oliver's Swedes are ready to drill, put a vast protective cyclone fence around here, turn elands in, keep the Bantus and their cattle out."

Then I gave voice to the next thought that flashed across my mind at this emotional moment. Into the rabble of other anxious voices which were trying to give Shylock a meaningful response, I shouted, "I'll be damned if we're not going to try to get Bush or somebody to look out for you wild Bushmen." This was probably the moment I became dedicated, to try to help these wonderful, but down-trodden and forgotten people.

Noishay continued talking animatedly. He was wound up and visibly frustrated and aggravated. Qui, as the eldest and therefore the clan's official spokesman, had lapsed into silence. In their egalitarian clan structure, however, there are no headmen or tribal chiefs. Everyone is equal. For Noishay to vent his spleen and speak out was totally acceptable.

"This gentleman," Shylock said, turning and gesturing toward Noishay, "he is now tired of all these questions which are being asked every day ... every night. He had decided he is here the last day today ... and tomorrow if you guys will be coming here to see him, it's bad luck, he won't be here. He has got to go. He is afraid you've asked so many questions that you might be leading to ... death ... to his death ... or something like that. So he thinks he better start getting out of this place, and go away. He is serious! Even now he is about to leave. He's just about full up of these questions."

We looked sheepishly at Peter, whose concerns over producing a form of cultural shock had obviously been well-founded. Our questioning session was over! We were crestfallen and ashamed that in our exuberance we might have angered Noishay and driven the clan away.

Then Keeme left the circle of people, the Bushmen and us 'aliens,' and stamped several meters off into the bush, his head carried low. He was obviously agitated and embarrassed. Keeme was, after all, by his mixed genes, a tamed half-Bushman and a herder, two huge steps removed from these still nomadic people belonging to one of Africa's most cloistered cultures. Keeme was able to see things in a broader light and seemed to understand that while we might make errors in Bushman protocol, our intentions were good. One could imagine he was feeling his share of responsibility for bringing his wild Kung cousins and us white strangers together. It would follow that Keeme, who found himself on the fork of the road toward civilization, would be more prone to want the respect and goodwill of white men like Peter and the rest of us, but would also be more aware than we of the nomadic San's decades of bad experiences at the hands of European and Bantu intruders. The clan really only wanted to be left unmolested to try against the odds to continue its traditional ways in the vast but ever-shrinking sanctuary of its remote and inhospitable Kalahari bush.

In our own culture, questions usually demonstrate an interest and curiosity to know and understand, but among the San, questions are considered a show of suspicion, demonstrating a lack of trust or even hostility on the part of the questioner. Among themselves, it is generally considered to be impolite to ask questions of the nature of some of ours.

Keeme rejoined the gathering and Noishay cooled down. Noishay's next pronouncements, as translated to us, closed the issue.

"About demonstrating how this snaring goes, we can welcome that. But we are a little fed up about all these questions about where we will be going from here and how we do this and that. We think you have too big eyes enough to see exactly what we are doing and how we live. There shouldn't be a problem. You shouldn't be asking all those questions."

After an uneasy pause, Noishay, like Qui, fell silent while the two continued preparing the sisal cords. Shortly thereafter, they had enough sisal cords to start setting snares.

As we followed Qui, Noishay and Keeme south down the slope, away from their encampment, Shylock said, "They are going to show us their waterhole. They've got some water."

Water! This was surprising news to all of us. We had naturally assumed they were completely without water; for wasn't it on this basis that we had brought them a gift of five gallons?

Their encampment was up on the gentle shoulder of the low sand ridge. We were descending into the ancient dry river bed or valley bottom toward the two-rutted vehicle track. Not more than 200 meters down the gentle slope was a round dry pan, some 150 feet in diameter. It was obviously a pond or oversized puddle which served to temporarily hold water during the annual rains, but now it was just a depression, baked hard and cracked. It turned out that when the clan had first camped at this location they had dug a hole three feet in diameter by four feet deep in the bottom of the pan looking for water, but found none.

They had come back and checked their well in the last couple of days, after the unseasonal August rain, and found eight to ten inches of water in the bottom.

Noishay removed a thorn tree branch that had been placed over the hole to protect the well from nature's intruders, and crawled down in the hole. Keeme handed him a hollowed-out tasama melon rind with which Noishay scooped up some water. Qui, Keeme and the two younger boys proceeded to drink. Finally, they offered their water to those of us who wanted to try it. This seemed a generous gesture on Noishay's part, as if he wanted up to know there were no hard feelings. Tom and I sampled it. It was cool and sweet.

The location of the clan's encampment relative to the waterhole is typical. San camp a reasonable distance from any water source so as not to foul it with their defecation in the sand close to camp. They also want to be far enough from the water so as not to invite conflict with predators visiting it at night.

As we proceeded on to set the snares there were several blackthorn acacias in full bloom, their white blossoms standing out against other thorn bushes still in their bare leafless winter attire. Qui and Noishay fanned out looking for suitable places for their snares. Their intended prey was the korhaan, a pheasant-sized bird. The bait was a bit of gum gathered off tree trunks. Each snare was set up near the base of a tree, at a site where a half-inch branch could be bent down to act as the spring to activate the snares.

They had cut small forked branches, like we'd cut as children to make slingshots. These were embedded in the ground, with the gum on one arm of the fork. The 'spring' branch was tied down to the other arm. The cord then continued into a loop which was supported three inches or so above the ground by vertical sticks forming a miniature cord corral. When the korhaan leans over inside this corral and pecks at the gum, it disturbs the tiedown string and the branch flies up, bringing the noose around the korhaan's body or neck.

Qui and Noishay worked rapidly setting up the five snares within a fairly close proximity, not further than fifty meters apart. We crossed back and forth between them to see the five snares go through different stages of completion.

It was interesting to see how these men were able to squat down comfortably, with their buttocks touching their heels as they worked. Elsewhere I had marveled at seeing bush Africans sit like this by the hour. Sitting this way from childhood, Africans' bone structure becomes deformed at the knee in order to accommodate this posture.

In the light of the too-many-questions flap and in anticipation of our final parting we wanted Peter to assure the clan that we were leaving in the morning. If they were to pull up camp now on our account and start moving and should not find water or favorable conditions, our inquisitiveness might just be the unintended catalyst that caused them to be drawn to the vices and misfortunes awaiting these last wild Bushmen at Xai Xai wells.

We knew that neither of the two days of hunting had yielded any game in spite of the number of tracks encountered. Still on our gathering day with them, they had found a profusion of melons and buried tubers no great distance from their encampment. At least for the moment they had water in the pan and snares set. It would be a shame not to give the snares and more hunting some time to produce results. By now the contrast between their life in the bush and that lived by the people at Xai Xai was so marked in our minds that we feared for their welfare if they were forced into Xai Xai. We in no way wanted to be responsible for such a move. When Jack put our concerns into words, Peter reassured us.

"Jack, I think they made their point. We are aliens who were starting to tread on their privacy, but they're not really that miffed with us. It's not their nature. We have made it clear that we're pushing off tomorrow, so there is no reason to believe they'll leave now."

The setting of the five snares accomplished, Qui now gave us a

Noishay shredding sisal for snare cord—using the thumb piano as a workbench. —BG

Qui braiding wild sisal for snare cords. —WT

117

Noishay preparing snare; note "African squat" with buttocks touching heels. —WT

After unseasonal August rain, digging in dry pan yielded some water. Tasama rind is the only cup the Bushman knows. —WT

Above: Noishay tests the snare's springpole. —JP

Right: A Bushman's snare. —JP

Right: Lean Bushmen sample Peter's biltong as the clan and Wheeler's group prepare to part company.
—JP

Below: Average build Bushman Qui is dwarfed by medium-build Dr. Wheeler. —JP

farewell speech, as translated through Keeme and Shylock.

"It has been like a blessing to me and my band to be close to people I never thought I'd be close to. I thank you for not having troubled me ... or troubled us, and I think from now on I will have a little knowledge as to what a white man is and how he can react and how he is supposed to be handled, having been with you for this short time ... or rather for this long time we have been together. I didn't have any trouble with you, though I didn't mean to have been with you this much time. With the other group that we have just mentioned, that is somewhere there," — as Shylock paused and gestured off to the south — "and that we might possibly see again, I will have to let them know of the experience that we have had with you, and maybe some time they will meet a group like you and won't have to have the anxious time that I had the first two or three days. For all it was going to be, I was going to put a big blame on Keeme for having brought you to me, but now I have found that Keeme is not an enemy to me as he has not brought enemies. I can rely on him from now forwards. Thank you."

Peter now produced a few sticks of biltong, dried game meat, and offered it to each of the three, Qui, Noishay and Keeme as a small gesture of appreciation. They tested it and looked at each other quizzically, then smiling ... then laughing.

"We make biltong like this but why is yours sour tasting?" asked Keeme. But they apparently did not find the biltong all that disagreeable and said they would share it with the rest of their clan.

Our party was jubilant. Our week with the Bushmen was coming to a close but with laughter, not animosity. Qui was most gracious in his farewell and we felt that our contact with the clan had informed both sides in a positive way. Perhaps we had helped show Qui and his family that white men were not necessarily all bad. Peter and Shylock turned and made off toward our camp. Jack, Joel and I hung back, transfixed, watching the three zig-zagging between leafless thorn bushes and finally fade out of sight behind a veil of trees. It was a spellbinding moment, as though they were walking away from a magical encounter to a time and place 10,000 years ago!

Soon after we got back to camp, Peter turned on his short wave radio. It was just after mid-day, the appointed time to listen for Map to call from Tsodilo Hills. Map, who had left Hyena Camp the previous day, confirmed he was camped at Tsodillo Hills and briefed Peter on conditions and what he needed. Meanwhile, the rest of us settled into our circle of camp chairs around the fire.

Salome listened to our account of Noishay's rebuke of our questioning. "There's an aspect of you as giants or oppressors descending on them," she said. "In their legends and stories the Bushman are for the little guy, the underdog. Their mythical heroes are apt to be the little jackal who through trickery or cunning narrowly escapes, rather than the bigger more aggressive animal like the lion, who would end up being duped, singed, cuckolded or killed. Perhaps

Noishay felt the little guy needed to stomp on the giants a bit and so he let you have it for being so nosey."

When van der Post was finally able to locate some wild San, and get acquainted and spend time with them in the 1950's, he notes they clammed up, or could not hear, when his questions got out of the tangible into more philosophical issues, questions about what they believe, invading their privacy. As Noishay had said, "What we are doing is obvious, why any questions?" But what's evident to them is not apparent to us, and vice versa.

"Here in Botswana, one of the conflicts that is coming into their culture is the push for formal education," Salome said. "But it seems that some early education could work, as they really don't start hunting or formally learning their culture from their elders that early. They could go to school and then if they so chose, come back to the traditional nomadic culture." It seemed a way to help prepare them to be their own advocates.

"Yes," said Jack. "That is more or less what is happening with the Aborigines in Australia now that they have some land and a chance to carry on their traditional hunter-gatherer tradition. They go off to school, get some education in post agricultural revolution ways, and more and more are now starting to go back to the outback and their traditional culture. Although there are conflicts, at least now there exists the possibility of having two options, rather than no choice at all. Isn't that also what we would wish for the Bushmen?"

"But, some of the Bushmen have had a bad experience with education," said Salome. "The kids have come back smart-ass and sassy, mocking the parents' backwardness and ignorance, as seen in the eyes of modern civilization and their non-Bushmen teachers."

Education can be problematic for primitive peoples, and there is many an example of young people becoming unfit or unwilling to live in their original ways after being exposed to the white man's or Bantu's schools. But by the same token it will be necessary for some individuals to learn how to work the system on their people's behalf. There would be no easy answers.

"These days there is an often repeated conflict between the Kung themselves," said Peter, "as they are forced by conditions beyond their control to transition away from their foraging life, as they are dispossessed of their land by the cattle and their traditional range becomes devoid of game and veld food. Let's say that the little clan here decided it was too tough to make it anymore out here in the bush, and they go into Xai Xai lured by water. Then so as not to starve, they seek employment as hired herders for the Bantus, Tswana probably rather than Herero, as the Hereros tend to herd their own cattle."

Dr. Megan Biesele, who wrote a chapter in the Tobias book, observed and reported something like this. She was living with the Kung Bushmen people temporarily at Kauri, to record some of their folklore. Kauri has a fairly abundant water supply like Xai Xai, and is thus a cattle post or center, down the track a ways past the caves towards Maun. With dwindling game and all, the Kung Bushmen had been lured into the cattle post by the water, and the prospect of the 'better' modern life. Biesele found there were two Kung groups. One had become disenchanted and had quit work for the Bantu cattle owner, but was still camped near the water source. The other Bushmen group was still working for the Bantu cattle owners. These 'contents' were living in Bantu type mud walled thatched roof huts, intermarrying with the Bantu. The 'malcontents' were camped a mile away, at campfires in front of their traditional flimsy grass shelters, discussing endlessly whether to go elsewhere to find employment more to their liking, or whether to return to the old ways of foraging in the bush. There was an uneasy relationship between the two Bushmen camps. But the two groups participated in one another's periodic trance or healing dances. That was the one element of their old culture that both groups still held to, and the Bantus also came to the dances to be healed. This was the one area where the Bantu did not look down on the Bushmen or treat them as inferiors. They respected the Bushmen's powers of spiritual medicine and submitted to it.

We could imagine seeing a similar type situation coming and tearing up the close knit band unity of Qui's clan. Imagine Qui feeling old in his bones, pitching it in on surviving off the land, and opting for the security of the Xai Xai wells, while younger, more independent Noishay might return to try to make it again in the bush, with the clan splitting up after many heart rending and acrimonious discussions.

Just then a dust devil whirled past, leaves and dust spiraling up into the midday heat outside of camp. We all turned to watch it. The San believe a dust devil is the restless spirit of someone who took his own life. The human despair that can lead to suicide is not foreign to them, especially since the incursions of recent history.

"What about names," asked Tom. "How are they named, with no written records?"

"The Kung don't have surnames, only given or what we'd call Christian names," said Peter.

The Kung men have the right and duty to name their offspring. Anthropologists have established lists of the forty to fifty names each for males and females, to which they restrict themselves and which are thus often repeated. Kung have a practice of not naming their children after themselves. Rather, the first son usually is given the same name as his paternal grandfather, and the second son for the maternal grandfather. If a man has two wives, the first son of each, the two half-brothers, would have the same name, that of their father's father. Polygamy is known but not extensive in San culture. If something happens to either Qui or Noishay the surviving man might marry the widow. He is obliged to hunt and provide for her anyway. But there would be resistance from a wife to a husband's interest in taking another wife.

Daughters are likewise named first after the father's mother, then the mother's mother, following the generation skipping in naming offspring. Later children are usually named after aunts and uncles or others of their parents' kin.

With the Kung, kinship is an important relationship in meat sharing and gift giving and everyday life. The Kung know who is related by blood and by marriage, but anyone who has the same name is considered to have a special or near kinship relationship, even if it cannot be traced.

Kung pick up nicknames, referring to individual characteristics, character traits, or occasionally events: Qui Stomach, for a big eater, or Toma Word for an articulate man of wisdom and peace-making abilities. Then Short Goa for an unusually short individual, or Goa Feet for a relatively large-footed individual.

A buzzing flutter of hundreds of wings caused us all to stop talking. A flock of several hundred small, sparrow-like, pink and grey birds descended on the pan of precious water that bird lovers Peter and Salome had placed just outside the shade of Hyena Camp's grove of Kalahari apple leaf trees, some twenty meters from our campfire circle. We marveled at how they flew in such tight formation and in perfect union.

"Red billed quelea," said Peter. "One of the most common birds ... a pest really ... seed eater. They have replaced the locusts as the main plague to the grain and seed growing farmers of southern Africa. They are not uncommonly seen in flocks of hundreds of thousands, even millions." Then as one, in a buzz of wings, they lifted again in perfect unison. One had to wonder how so many birds could fly so close together without colliding. Or how they found feed enough for so many in such a seemingly barren place.

There is another curious family of African birds that is found in the Kalahari, called the honey guide. These birds attract the attention of the ratel or honey badger and sometimes of humans as well and will guide them to bee hives in the bush. There is a legend that if you follow a honey guide to a bee's nest but don't share the honey with the guide, the next time he will take his revenge by leading you to an encounter with a mamba.

Honey is very important to the San and they thus have a certain reverence for the bees. Bees, like the eland, hold a special status. The wife of the Great God is called the Mother of Bees. During the rainy season the San begin gathering honey and can be seen at night stopping and watching and tracking bees as they make their bee line back to their hive in a hollow tree.

There are stories of the San killing anyone who dares to poach their hives; for, once found, a hive is considered to belong to the finder. "Others have cows and sheep that live off what was our land," they have said. "We now have none. But we still have the right to the bees that live off the flowers."

124

Peter's call to shower and Salome's to dinner came and went as we continued to talk around the fire.

It has been shown that the hunter-gatherers have near perfect health. They suffer none of the health conditions that trouble people in developed societies like high cholesterol counts and high blood pressure. They have cholesterol counts around 120, while we are trying to reduce our 220's to 180. They eat a wide range of vegetables and only lean wild meat. Obesity is virtually unknown, and they have good teeth, no hearing loss and no evidence of coronary or hypertensive heart disease. The one 'vice' they have is smoking, which doctors have found leads to a prevalence of chronic bronchitis and emphysema.

There are some taboos related to food that vary with particular groups and seem to override the general rules of food sharing. Large male antelope are taboo to girls and young women. Ostrich eggs are reserved for the young and old and are not partaken of by hunter-aged males. Tortoise and Kori bustards are also reserved only for young and old. Married adults with children under one year old don't eat spring hare and steenbok, two of their most common prey. And the San generally don't eat the meat of predators that are known to eat man, such as lion, leopard, and hyena. Usually only old women eat snakes.

However, researchers have found that the Gwi San in the Central Kalahari regularly eat several varieties of snake, including puff adder and mamba, and the Marshalls refer to occasions when these two snakes, among others, were consumed. Snakes may well be a target of opportunity, utilized when found near the encampment but passed up on a long walk or hunt when they would be a burden to carry and susceptible to spoilage in the hot sun, as Qui and Noishay had shown no interest in the puff adders encountered on our hunt.

Peter and Salome and Liza were very knowledgeable and forthcoming in answering our questions. What we were coming to know about the life of these people was gleaned from many sources, from our guides, from each other, from our camp library and from what we could see with our 'too big eyes,' each bit woven into the larger tapestry that was the San. This was our last night at Hyena Camp and none of us was quite the same as we had been when we arrived. Our experiences with the clan and our discussions around the campfire contributed to a new awareness and understanding of a people who had captured our hearts. Their plight gave each of us much to think about.

"So, it's the feathers for me," I said as I vacated my chair and headed for my bed. Soon the bright, full moon was casting its shadow on the empty chairs as Hyena Camp fell quiet.

—9—
Tsodilo Hills

It was our last morning at Hyena Camp. I revived the campfire just as the sun broke the horizon on another crystal clear Kalahari morning. We had to leave camp by eight to make the hour and a half road trip west to Xai Xai, to meet bush pilot Andre and the Islander aircraft for the shuttle to Tsodilo Hills. Nothing in camp stirred. The moon was suspended large and pale in the western sky. Birds, apparently also happy with the unfolding morning, added to its beauty with their chattering and chirping song.

I felt sad at the thought of leaving this now familiar camp, the focal point for our idyllic visit with Qui's clan. I went into the sparse bush surrounding the camp to haul in one last log for the fire. The supply of wood close to camp was becoming depleted. Our robust fires had taken their toll.

Soon the camp began to stir. George stoked the cooking fire and prepared coffee. The aroma drifted across the cool morning air, reminding me of my joy of being in the African bush.

I gave voice to my glee at not being confronted with the concerns facing all the poor souls in the world, rushing around this Monday morning, getting into their coats and ties, enduring traffic jams, smog, the stressful world of plastic, steel, electronics and disturbing news on blaring radios and TV's.

Salome would be driving us to Xai Xai in the Toyota, then returning to load up the camp. She and Peter were expressing concern whether there was enough gas left to get her back to Maun, as there was not a gas station anywhere on the way!

About a half hour before we were to leave Hyena Camp, Keeme materialized. Peter and Shylock went out and joined him for a last discussion.

Keeme reported that everything was fine with the clan. Around their campfire they were giggling about their visit from the giant strangers from far-far-far away. They were going to stay on here, and the men were going out hunting. The previous afternoon they had already caught their first korhaan in one of the snares.

Yes, Peter had taken a risk bringing us together and while we may have stressed them a bit, presumably no permanent damage had been done. Perhaps our visit would even turn out to be an event they would recall and talk about for years to come.

Bushmen do not have a calendar; they don't know or remember what year they were born in or how old they are. No birth certificates. They tend to tie their age and their life to major natural events or things that are especially memorable. In future years this little clan might well tell the clan's youngest, "You were a baby when the white strangers came and asked all the questions."

As we got ready to abandon Hyena Camp, I carefully packed the two sketches Liza had made as she sat in on the campfire discussions. The 'Bush for the Bushman' drawings were treasured mementos of our campfire discussion and symbolic of our desire to do something to help Qui and his clan maintain their way of life. I also found a safe place in my gear for some of the quills left by the hyena after his dinner of African porcupine. These quills dwarf those from any porcupine I had seen in North America, some being almost a foot long and a quarter inch in diameter.

"Good-bye you all," we shouted to Liza, Shylock and George as we drove away from Hyena Camp. *"Kwaheri"* replied George, in Swahili which he'd learned in earlier years, hunting seasonally with white hunters in Kenya. A part of me wished I could stay there forever and another part was eager to get to Tsodilo and see the rock paintings. The track west to Xai Xai passed within three hundred meters of the Bushman's encampment. As we went by, we could just see their grass hut shelters.

Joel put our thoughts into words, "Good-bye, you lovely people. Thanks for an unforgettable experience, and may you endure."

"And may we or somebody get off our duffs and do something to ensure that," added Jim.

Peter paused periodically to point out birds: longtailed shrike, buffalo weaver, swallow-tailed bee eater, yellow-billed hornbill, brown snake eagle among many others. On the remoteness, Salome remarked, "A week here, and only one other vehicle passed, a Landrover from a mission." Otherwise we were all lost in thought. I was surely not alone in reflecting with some melancholy sadness on leaving our once-in-a-lifetime rendezvous with the valiant band of still-skin-wearing, civilization-avoiding, hardy, healthy, adorable Bushmen.

Then there was Xai Xai. As we drove toward the open glade in the ancient dry river valley where the plane was to land, the two-rutted track took us past a collection of grass-thatched mud huts. Brightly dressed Herero women came running out and tried to flag us down, then continued running down the track after us, hoping to sell us the dolls they had made that were colorful replicas of themselves.

As we stopped at the Xai Xai airstrip near one of the town's single-bucket wells, there materialized beside the Herero hawkers the usual kaleidescope gathering of gawking village dwellers. Among the assortment were many showing San features, but they were all dressed in tattered European clothes, not in skins like Qui. Keeme's Bushman mother, married to a Herero, could well be among them. Some are employed by the Batawana or Herero cattle owners, some are their kin living off their poorly paid mates. Most of the men would be off in the adjacent bush grazing longhorn cattle for cattle owners. We had come to see cattle in a new light, as the innocent pawns in the rivalry between the recently-arrived cattle owners and the dispossessed aboriginal hunter-gatherers and their wild game animals. Each needed land to survive.

The whole cattle post had turned out before our plane arrived, small children not old enough to walk were slung on their mothers' backs or carted by older siblings, while the ever-present scroungy mixture of gaunt dogs milled about inquisitively.

The low level flight from Xai Xai north to Tsodilo took about thirty-five minues. The world in all directions had an immense flatness to it. After the one break, the shiprock outcropping of Aha Hills rising above the acacia thorn scrub, there was only the otherwise monotonous flat horizon northeast of Xai Xai. On our flight path north, the west edge of that wetland jewel, the Okavango Delta, would be some sixty or seventy kilometers off to the east, too far away to change our view of flat dry sparsely-covered Kalahari bushveld. Jack, up front spotting, cried out on two occasions, "There's a bunch of wildebeests down there," as in each case he drew our attention to a black herd of six to ten animals grouped under the meager shade provided by the Kalahari's sparse trees.

The country off in the distance took on a hazy blue-green color as the meager trees and bush cover lined up, but, looking more directly down, the country had a distinctive yellow color, the unending Kalahari sands broken by skimpy well spaced splotches of green.

Jack shouted back over the sound of the engine, pointing out one exception to this color scheme. "Those yellow stripes against the green stretching off into the far distance—they're continuations of what we saw between Maun and Xai Xai, million year-old fossilized sand dune bases which extend clear on up to the Caprivi Strip and the Angola border."

Then something started to break the horizon ahead. Out of the haze, a dark form, like a ship materializing out of the sea.

"That's Tsodilo Hills, legendary birthplace of the Bushman," said Peter. "One can imagine how this singular prominent feature in the otherwise vast flat expanse would attract people from a great distance."

The silent, brooding hills, lost in the vast expanses of the heat-shimmering Kalahari, are surrounded by an aura of mystery.

Before landing at the airstrip south of the hills, Andre gave us an aerial tour as Peter pointed out the features of Tsodilo Hills. "This biggest and highest rocky ridge in the south is called the male mountain." There was a slight break as the first outcropping ended, then the next one started as we flew north. "Now we have the slightly smaller female mountain. It's on the female mountain where the permanent water is and most of the rock paintings. That much lower and small outcrop is the outcast woman, and the other smaller outcrops sprinkled about are the children." At their highest, the rock structures of micaceous quartzite schist rise about a thousand feet above the surrounding terrain with many sheer vertical walls ending in rough crags.

The imposing hills drew us to ponder their mystery and myth. The names Peter related came from one Bushman legend surrounding the hills. It tells of a man who had two wives and was showing more attention to his younger second wife. The jealous first wife hit him over the head and fled into the desert. Because there was no peace among them, God punished them by reducing them all to stone.

As we landed we noted considerable activity, people and animals at the community water well to the south. Permanent habitation at Tsodilo has occurred only since two wells have been installed. When van der Post first visited here thirty-five years earlier there were no man-made wells and no one lived here. Then Tsodilo was visited only seasonally by nomadic San. They obtained water from the prehistoric permanent spring located in a cleft of rock on the side of the female mountain, inaccessible to cattle or game, which we would visit.

Our Toyota was at the airstrip, the sole vehicle we were to see in the Tsodilo area. Map whisked us off to the north, toward our camp on the west side of the female mountain.

"There's a pair of leopard about," said Map. "I've heard them coughing at night and seen their tracks in the morning. Looks to be a big male and his female. Then there's the odd hyena around, and Gowi says there's greater kudu here around the hills." Van der Post makes mention of kudu on his visit to Tsodilo in the 50s. It was reassuring to know that they were still to be found.

The greater kudu is an antelope, a bush browser rather than a grass grazer. Bulls attain five hundred pounds or better and are majestic animals having great spiraling horns. The females have no horns. Both are a greyish-brown with a distinctive white stripe down their back bone, and vertical white stripes down their flanks. This white striping is the bush buck family emblem, seen on eland, bushbuck, bongos, nyala, and lesser kudu. The greater kudu and sable are the most sought-after African trophies. Hemingway spent considerable time hunting the two in Tanganyika. I had successfully hunted both kudu and sable in his tracks in what was by then called Tanzania, but not without sharing

Hemingway's great effort and frustrations.

We pulled off the track into our new camp in a pleasant, heavily shaded, grove of trees. Tsodilo Camp was a cut-down version of the layout at our Hyena-Porcupine Camp, located very close to where the ground sloped up to the sheer rockwalls of the female mountain towering some several hundred feet above the surrounding flat terrain.

We gathered around the fire in our circle of canvas chairs. Map briefed us while Mansu prepared lunch.

When van der Post came to Tsodilo back in the mid-fifties he found no one. Only nomadic San came seasonally or on occasion for a conclave or visit, but van der Post found only their cold camp fires. Van der Post had grown up in South Africa, been through World War II; in his case a long war stretching from Abyssinia through the war in the Pacific. He had been in a Japanese prison camp and then stayed on with the British who had military operations in Malaysia after the war.

Not too long after the war he had concentrated his interests on the Bushmen. He came from South African Dutch-French Huguenot ancestors who in earlier generations fought wild Bushmen, then later he was exposed to tame Bushmen as servants and workers. He had read Bleek and Stow, South African writers who were alone among academics before the twentieth century to take an interest in the Bushmen's history, culture, language, rock paintings, folklore, legends and mythology. By this time the free-roaming nomadic Bushmen had long since been annihilated in South Africa. Bleek and Stow gathered most of their myths and history by talking to Bushmen prisoners working on a jetty in Cape Town. Van der Post raised some sponsorship money to travel up into what was then Bechuanaland's Kalahari to try to learn if there were, in fact, some surviving hunter-gatherer San and, if so, to film them for the BBC. Even back then he was apprehensive about finding Bushmen still wild enough to merit photographing.

Van der Post's travels, documented in his first book, *The Lost World of the Kalahari*, took him to three places in the Kalahari: inside the Okavango, Tsodilo Hills and finally the Kalahari east of Ghanzi. He went into the Okavango looking for river Bushmen, but found none and became convinced they had perished. During his Okavango ordeal his black African guide, a mystic healer or shaman, told van der Post of Tsodilo Hills as a place where nomadic wild Bushmen gathered. So van der Post set out to investigate.

He had four Landrovers that had come out from England especially rigged with extra fuel and water tanks. Samutchoso, the African Bantu guide and shaman, had promised to take van der Post to Tsodilo even though he had a great reverence for the place. However, he made van der Post promise no game would be shot on approaching the hills, so as not to anger the Tsodilo spirits, until their permission could be obtained.

Van der Post had two European friends who were assisting him on the expedition and providing camp meat. With his other preoccupations, with camera malfunctions and cameraman problems, van der Post had to leave the expedition temporarily and return to Johannesburg, and had forgotten to tell the two about not killing anything. Approaching Tsodilo, they shot a warthog and some other small game. The guide was horrified and furious, but the group eventually continued on. At Tsodilo they were repeatedly swarmed and stung by bees, and their new movie camera failed to work. Samutchoso started to kneel at the hillside spring and experienced being jerked over backwards by an unseen force.

A couple of days of recurring bee attacks and camera malfunctions convinced van der Post that the Bushman Gods were angry with his party and he decided it would be best to leave Tsodilo. On the mystic's suggestion van der Post wrote an apology to the Tsodilo spirits and had all his companions sign it and he buried it in a lime juice bottle below one of the more spectacular Bushman painting sites now referred to as the van der Post panel. The bottle has since been recovered and is in a museum in Gaborone.

Van der Post wasn't having much luck. He had seen no river Bushmen and now he was leaving Tsodilo with nothing more than some footage of rock paintings. He had to make yet another trip to Johannesburg to sort out the camera problem and then traveled on to a third location in the heart of the southern Kalahari east of Ghanzi. After anxious searching he finally found some Bushmen in a remote, trackless corner of the Kalahari where they were camped near a sip well, and got some film footage.

This central Kalahari area was even drier, and more desolate, than Xai Xai, but the San people had found a way to locate underground water. They had an uncanny knack of identifying a promising spot, and would run a hollow reed several feet, or even meters, down into the ground. They would then suck on the reed, pulling a vacuum. The water would be forced up the reed and into their mouths, then would run out of their mouth down a grass stem, drip by drip, and collect in an ostrich eggshell. They were then known to cache or bury water-filled ostrich shells for later survival needs.

In the northern part of the Kalahari the Kung talk about water rights. In the harsher thirstland of the central Kalahari the Gwi Bushmen talk about melon rights. Each person eats up to ten pounds of melon per day to get his required moisture. A sad time comes at the end of the dry season or in droughts when the tasama melons have all turned yellow and become bitter and are no longer a dependable source of moisture. The Gwi sing laments about the 'bitter melons'.

We were accompanied by our local Bushman guide, Gowi, as we marched off after lunch to get our first look at the Bushmen's paintings. Gowi is a hunter, who is now working more and more as a tourist guide. He lives in the village in the morning shadow of the male mountain, which we passed coming from the airstrip. He wears shoes and European clothing.

The paintings are breath-taking to see. They are of the Bushmen and their animals. At the first site was an elephant, a giraffe, and their sacred eland.

Seeing these paintings gave me the same eerie, haunting, feeling I had experienced when visiting Bushman painting sites at the Giant's Castle Game Reserve high up in the South African Drakensburg, wondering about these long-departed spirits who painted rock walls and caves all over southern Africa. Our group was incredulous and angered when reminded that as late 1910 a cash bounty was paid for shooting these gentle people. The bounty was discontinued, but throughout the twenties there was still no ban on such killings. It was not until as late as 1952 that laws were written that identified the San as members of the human race and deserving of civil rights.

"Bushmen got a bad name for killing cattle," Map told us. "They wouldn't give up to the encroaching whites." Early whites and especially the Dutch Afrikaans farmers and cattle herders declared war on the Bushmen, deeming them vermin to be shot on sight. People were afraid of their poisoned arrows, since there is no known antidote for the poison. Once hit, you were dead. John Campbell, a missionary in the early 1800s, chronicled the lingering death and the great pain that accompanied it when a white companion was wounded in the shoulder.

In the early years of white encroachment, the firearms of the whites were effective for only short distances—about the same as the Bushman's poisoned arrows, and the invaders advanced, protected from arrows by heavy oxhide screens or shields. Two hundred years later the more modern firearms could dispose of the Bushman from positions well beyond the range of his arrows. And it is only recently that in the slowly changing attitude toward the Bushmen, they are protected by law from being shot.

The paint seemed to be enduring well on these exposed walls, generally without any protecting overhang. No one knows for sure what the paint is made of. Unfortunately, with the disappearance of artists have gone the secrets of how they made up their paint. One theory is that the Bushmen got their pigments from mineral oxides, shades of yellow, red and brown from iron, black from manganese, and white from zinc. The minerals were possibly bound by blood, urine, milk, animal fat or honey. One of the last known painters was slain by mounted Dutch in Basutoland, now Lesotho, in about 1866, and was found to have ten small animal horn containers around his belt, each with a different color.

Tsodilo is one of the major rock painting sites in both the current and the former ranges of the San. There are also paintings all through the east coast areas of South Africa, the Drakensburgs, Kruger and up into Zimbabwe. They extend into Angola and Namibia, some even in Mozambique, Zambia and as far north as Malawi. Paintings have been discovered in over six thousand locations in southern Africa. At Tsodilo not less then thirty-five hundred individual paintings, clustered over more then two hundred separate locations, have been found.

Mansu cooked the evening meal over our campfire—no separate cooking fire like at Hyena camp. Our conversations inevitably returned to the Bushmen and what could be done for them.

After dinner, we were sitting in the dark in our usual circle around the fire, continuing our Bushman discussions. My eye caught something moving across the ground toward Joel.

After our snake scares, Joel caught the direction of my glance and instinctively raised up his bare feet. A large—four inches in length—black scorpion was not six inches from Joel's toes and headed his way. Stinger up, claws out, with the light from the fire dancing across his profile, the scorpion stopped dead. Minor pandemonium broke out.

With all our movement the scorpion had stopped and circled around on guard. I grabbed an empty tumbler from the table and scooped it up, saving it from being stomped on by some of my mates. I set the glass temporarily on the camp table nearby, and we went on with our campfire discussion. But a little later, as Mansu made his rounds picking things up, he scooped the glass up, not knowing about the scorpion.

"Look out Mansu," I shouted as he pitched the glass away onto the ground. The scorpion was on the loose again.

About an hour later, Wally stepped out back of the tents for a call of nature and cried out, "Here's the scorpion."

I proceeded to recapture it. At least it looked to be the same one. This time I put the scorpion in my empty water bottle, secure under a lid.

Later, as we were sitting around the fire with the scorpion incident behind us, there was a rumble of thunder in the distance. Lightning flashed, illuminating towering cumulus thunderheads. A storm was fast approaching from the southwest. "It never rains in the Kalahari in August," we mockingly shouted out in unison.

This was another male rain. For the San, rain with thunder and lightning is a male rain. A quiet gentle rain without lightning is female. They think of the leopard as the creator of male rain. The lightning comes from flashes from the leopard's eyes, the thunder is growls from deep in his throat.

The violent storm put a stop to our conversations for the night. We had to seek the shelter of our tents.

Joel and I listened to the sharp pounding of rain on the canvas. No doubt about the masculinity of this rain. The leopard was doing his thing, the echoing sharp crash of thunder and flashes of lightning went on and on. One feels a bit insignificant in the remote Kalahari in a violent thunderstorm, with nothing overhead but thin canvas.

Then, eventually, I could hear Joel's light snoring. To induce sleep, I decided to count sheep the way an engineer does it, by counting the seconds between the flash of lightning and the thunder clap—light being nearly instantaneous; sound taking five seconds to travel a mile. Ten seconds between flash and bang, the lightning is two miles away. This storm was here and around us. There were several flashes followed by deafening thunder separated by much less than a five second count. Eventually the interval increased and the noise level receded as the storm moved away. But did it rain! As I listened to the pounding of the rain on canvas, I wondered if this amount of rain in August could be signaling an end to the several years' Kalahari drought. If so, it would make Qui and his clan happy, allowing them to stay in their bush and avoid Xai Xai!

As I awaited sleep, I reflected back on our campfire discussions, looking for a solution to the Bushman's plight. Traditionally, when confronted by advancing civilization, the San have taken refuge deeper into the bush or the thirstland of the Kalahari. Stories of savageness and poisoned arrows and the logistical problems of finding them have discouraged curiosity. Because of this, most people are not aware of the San's current situation; out of sight, and out of mind. Except for the popular movie, *The Gods Must Be Crazy*, many Americans and other western people might never ever have heard of the Bushmen. There are anthropological studies, but these are not available in the popular press. Suggestions by anthropologists on behalf of the San tend to get swept under the rug by adminsitrators with the power to act. Most politicians, conservationists, cattlemen, miners, industrialists and their well-financed lobbies have never seen the likes of Qui and his band, but are all, knowingly or unknowingly, competing for the San's traditional land.

Certainly, much could be done for the Bushman. As a beginning, the edict evicting them from the Central Kalahari Reserve should be reversed, ensuring that the few that are still hunter-gatherers, like Qui and his band, have land, their own bush. Land for the San need not mean that some other entity must lose land. With 17% of Botswana dedicated to reserves, there is certainly room in the parks for both animals and a few clans of hunter-gatherers. In the Central Kalahari alone, tens of thousands of wildebeest die up against the hoof and mouth disease isolation fences. In comparison, a small number of hunting Bushman harvesting a few animals for food would have minimal effect. To complicate matters, any effort on Qui's behalf should also focus on the majority of San, the tame Bushmen. They also need land and water away from the traditional Bantu herders, where they can integrate into modern society following a transitional mixed economy.

The government needs to listen to these people, find out what they want, then let them participate in organizing and administering the solutions. But who really knows about them, much less will speak for them?

"What beautiful fresh air after last night's downpour," Wally's voice broke the early morning stillness. "No Los Angeles smog or air pollution here." The birds around Scorpion Camp—Cape turtle dove and bleating warbler—seemed exhilarated too, in the aftermath of the unexpected, but welcome rain.

As more of our group gathered around the fire to ward off the early morning chill, Joel asked Map if, like van der Post, we had angered the Gods. "We had a sprinkle, then the downpour at Hyena Camp, but last night's unseasonal August lightning and rain tops them all!"

"The Gods are not angry," Map replied. "If anything they're paying us a compliment. Rain means life to the Kalahari people who struggle to survive with little or no water. You won't see them turning down a rain anytime. The unexpected August rain is why Qui and his clan's dry well went wet."

Our visit to the Kalahari in late 1988 did in fact come at the end of a five-year period, 1982 through 1987, of poor rains, a severe Kalahari drought.

"Do you guys know what *Pula* stands for?" Peter asked.

"That's the local money here in Botswana isn't it?" Tom answered.

"Right. But *pula* is also a greeting in Setswana, the Bantu language of Botswana. But more important, it is the word for rain. Think of it. To call your money rain, and every time you greet one another you say "rain," not hello. This Kalahari thirstland lives and dies over rain, and to the Bushman rain is a life thing, as opposed to the sun which is a death thing."

The scorpion from the previous night was still in my plastic water bottle. Years before, in Libya, I had kept pet scorpions in a bottle on my desk, feeding them flies. There were a few flies about, but these had not been bothersome enough in this winter season to make catching them, to feed to the scorpion, worthwhile. So I went a short way out in the bush and turned Blackie loose. After the van der Post experience, I didn't want to bring down the wrath of the Tsodilo Gods by harming any of his creatures.

Both the Kung of the northern Kalahari and the Gwi of the Central Kalahari have similar, if somewhat varying, religious beliefs that involve a greater and a lesser God. In their many myths and legends, the good Great God lives in the eastern sky and the secondary, sometimes mischievous or bad God lives in the western sky. The Great God in the east created the earth and is the giver and keeper of all things—children, water, the rains, the sky, all the plants, all the animals. He created the people and gave them the knowledge to make all their weapons and tools and the poison for their arrows. Thus the hunting and gathering ways were decreed from the beginning, as was the Bushman's affinity for nature: their nomadic, foraging culture *is* their religion.

In their myths there is a contrast between the Gods; the Great God in the east is the tallest of men, with supernatural powers and capable of assuming the form of animals or objects as he chooses. He can change people into animals. He has great power and does not reveal

The Bushman's Louvre, the female mountain, Tsodilo Hills. —JP

The craggy, lichen-covered rock adds to the mystery and aura of Tsodilo Hills— legendary birthplace of the Bushman. —BG

A Xai Xai one-bucket well. —JP

Right: Tame Bushman at Tsodilo well. —JP

Below: The "despondent" tame Bushmen at Tsodilo Hills. —JR

Right: Five dirty-faced urchins at Tsodilo tame-Bushman village. Note the varying genetics from Bushman to Bantu. —JW

Below: Young Bushman girl with traditional right-shoulder tie of gameskin kaross. —BG

Victorian-dressed Herero women, out to hawk doll replicas of themselves to visiting strangers, tower over the squatting lone tame-Bushman woman at Xai Xai. —JP

Bantu cattle, the Bushman's nemesis, hanging around a Tsodilo well. —JP

Tame-Bushman Gowi, our Tsodilo guide, practices a mixed economy, still engaging in traditional foraging when not guiding tourists. —JP

Bantu woman at Tsodilo. When van der Post visited in the mid 50's before well drilling, this was the exclusive domain of the Bushman. —JP

Except for among the wild Bushmen, rural African women's daily routine normally includes transporting water on their heads. Tsodilo Hills in the background. —JP

Above and below: Dr. Jack Wheeler at van der Post panel at Tsodilo Hills. —JW

141

Right: River Bushman plays a tune on his thumb piano. —BG

Below: Clan's three girls and young unattached woman. —JP

himself to ordinary living people.

By contrast the lesser God in the western sky is depicted as a very small, incompetent fellow who brings misfortune, more like our devil. He is subservient to the Great God but often acts on his own. Traveling in a whirlwind, he can mischievously cause sickness and death to those he touches in passing. He is occasionally glimpsed lurking in the shadow of trees.

As eggs cooked over the open fire, Gowi, our guide, appeared. He had the obvious San features, short stature and light build with the prominent high cheek bones, apricot yellow skin, Asiatic eyefolds, broad flat nose and wiry hair in spiral curls. He was about the size of Noishay, perhaps more sturdy. He was dressed in a short sleeved shirt and long pants and what looked like game department or military issue boots, complete with socks. The previous day he'd worn shorts and a shirt jacket. Most bush Africans I had seen through the years were lucky to have a single tattered suit of European clothes.

"Wow, two days, two changes of clothes for Gowi," I remarked to Map, "Is that affluence?"

"With some tourists visiting Tsodilo now, he survives as a part-time guide," Map explained. "But he's a renowned hunter as well, and you can bet he still hunts seasonally. Gowi is one of the lucky exceptions who seems to have made the transition with minimal scars."

Gowi spoke enough Tswana to communicate with Map and to a degree with Peter. Shylock's and Keeme's services were no longer available to us. We were preoccupied as to whether Shylock, Salome, Liza and George had made it back to Maun by now and were not out of gas along the track.

We drove to several of the more distant rock painting sites, bailing out and hiking up into the hills of the female mountain, the giver of life. Even though the male mountain is bigger, it is the female mountain that the Bushman have chosen for their paintings. One panel in an angular nook on a vertical wall was of two rhinos in silhouette joined by a domestic bull. Further on in another vertical crevice were rhino and several spring hare. Rhinos are not animals that have been reported in the Tsodilo area in recorded time.

"And that up there is the famous van der Post panel," said Map pointing over tree tops to a grouping of animal figures at the top of a vertical wall some hundred feet above. Van der Post was the first European known to have discovered and reported it, and it has since become one of the most frequently visited and photographed. "It's here he reportedly buried his bottle with a note pleading for the God's forgiveness before beating a hasty retreat from Tsodilo," Map informed us.

We scaled the rock wall to get up to inspect more closely the van der Post frieze. The main grouping was of four eland and a giraffe painted in silhouette in a reddish-brown color on the weathered wall with its soft hues of grey, buff, pink, and lavender. "Look where the artist has signed one eland and the giraffe with his hand prints," Map noted.

"There's an interesting parallel between the Bushman and the Australian Aborigine," observed Jack. "The Australian Aborigines also leave their hand prints on cave and rock painting areas, but they stencil it. They put their hand on the rock and blow a white paint from their mouths onto their hand which leaves their hand imprint bordered in white."

For a different interpretation, in 1973, while doing a *National Geographic* video in Botswana, John Marshall met with some of the Nyae Nyae Kung that he and his family had befriended and studied, but whom John had not seen for almost fifteen years. Marshall took Toma, one of the prominent members of the Nyae Nyae clan to Tsodilo. Toma thought that the hand prints near the eland were not a signature of the artist, but rather the artist depicting the way the hunter approached the animals, by stalking it on all fours.

"Tsodilo has been called the Bushman's Louvre," said Map. "There are thousands of rock and cave paintings throughout southern Africa. This is one of the more important sites but there's no mention of it prior to van der Post's coming here in the mid '50's."

Hidden deep in the bush, far away from the musty museum corridors, glass cases and electric lights, Tsodilo Hills is one of the prehistoric art wonders of the world.

"How can it be that nobody discovered it before that?" asked Jack.

"Well, from the mid-1850's on, Livingstone and others came through Botswana, but the early guys all passed east of the Okavango. Tsodilo was on the wrong side of the Okavango and too far north of Ghanzi. Gcwihaba caverns were only first visited by a European in 1934. Tsodilo was that much further away, and in *Testament to the Bushmen*, Jane Taylor says that van der Post is the first white man reported to have set eyes on the hills or their paintings."

In the '50's. the Marshalls in Nyae-Nyae found a huge baobab tree with carvings made by early Europeans who were passing through the remote Kalahari plateau. This tree chronicled that there was some movement through the vast area to our west by German military at the turn of the century during their Herero wars, and a few Europeans, possibly hunters, came before and after. Still, the Tsodilo area is a quiet cul-de-sac of the Kalahari, well off the beaten track when van der Post visited it in the 1950's, and continues relatively so today.

Local legend has it that the Great God created the Tsodilo Hills and lived there, creating the San people and the wild animals of their domain. Up on the west side of the female mountain is a permanent spring the God created where he knelt to drink. Legend has it that two depressions in the rock are his knee prints left when he kneeled down to drink, all endearing the hills to the San.

We climbed out of the Toyota and started up the steep rocky trail to the spring several hundred feet up the side of the female mountain. The stepping stones were worn smooth, and one imagined untold numbers of bare feet passing here over the course of the centuries. Gowi and the other Bushman believe that the "everlasting water", as van der Post refers to the spring, is guarded by a large serpent. Gowi cast some stones up the path as he approached the well to scare away the mythical serpent.

Bud, one of the first up the steep trail called out, "But there *is* a big snake here!" And there was a python of some eight to ten feet in length staring up at us from the water surface. The permanent source of water is in a cave-like depression that runs back into the hill at a forty-five degree slope. At the bottom is a pool of standing water some ten to fifteen feet below the rock rim. The surface of the pool, where the python was, is some eight to ten feet across.

"But this is not the serpent Gowi talks about," Map said. "The guardian serpent is not visible even to the Bushman."

Anthropologists have found that the San have a rich repertoire of myths, fables and legends. Some revolve around the roguish trickster God, his wives and his heroic daughter-in-law. Basic themes deal with living, marriage, sex, food quest, sharing, family relationships, divisions of labor, birth and death, murder, blood vengeance, and the creation of the present world order and the people's relationship to other more advanced societies and economies. An example of a Bushman legend was brought to mind by our encountering a python in the well.

Python is a beautiful heroine, married to the Kori Bustard. Python's jealous younger sister, Jackal, tricks Python into climbing a tree for some veld fruit. The limb breaks and she falls into a deep well beneath the tree. Having disposed of Python, Jackal puts on her sister's discarded clothing and ornaments and struts off to the encampment to alienate the affections of Python's husband. Kori comes back from hunting and misses his wife. Imposter Jackal appears doing a poor job of imitating the smooth regal step of Python. Kori greets 'Python' by passing a wildebeest tail whisk dipped in fat across her forehead. Imposter Jackal, not being accustomed to this high-class greeting courtesy, greedily licks the fat, tipping off Kori Bustard to the sham, and he immediately schemes to kill Jackal.

He arranges the evening sleeping place by putting poisoned arrowheads in the sand under Jackal's bed of skins. Jackal complains as she is pricked, but Kori responds, "This is where you have always slept since we were married. Why complain now?" Jackal holds her tongue and by dawn succumbs to the arrow's poison. Kori Bustard gets up and goes hunting. The grandmother and young child find Jackal dead, and proceed to roast and eat her.

Eventually Kori Bustard goes to recover his real wife from the depths of the well. He calls all the animals to assist. Tortoise offers a leg, but it is too short for the deep well. Eland tries. Still too short. Kudu and gemsbok try, but can't reach Python at the well's bottom. Then giraffe is called. Only his long leg will reach the bottom. Python has given birth, and giraffe pulls her and her children out of the well on his leg. They all proceed back to the encampment on a carpet of skins provided by Kori where they rejoice with relatives over the demise of Jackal and the rescue of Python.

We looked out over the flat dry Kalahari from the vantage point of the spring well. Looking south toward Hyena Camp then sweeping east toward Namibia and north toward Angola, the desert stretched in an unbroken monotonous expanse to a far flat horizon across a sea of bone-dry, heat-shimmering sand, sparse bush and low trees giving it a green-grey hue. There was an immensity and absolute flatness to the panorama. The attraction of this spring in the waterless Kalahari expanse was apparent, for its spiritual as well as its survival value.

To see all the paintings at Tsodilo would take several weeks, and it is not yet certain that these all have been discovered or included in the estimated count of 3,500 individual images at 250 locations. We had visited a cross section of some of the more representative ones, and now the sacred spring. Next we would go to Gowi's village to see for ourselves the state of the tame Bushman.

We drove back south to where the village lay against the west side of the male mountain. We stopped the Toyota in front of the village and a group of five dirty-faced urchins, boys of eight to twelve years of age, materialized to greet us. Two of the boys had the high cheek bones and apricot complexions of the Basarwa, two had Bantu features, and one fell somewhere in between. The genetic lines were obviously blurring.

The village was inside a small compound enclosed by a rustic four foot high picket fence constructed of slim tree trunks or limbs driven into the ground and lashed together at the top by a pole railing. There were less than a dozen round dwellings, some thatch-roofed, mud huts of the simplest Bantu construction, then some leaning more to the 'stick and straw' Bushman style.

The friendly group of boys escorted us through the narrow entrance in the enclosure. I had to turn sideways to squeeze through. One presumed it was constructed in this way to keep cattle out. Despite having access to a well nearby, some of the children obviously had not had water on their faces in a long time. They looked much dirtier and more unkempt than Qui's proud clan in the waterless bush. There were gaunt dogs and chickens foraging in the general filth and clutter inside the compound.

"You're a real ham," said Tom to one, as the lad danced around trying to place himself in front of Tom's Polaroid camera. As usual the Polaroid pictures were a big hit with the children.

There were several new arrow quivers hanging from a post nearby, probably intended for Beth Oliver. One middle-aged lady with huge breasts, bare to the waist, with a bright orange skirt, was seated on the ground near the entrance busily making craft items.

Three men in tattered European clothes were lying on the ground at the back of the compound. They looked at us with rather vacant, lost looks in their eyes. Flies crawled over them at will and an aura of despair and gloom hung over them. They had the distinctive Bushman features but lacked the sparkle, vivacity and industry of Qui's clan back near Hyena Camp. So these were the suffering tame Bushman we had been hearing about. We felt truly sorry for these individuals, who no longer knew their forefathers' secrets of the hills, and who were at a loss to adapt to modern culture. They were left to suffer in a no-man's land.

Surely they were not in this state by their own choice, but as a result of losing their land and with it their nomadic existence, heritage and culture. They were people lost in a rapidly changing modern economy, forced to take up permanent sedentary life here near a water hole. This was what Peter and Map had been talking about. The men appeared to be living worse than prisoners, unable to bridge the distance between the free nomadic lives they had known and the cattle herding culture of the more sedentary people who now claimed their land. It could not be an easy leap for the Bushmen, requiring them to make, in a generation or so, a change that had taken thousands of years and many generations for their new masters to accomplish.

We drove across to the south side of the airstrip to visit the well, a beehive of activity. San and Bantu girls and women were queued up, waiting their turn. Two girls were industriously turning the crank which simultaneously reeled in and out a double chain that lowered an empty five-gallon bucket deep into the well as it raised the full one, like a crank handle operated elevator. We queued up and waited our turn to draw some water. Most of the women carried their youngest child slung on their backs or at their side to be nursed on the spot whenever the small hand searched for a breast.

I tried to capture on film the profile of a woman leaving the well. This was a typical scene being repeated throughout Africa's rural bush—a woman with a full five-gallon bucket of water adroitly balanced on her head, a baby slung over her back, moving at a fast pace on the long walk back to her mud hut.

Bud captured the scene with, "WOW—look how her hips, shoulders and neck are moving all over the place, while the top of her head is straight and level, with not a slosh of water out of the plumb full bucket."

There was a herd of cattle hanging around the well. Among them a couple of bulls whose body size and huge horns would have put most Texas longhorns to shame. Except for this and one other well, modern man or domesticated beast would not be here at all, and Tsodilo would still be the sacred sphere of only the traditional nomadic San. In 1987 when van der Post returned to Tsodilo with Prince Charles he remarked at finding nothing to his liking in the changes there. In the thirty years since his first visit the wells had been drilled, attracting the cattle owners to its steady water source, and effectively dispossessing the Bushmen.

Later in the evening we were gathered around the fire discussing the Bushmen and their game, and their nemesis, land grabbing Bantu and their environmentally destructive cattle, threatening the Bushmen's domain and nomadic culture.

"You saw a bow and arrow hunt, and snaring, but you missed spring hare hooking," said Map. One of the Bushman's 'how things are' myths is about his spring hare hook. The Bushmen's great God became angry because the spring hare borrowed the God's son's duiker loin cloth to dance in and did not return it. To punish the spring hare, the God devised the first spring hare hook, so that men could capture the spring hare as food. Big antelope like eland, gemsbok, kudu and wildebeest, that the Bushmen hunters kill with their famous bows and poison arrows, are few and far between. They spend a lot of time snaring and capturing smaller animals they can get out of burrows, like warthogs, honey badger, ant bears, porcupine and the spring hare. The spring hare is a little like a large kangaroo rat in appearance. It bounds along on its back feet, zigging and zagging along on its nocturnal feeding. The spring hare pole has a 'branch hook' on the end and can be up to six meters long, usually of several branches spliced by notching, and bound with animal sinews. The Bushmen track the hare into one of its burrows and run the pole down after the hare with a stroking motion, listening to the end of the pole to see if they have the hare. The idea is to place the hook beyond the hare to keep him from escaping via one of his several other burrows. Once he is hooked, the hunters dig down and capture him. When they go on a spring hare hunt they often tuck the hook end and a portion of the poles through their waist band, and let the long slender pole drag on the ground behind them.

As we sat in the dark, with only the dancing light of the campfire, my eye caught a movement. It was another African-sized scorpion, silhouetted in the firelight! But it was not the previous night's black scorpion visitor, rather a yellow one. It was moving resolutely toward the place in the circle where Peter was wearing only shower thongs on his feet. "Look out, Peter, headed toward your feet," I shouted.

Dr. Wheeler muttered, "Enough of this scorpion nonsense," and stomped it dead under his boot. Would the spirits of Tsodilo be angry at us for killing one of their creatures? I wondered. If the bees swarmed us and our cameras malfunctioned the next day, we would know why.

Map reminded us of the parallel between us and Qui and Noishay sitting around their campfires with their families. They would be exchanging hunting stories for the benefit of the youngsters and to relive the excitement of the hunt. As Jack had observed, story-telling is a lost art to most cultures, but is still retained by the Bushmen in lieu of our often misleading TV, radio, and newspapers, which rather than pass on our culture, often confuse and corrupt us.

Then our conversation was interrupted by flashes of lightning off to the southwest.

"Here comes the leopard, lightning out of his eyes, thunder from his throat," Map said.

On came the lightning flashes and rumbling thunder, another male rain. Peter and Map took more ribbing about its 'never raining in August'. "Rain in September is possible, but never in August, no never," Peter had said.

"Well you're getting close, Peter. Tomorrow is the last day of August," Joel observed as we retreated into our tents.

I drifted off, lulled by the patter of rain on canvas, happy that surely there were Bushmen in the vast Kalahari for whom this never-in-August rain was an answer to fervent prayers. And understanding their situation, we now looked at this rain as a blessing, an end to a long drought, rather than a temporary inconvenience. Let it rain!

—10—
River Bushman

It was dead quiet when I woke to the smell of rain-cleansed air. A bright and clear August 31st unfolded. What a contrast with the crash of thunder and lightning of the previous night, now a fading memory. We assembled around the fire to cut the Kalahari winter chill on the shaded west side of the female mountain.

The campfire discussion turned to the similarities between our trip and van der Post's. Both included the three similar stops, but in reverse order and, in our case, a much compressed time frame. We had come as casual observers, but now we wanted to see more, to know more, to contribute actively to the preservation of the San and their vanishing way of life.

Traditionally the San have avoided civilization, retreating further into uninhabited areas rather than going to the feared and foreign police or authorities to seek retribution when one of their number was shot or abducted. They grieved and moved off into the most remote areas they could find. They have tried to run away, but civilization has continued to encroach upon them.

In order for Qui and his clan, and others like them, to maintain their traditional hunter-gatherer life style, they must have land. They need a benevolent government that actively watches out for this small minority against the onslaught of larger and more vocal lobbies.

And their supporters will probably have to be outsiders. No local Bantu is about to go out on a limb for the San in either Botswana or Namibia. The Bantu were themselves just recently emancipated, but do not yet have an encompassing world view that allows them to see the San as a culture globally, important in its own right, rather than as the dispossessed beggars, thieves and general nuisances as many of them have come to be viewed.

Map pointed out an indication of the past low regard for the San in the local language. Bantu languages are structured around noun classes, as opposed to the verb classes we have become accustomed to in European languages. Bantu languages have a man class, an animal class, a thing class and so on. The prefix of a noun indicates into which class an object falls. Until well into the twentieth century the government continued officially calling the Bushman the Masarwa. The Ma- is an animal class prefix in Setswana. Today in Botswana they have officially been renamed Basarwa by the government and the press and by anthropologists, the Ba- prefix indicating an elevation to a man or human class versus the earlier animal class. All the other eight major tribes of Botswana have always had the Ba- prefix. But the stigma of the San being less than human still lingers.

One thing the Botswana government has done which is very useful to the San (Bushmen) is to extend the special provisions of the Fauna Proclamation Act of 1961, allowing them to hunt without licenses providing that they use only their traditonal weapons: poisoned arrows and snares, not firearms. There are many earlier horror stories of Bushmen being put in jail for breaking game laws that they neither knew existed nor understood. Many died in jail of extreme depression, like wild animals that cannot live in captivity often do.

Elizabeth Marshall Thomas in her book *The Harmless People* relates of talking to a mature young Bushman in the southern Botswana Kalahari in the 50's, who as a child several years before had witnessed his father being led away with his hands tied behind his back by a white and his two black Bantu 'police boys', all on camels, in the days before four-wheel drives. The father had a rope around his neck, was being pulled cruelly and unceremoniously behind one of the camels. The authorities had used another chagrined and downcast Bushman to track down his father who was guilty of shooting a giraffe. The giraffe was 'royal' game, or protected in the white man's scheme of things—a system the Bushmen did not know about or understand. And white man's laws change! In Teddy Roosevelt's time, shooting a bull giraffe was the thing to do. The Bushmen had hunted giraffe, one of their 'God given' animals, for thousands of years. The young Bushman never saw his father again. The family only later heard that the father had drowned when the camel forded a stream. Bushmen had their reasons not to want to fall under the white man's rules and justice!

The Namibian Bushman is faced with a different situation as to traditional hunting. A 1927 act made it a criminal offense to carry a Bushman's bow. A 1976 law pertaining to nature conservation in certain native areas revived the 1927 law. Today, the hunting of any animal in Bushmanland by bow and arrow is officially prohibited. Only hunting with firearms, which requires a permit not issued to Bushmen, is allowed. Thus the Ju/wa Bushmen in Bushmanland, who still hunt with poisoned arrows, are subject to prosecution at the discretion of local officials.

Peter pointed out the paradox here. The Bushmen are being thrown out of the Central Kalahari because they are human and a threat to the game (in their myth and culture, their game), but San are still treated as less than human and denied human rights in most other ways.

Botswana's Vice President has basically said, "We've got to civilize them, whether they want to be civilized or not," But, the Member of Parliament from Ghanzi, Mr. Jankie, has said he will resign his post in government if it carries through the 1986 edict to remove the Basarwa from the Central Kalahari against their wishes. The Basarwa are a knotty problem for the young Botswana government and their status is a long way from being resolved to anyone's satisfaction. While the politicians debate, time is running short for the Bushmen.

We were to fly a short distance to the southeast from Scorpion Camp, landing us in the upper panhandle of the Okavango delta on the Boro River. The Okavango delta is a unique geographical phenomenon, the world's biggest oasis, or wetland, smack in the middle of the world's fourth largest desert. The Boro is the middle of the three rivers which upon entering the delta fan out to split off from the Okavango River which is fed out of Angola. Most rivers are made up of many tributaries flowing into a trunk river, like the Nile, the Amazon or the Mississippi, which then flows on to the sea. The water of the Okavango River first flows in quantity and then fans out into smaller delta rivers that eventually disappear into the Kalahari. The situation is more like a tree than a river, where the water flows up the trunk from the roots, then out through the branches to the leaves where it evaporates. The Okavango delta streams get smaller as one goes downstream and as the rainwater from Angola's highland dissipates and spreads out, in its slow three kilometer a day journey from northeast to southwest, to dwindle and disappear into the sands of the Kalahari.

"Okay, you scorpions, the camp is all yours," said Jim as we drove away. As we passed Gowi's village we were again touched by the plight of the Bushman people there.

Our Islander aircraft appeared on the horizon, to shuttle us to the fishing camp at Gedibe. We said our goodbyes to Map, and thanked him for being such an informative guide, contributing to our 'once in a lifetime' experience. And even for Map, a native Botswanan, this had been a unique experience. Map and Mansu would break Scorpion Camp and head back to Maun. From there, Map would go back to his more mundane activities in Francistown.

When the plane landed, we spotted Salome up front with the pilot. She had come out to rejoin us for this third and last leg of our version of van der Post's search for surviving Bushmen.

"Salome, we've been worrying about you. Did you get into Maun on your gas?" Jack asked.

"Just barely. I was driving on the fumes," said the ever-cheerful and smiling Salome.

We were a full load for the small, highwing, two-engine Islander. It had handled the seven of us plus Liza from Maun out to Hyena, then our seven plus Peter from Hyena to Scorpion. Now we would squeeze in one more.

"We haven't learned, or through the centuries we've forgotten how to travel as light as our Bushmen friends," Jack apologized for us, as our pilot Andre stuffed the mountain of gear into the Islander.

From Tsodilo Hills we headed southeast, over the grey-blue haze of the Kalahari. Then abruptly the dryness ended. Water everywhere! We were in the Okavango. Soon we approached the landing strip servicing Gedibe fishing camp. We witnessed that magical transformation of abundant water, the emerald green of lush foliage, a profusion of colors and forms of life, the Okavango wetland's maze of braided streams, ponds, sloughs and backwaters, around the sprinkle of islands, many formed by sediment carried from Angola, settling out first around the termite mounds.

The airstrip servicing Gedibe is less than fifty meters from a village. As we approached to land, a dog stood smack in the middle of the strip, staring up at us. We all held our breath, but Andre flew in to land as if the dog was his usual greeting party. At the last moment, when he had disappeared from our view, he had evidently moved, as the crash we were all braced for did not come.

As at Xai Xai, the local black villagers all dropped whatever they were doing and came to greet the plane. Our cameras caught the colorfully-dressed young women, most with babies in arms or slung on their backs, and the kids running around accompanied by the usual inquisitive mixture of lean, hungry looking dogs.

We walked a short distance through the village under heavily canopied trees, making our way through the milling crowd of about sixty villagers to the water's edge where we found a couple of aluminum boats next to several *mekoro* (mokoro, singular; mekoro, plural), hand-hewn African dugout canoes that are the traditional Okavango transport.

We were relieved when we were directed to pile into two aluminum boats, not the rustic mekoro, for the short crossing to the lodge. We landed at Gedibe's wharf, gliding in between emerald carpets of water lily pads, and stepped from our boats directly onto a veranda leading to the bar and dining hall. What luxury! No Hyena or Scorpion bush camp this. Gedibe is a well-established tourist camp. In the center of the veranda, looking very inviting, was a camp fire surrounded by canvas chairs. There were no other guests, so we had the spacious lodge to ourselves.

Two-bed tent accommodations were along the curving shore, cut off from view by a heavy stand of trees growing down to the water's edge. The tents were huge compared to our small bush tents. Out back was an open-air reed-fabric enclosure with latrine and showers, with an unlimited water supply. No more rationing to one gallon showers. After our dry Hyena and Scorpion Camps, and for the rest of our lives, we were to be more appreciative of what a difference unlimited water makes!

We had lunch and a rest while waiting for the mid-day heat to subside. Peter briefed us on the van der Post parallels.

The first episode of van der Post's book covers his search for the river Bushman in the Okavango. Van der Post had gathered a group of locals with *mekoro*, thinking they would take him into the swamp. The Africans were horrified, afraid of going long distances in the deeper watercourses where hippos were apt to upset their little canoes in crocodile infested waters.

Van der Post then hired a river ferry that crossed the upper Okavango once a week. It transported his party deep into the swamp and dumped them off, and was to come back later and pick them up. But, the ferry broke down and when the appointed time arrived, they were left marooned deep in the Okavango. Again, natives refused to risk the return in the *mekoro* and van der Post could only wait. Eventually the ferry showed up and took them out. Van der Post's experience made us a bit anxious about venturing out in the dugout canoes for afternoon game viewing, as Peter had planned.

Our host assured us that we were in no danger. "In these backwaters and shallows off the main river course there's not that much of a problem. However, there are crocodiles and hippos in the deeper main channel. Tomorrow, to visit the river Bushman, we'll be going down the Boro River, but we'll go in the aluminum boats that brought you across from the airstrip. Even with the much faster craft it will be over a three hour trip each way."

The Okavango River, at its March and April Angola rainy season flood peak flow, delivers ten times the amount of water into the top end of the delta as it does at its low flow in November. The flooded 'wet' boundaries of the huge Okavango wetlands double when the peak river flows arrive some three months later in the heart of the delta. Water levels were now receding toward their post November inlet lows.

At about three-thirty we set out for the evening game run in five *mekoro*. The construction of a mokoro can take up to six weeks, using an adze, or 'wood hoe'. Mekoro are fashioned from such Okavango species as the sausage tree, the jackal berry, or the African ebony. Each of our dugouts was powered by an African poler who stood upright in the boat. We were two passengers to a dugout and one in number five.

"Well, Big John, guess what," Jack needled, "You get one by yourself."

I settled into the bottom of one of the crudely hewn *mekoro*. It had only about two inches free board and was leaking. It rocked from side to side and let little gulps of water come in over the gunnels. 'Not to worry,' I thought, 'I'm a good swimmer.' But wait, did I really want to swim if those crocs and hippos were about?

We glided away from the dock, the silence broken only by the sucking sound of our fleet of *mekoro* cutting through the water. It was beautifully placid on the glimmering water, with patches of lily pads floating on the surface. The airstrip and the lodge were on separate small islands. Most of the rest of the area was wholly or partially covered by water, much of which was in turn covered by heavy floating reeds, or tall patches of papyrus, fringed by lily pads.

My mokoro was not only down in the water but sinking lower by the minute. There was a rotten place in the boat's bottom, well below the water line. A little water spout shot vertically up into the boat. After a good sized puddle of water had formed in the bottom and I was showing some concern, my poler jammed his pronged pole into the swamp bottom, twisted it and brought up some grass and mud which he pressed into the hole. The leaking nearly stopped, but the accumulated puddle continued to slosh around.

Our guides couldn't speak English and we couldn't communicate in either Tswana or their local tribal language, but since the idea was to be absolutely quiet so we could see game, it did not much matter. Unfortunately, sitting so low in the dugouts, we could not really see much. There were a couple of times when we heard game, either sitatunga or lechwe, two swamp antelope, splashing as they moved across the floating beds of reeds in view of the polers but concealed from us. I, for one, wasn't about to jump up quickly in the narrow, frail, unstable little dugout and risk turning it over in the hope of catching a glimpse of game.

It was a peaceful time for reflection, floating on the quiet water and keeping silent to avoid startling any animals that might be present. With each turn of the meandering open waterways, bordered by dense papyrus or alternately paragmite reed beds, we might come across a lechwe or a sitatunga. The sitatunga is the most aquatic of antelope, living more in the water than out, walking on the muddy bottom or floating reed beds with its exceptionally long, widely splayed hooves. It is an excellent swimmer, and when wounded or alarmed can submerge completely with only its nostrils out of the water.

I had a strong sense that this game watch, looking for the shy and seldom seen sitatunga, was similar to how it could be in the parks and arid places of the Kalahari if the small, shy clans of wild nomadic Bushmen were allowed to remain. They would be as elusive as the animals, shying away from visitors as they pursued their solitary ways. If allowed to stay in the parks with their animals there would always be the chance that they were over the next rise, out of sight of the visitor, but safe from encroachment and disturbance.

We made a two-hour tour across the floating lily covered glades, through narrow-water passageways flanked by towering papyrus and on to yet other ponds and backwaters. The circuit brought us back to the lodge while there was still good light, to settle in around the campfire.

At Hyena Camp Salome had been busy cooking and keeping camp and hadn't been able to sit in on the campfire sessions, only getting involved in occasional snatches of the conservation. Now she could relax and join in. Salome related a 'how things got to be' myth ... of how, in the beginning, the Bushmen and the animals originated together, issuing out of a hole in the earth, all speaking the same language. They came out from between roots of a great shade tree and as they gathered beneath the tree for the night the Great Bushman God warned them that no matter how cold it became no one was to light a fire. It got bitterly cold before dawn and one of the humans lit a fire. All the animals took fright and stampeded away, losing their power of speech in their panic. Ever since that day animals have been speechless, and have fled from fire and man.

Peter reminded us that different language groups have similar but varying myths. He related the legend about how the Kung came to have fire. In this version there was a time when there was no fire and people ate their meat raw. One ancestral Bushman discovered that by twirling a stick he could make fire, but he did not share this knowledge beyond his clan or with the Great God. One day the Great God visited the encampment while the hunter was away and his children gave him cooked food. It was so delicious that God came the next day for more, concealing himself at a distance to observe how fire was made and noting where the selfish man hid his fire sticks. Then the Great God entered the camp pretending he had seen nothing.

He suggested that they play a traditional Bushman game called *djani* in which the children take a small piece of reed with string and a weight at one end, and a feather at the other. It is tossed high in the air and comes spinning down while the people run under it and see who can intercept it on a stick and hurl it skyward again. After a while God changed the guinea fowl feather with a larger bustard feather and blew, causing the *djani* to drift well out of camp where the people followed. The Great God then unearthed the fire sticks from their hiding place, broke them into pieces and threw them into the sky, spreading them over the world. He changed the man into a bird as punishment for his selfishness. And from that time forward everybody has cooked their food and enjoyed the heat of the fire as there has been fire in every piece of wood; the Kung explanation of how a 'twisted stick' now produces fire.

A shy, nocturnal Pel's fishing owl was discovered perched fifteen feet up in the dense foliage of trees at the water's edge, near our sleeping tents. We all quietly observed the owl, half the size of a barn owl, the color of Kalahari dunes with darker brown speckles. It peered down at us with innocent, unfearing black eyes.

As the sun went down, the wetland surrounding our small island came alive with pleasant relaxing sounds. After dinner, the lively campfire discussions went on. North Pole visitors Wally and I encouraged Jack to brief our group on the Arctic Inuits and their parallels with the Bushmen.

"Parallels are many," started Jack. "They are each one of the few

Keikanamang, the river Bushman.
—JP

Baobab and vegetable palm trees shelter the river Bushman's camp.
—JP

Left: Bream hanging at the river Bushman's camp. —JP

Below: Mekoro are the traditional means of transport in the Okavango except in the main waterways where hippos may overturn them in the crocodile-infested water. —JP

quintessential hunter-gatherer societies that have survived until recently. They shared in the development of unique survival cultures to exist in extremely harsh climates, the frozen Arctic for the Inuits, the thirstland Kalahari for the Bushmen."

Over the soft chorus of Okavango frogs and insects Jack gave our group a thumbnail sketch of the Inuits, one of the most interesting hunter-forager cultures on the globe ... the upper Arctic dwellers above the tree line along the Arctic seaways.

Authorities now believe the North American Arctic people first came from Asia something like 8,000 or 10,000 years ago. They were the last aboriginals to arrive in North America. There are indications that the first of what we call Indians came earlier and moved rapidly south, settling from the northern Canadian and Alaskan tree line south to Argentina. They crossed the shallow Bering Straits when the seas were lower during earlier ice ages, when sea water was piled up on land in the form of glaciers.

Australia was first inhabited by the Aborigines migrating from Asia, probably southern China, maybe twice as long ago as the first Americans. This makes the Americas the last continents, besides still uninhabited Antarctica, to receive the spread of man starting from Africa some three quarters to a million years ago.

Archaeological findings give reason to believe that there were several waves of the Inuits' ancestors, of Mongoloid or Arctic people, over several thousand years, as they perfected more advanced stone age technologies in Siberia, then carried them across the Bering Straits, and slowly 6,000 miles east as far as Greenland. Each more advanced wave assimilated or replaced its forerunners. Recent blood typing has confirmed that the Eskimo, or Inuit, is much more closely related to the peoples in northeastern Siberia than to the rest of North and South America's aboriginal Indians.

The Arctic is a savage, unforgiving land; in its way as, or more, formidable than the near waterless Kalahari thirstland. The Inuits and their Arctic forerunners were brave, hardy, innovative people who survived by adapting to living by hunting predominantly the sea mammals: whales, seals, walrus, sea lions; then salt and fresh water fish, then migratory land birds, and finally animals like the caribou and musk ox.

According to the season, a typical hunter and his family or immediate clan might hunt alone, or with others outside his clan. In spring and summer clans converged to join groups hunting for seal or caribou. Then individual clans often moved to a summer fishing site, and then would set in for the long winter, individually snaring seals under the ice. They used a retrieving harpoon on sea animals and bow and arrow on land animals. The men hunted, built the homes, made the tools. The women prepared the food, cured the skins, and made the clothing. Like most hunter-foragers they were well dispersed and organized in a semi-nomadic family clan culture roaming over a large territory not unlike the Kalahari Bushmen or Australian Aborigines, rather than larger concentrated post-agricultural revolution sedentary tribes residing in villages.

The Inuits, like the Kalahari Bushmen, needed to spread themselves thin over the territory so as not to overtax the resources in any one area, but they did need enough people together to get mutual support and to survive the inevitable disasters, such as hunting accidents. There is a consistency of the Inuit language from Alaska to Greenland indicating a mobile people who have maintained continuing contact with one another. This contrasts with Australia's Aborigines and Africa's Bushmen, in which widely dispersed people have a similar language group but it has developed in isolated pockets, so that today there are many mutually incomprehensible languages and dialects, versus a currently more universally understood language as with the Inuit.

The school book stereotype 'Eskimo' lives in an igloo. Actually, these people were more likely to live most of the year in more permanent semi-subterranean sod houses with driftwood and whale bone framing, and then game-skin tents out on the tundra in summer. The quickly constructed and easily abandoned igloos were made to support nomadic winter hunting. The Inuits' transport was the dog sled in winter and the kayak or an open skin-covered whale boat called a umiak in spring and summer, with both types of transportation always being supplemented by a considerable amount of walking. Special Arctic survival clothing in the form of waterproof boots, pants and the upper parka were made of two layers of animal skins sewn back to back with a natural fur exterior and fur against the body for insulation.

There were and still are other Arctic people across Europe and Asia, from Lapland through western and central Siberia, who were Caucasian, as opposed to the Inuit, who were Mongoloid. These Caucasians were more post-agricultural revolution pastoralists in that they domesticated herds of reindeer which are closely related to the caribou the North American Inuit hunted.

Despite the demands of developing the technologies of Arctic survival the Inuit found time to develop a culture in singing and in carving stone, bone and ivory, and they were great story tellers ... what with the long winter nights. Their myths and folklore indicate a desire to preserve a harmony between man and the environment to avoid antagonizing the spirits of the animals and nature, with close parallels to the Australian Aborigines and the Kalahari Bushmen.

Tom asked, "Is it a fact or a myth that the Eskimos offered their wives to explorers and outside visitors?"

"There is some basis in fact for that in the Inuit culture," Jack continued. "Their geographically dispersed small bands or family clans were related through blood ties or marriage ties, small isolated groups living and surviving together. Anyone outside the small local group was a potential threat to their game resources, or competition for women and mates. Inuit men did trade wives to others outside their blood and marriage groups to show hospitality to a potential enemy and to assure friendly reciprocal alliances, as in, 'You sleep with my wife in my village and I'll sleep with yours in your village, and we'll be allies and face the austere and unforgiving environment together.' Basically, it cut down on an element of competition, increased their odds of survival."

Then there's the 'song duel.' Two Inuit antagonists, or suitors, would insult one another in public gatherings using extemporaneous song. The loser was often forced to leave the community. This is an offshoot of the blood feud. Inuits, being in small egalitarian clans, not tribes, had no tribal chief or authority to keep order or arbitrate disputes. Under the concept of 'blood feud' anyone wronged in a clan or small organized group could go after not only the guilty individual, but any member of the other clan or group. As a result one thought twice about taking on a whole clan, or alternately, the clan exerted restraint on its own members, to avoid initiating a feud which could expose the entire clan to the wrath of the other group. This concept is not unusual in primitive aboriginal societies. The Australian Aborigines still have it, as do the people of New Guinea, where it is called 'pay back.' In 'pay back' one is more likely not to go after the one who perpetrated the offense, but rather his more defenselss children or women or other kin. In a blood feud anyone of the same blood will do.

The Inuit are one of the unique peoples of the world, surviving in the harsh Arctic where no other culture or society would venture, not unlike the Kalahari Bushmen enduring in the arid Kalahari, where only they have adapted to survive successfully. Both groups are now experiencing extreme cultural shock; a result of a rapid breakdown in their 'stone age' cultures as they give up their close-to-nature, hand-to-mouth-subsistence methods of survival, of living off the land and meeting all their simple needs themselves. They are forced to try to adjust to our modern capitalistic, materialistic, money-oriented society, and find that they have little or nothing to barter or sell to outsiders. They are caught in the middle, often suffering the worst of both worlds. Once the Inuit get away from their demanding 'on the edge of doom' hunter-foraging culture, their traditional technologies become lost to them forever and they have to adjust to completely foreign cultures, to make a huge jump or extreme adjustment in the matter of a generation or two. The Inuits', the Bushmen's and the Australian Aborigines' way of life and traditions have changed more in the last 200 years than in the previous 10,000.

"It hasn't been easy," added Jack, "And the day the first Inuit took a ride on a ski-doo, the Arctic and the Inuit's hunter-gatherer culture were irreversibly changed."

"But as you yourself have said, Jack, you can't uninvent the wheel!" added Joel.

Then finally the camp chairs were empty and the fire burned low to a soft chorus of Okavango night noises.

I awoke next morning to the piercing daylight cries of two water habitat birds ... very distinctive African sounds! Nature's alarm clock was the fish eagle and hadeda. The black and white fish eagle has habits similar to our American eagle and osprey. The hadeda, a buff colored member of the ibis family, nests and roosts nocturnally in trees near water and makes its shrill cry as it leaves its roost at daylight. The cry of the fish eagle can be heard throughout the day.

Over breakfast, our discussion focussed on the hope that we might be more successful than van der Post in finding the river Bushman. It was still early as we departed from Gedibe Lodge in the aluminum boats in quest of the solitary river Bushman reported to live down river deep in the Okavango. Initially, the water courses we followed were narrow passages flanked by tall reeds and papyrus, no wider than the aluminum boats. Parasol-topped papyrus drooped out into the narrow waterway, slapping our faces gently as we negotiated sharp turns. We had to break through some floating dams of swamp reeds and papyrus. "This is like a ride through a tunnel of fun," commented Tom.

"That's one of the hippo's contributions to the Okavango, he's nature's dredge, keeping waterways open," said Peter.

After a quarter hour we reached a deeper and wider main stream of the Boro River and were able to throttle up. As we headed downstream, Peter gave us a running commentary on the Okavango birds, "yellow-billed kite ... reed cormorant ... malachite kingfisher ... carmine bee eater ... African skimmer ... saddle billed stork ... green backed heron ... spurwing geese ..." With some 400 recorded species, the Okavango is an exotic bird watchers paradise. We glimpsed a crocodile, but no one could catch it on video before it left the floating reed bed and submerged.

After about three hours, we turned off the main water course through a fringe of reeds into a shallower backwater and worked across it toward a prominent island a half mile off the Boro. We had to do some aquatic 'bush bashing' when we got hung up on heavy reeds and papyrus and some of us got out and pushed, making our own waterway by walking on and breaking through the thick mat of floating reeds.

"We need hooves like the sitatunga," said Peter. "Nature has given them long hooves to skate across the floating reed beds."

Our effort got us through to a clear backwater, surrounding the island, on which was a large grove of tall trees. As we approached this solitary island, a black man appeared, standing upright and poling his handhewn mokoro.

"That's Keikanamang, our River Bushman," said Peter, as the man preceded us into a cove with a sandy beach.

Keikanamang had been out checking his nets and was returning to his fishing camp on this isolated island. We had not seen another soul since leaving our lodge. From the small entry cove bordered by reeds and papyrus we landed onto a narrow, sandy beach which opened into a secluded clearing, shielded from outside view by a border of large trees, towering baobabs, and some palms. The baobab, the seemingly upside down tree, has generated much myth-making among Africans trying to explain its odd appearance. The baobab is to the world's trees what the prehistoric looking rhino is to its mammals.

An abandoned and rusting refrigerator lay on its side with its door ajar. We wondered how and why this relic of civilization would be here. Keikanamang wore tattered western clothes, a short-sleeved blue shirt and store-bought cotton trousers.

There was a string of fresh-caught bream hanging from a tree. We observed the fish being handed over to one of our boat drivers in exchange for the flour and other foodstuffs they had brought. Further on was a string of drying catfish. The people of the Okavango live by fishing and some agriculture. The Okavango is off-limits to domestic livestock, even though such animals could now survive here since the recent virtual eradication of the tsetse fly. The fly carries sleeping sickness, fatal to domestic animals, but not wild game. The Botswana government has wisely chosen to continue to bar domestic animals, to protect the natural quality of the delta.

"Some conservationists lament the eradication of the tsetse as 'nature's game warden', protecting the Okavango from incursion by domestic animals." said Peter.

Then there is the controversial buffalo fence, which circles 150 miles of the south Okavango delta. It is to keep the buffalo from spreading their highly contagious foot-and-mouth disease to the domestic cattle, placing an important Botswana export in jeopardy. Naturalists applaud its function of keeping domestic animals from invading the delta.

"When you fly over the buffalo fence," said Peter, "There's a stark difference. Overgrazing on the domestic cattle side, still lush on the wild buffalo side."

Keikanamang had pots and pans, and he spoke Tswana. In his youth he'd been recruited to South Africa for work in the gold mines around Johannesburg.

"He speaks a bit of Fanaglo," said Peter. "It's the pidginized form of Zulu, used mostly in the mines. It's a simple *lingua franca* for all the varied tribes from scattered locations across southern Africa that the gold mines bring together."

He was taller and blacker, showing fewer of the classic Bushman features than Qui and his clan. How much of a Bushman was he? Still, he did have enough characteristics to indicate San genes. He is married to a black Bantu Tswana woman, so any San genes are being further diluted.

Keikanamang picked up his thumb piano, played it and sang us a tune. Eventually Peter indicated that we should move off in our aluminum boats across the lagoon to a pleasant sand bar to have our picnic lunch. From there we saw him put out in his mokoro. A young teenage son whom we hadn't seen before appeared in his own dugout canoe. The two were making their rounds, checking the fishing nets.

So some 35 years earlier van der Post had failed to find any River Bushmen. But had we?

After our Okavango picnic, we started the trip back up the Boro River to Gedibe lodge, stopping a couple of times to fish. Joel caught our only fish, a bream. Back at Gedibe when the fellows went for an evening fish, Joel again had all the fisherman's luck and the only catch, a tiger fish which Map had talked so much about. "Not an edible fish, but a real fighter," Map had said of the small, colorful creature with red spots and stripes, and teeth like a piranha. This sleek, ferocious predator is the sport fisherman's prize 'par excellence.' The men stayed out fishing until almost dark, when a hippo moving nervously in the rushes convinced them it was time to head for the lodge.

Then it was campfire discussion time. We were all finding this visit to Africa pleasant, game-viewing by day and storytelling by night. No radios, television or daily newspapers.

Could we leave now without trying to do something to help preserve the threatened Bushman? We all realized, of course, that there were competing interests, that the governments of Botswana and Namibia had myriad problems to solve as they worked to bring their countries into the modern age, to catch up with the advances of many centuries in a single lifetime, and that the survival of the San was not high on their lists of priorities. But the San's survival need not be contradictory to the progress of the larger society. The Bushman had always lived with the animals and if the animals could be protected, why not a few people who were still living nomadically? The very problem might be part of the solution. There are so few "still-nomadic" San hunter-gatherers, not enough to threaten the goals of game conservationists or of the government. It seemed so logical and simple to us. We found hope in the great and abrupt shift in priorities that had occurred in Australia to the benefit of the Aboriginal people there. They had beaten *terra nullius* at the ballot box by swaying public opinion with their Aboriginal Embassy. How could we contribute to such a change for the gentle people of the Kalahari? A Bushman Embassy movement in Gaborone or Windhoek? What could be lost in trying?

—11—
Chobe to Etosha

Our last morning in Gedibe we made a final sunrise run in the rustic *mekoro*, again hearing rather than seeing the shy sitatunga skating away across the floating beds of reeds. The beautiful and reflective cool and quiet of the morning was broken only by the sucking sound of the dugouts cutting through the water, and the occasional shrill cries of fish eagles and hadedas.

During the trip we asked Peter's recommendations on other places to visit in Botswana. Peter related how he and Salome had recently visited the Makgadikgadi Pans Reserve east of Maun, and found there were large concentrations of wildebeest, zebra, springbok and ostrich attracted by small pans that still held rain water. After the coming rains, and seasonal changes, they would migrate north across the Maun-Francistown road to another reserve, Nxai Pan National Park. "If these unseasonal August rains continue the animals will shift over to Nxai Pan, but I trust they'll be there in the Makgadikgadi for a few weeks yet, and if so it's well worth the visit," Peter said.

From Maun, Joel, Jim, Bud and I were going to Chobe National Park and on to Victoria Falls. Then I planned to fly to Windhoek, and drive up to Etosha game reserve in northern Namibia.

"What's the possibility of working something out with you, or renting a vehicle on my own to get to Makgadikgadi?" I asked Peter.

"It's a fairly easy camp-out trip from Maun, I'd be happy to take you," he said.

The deal was done. It had taken me four years to get back into the heart of Africa. The rest of my compatriots were leaving, even as I was plotting to stay on.

After breakfast several of us went out in the mekoro to watch the feeding of Joel's tiger fish to the fish eagle. These relatives of our bald eagle are often seen having midair skirmishes and dogfights

165

establishing their territorial rights to fish sections of waterways. As we approached the eagle's perch high up on a dead snag, the tiger fish was thrown out onto the open water well away from our boat. The eagle-eyed bird immediately swooped down with his talons stretched forward and, without pausing, took the fish off the water. The slippery fish was no match for the long claws and the spicules on the pads of the eagle's feet. It all happened too fast for me to keep the swooping bird in the restricted field of my Hasselblad's 250mm lens. Then all too soon it was time to get ready for the 11:30 arrival of the now familiar Islander which would carry us back to Maun. With our assorted bags ready, we gathered around the fire area on the veranda for the last time, reflecting on the trip.

"Peter, tell us something," said Jim Reed. "How do you feel now, in retrospect, about organizing a trip like this to put people like us in contact with some of the few remaining nomadic Bushman?"

"Well, going in I had mixed emotions," said Peter, "And I still do. As you all can now better appreciate, it's a delicate undertaking. For me, it's a one shot effort I don't see repeating. If we were to try to commercialize on them, to bring masses of people out here, we couldn't find enough traditional wild Bushmen to show them. If we were to keep on the track of Qui's little clan, they would quickly fade away. It was a high wire walk to get you as much exposure to the Bushmen as possible without overwhelming them.

"As far as your broad 'Bush for the Bushman' idea, well, you're dealing with a very complex situation. Map and Salome and I are all for whatever can be done for the Bushmen to ensure that this last thread back to the past does not perish. But there's a paradox in the situation. You want to ensure that their traditional culture goes on. You can't bring throngs of people out here to gawk at them up close. Tourism would soon destroy what the tourists came to see.

"Say that things can be turned around and the Bushmen not be ejected from the Central Kalahari Reserve. What if Bushman were allowed to stay or be reintroduced into the Botswana's huge Gemsbok National Park and South Africa's adjoining Kalahari Gemsbok National Park? The good news is that, except for limited parts of South Africa's Kalahari Gemsbok Park, these areas are currently off the beaten track and hard to get to. I would envision only small, specially-picked groups of anthropologists and professional photographers being allowed in. But they could take pictures and videotapes from which the general public could benefit without there arising a situation of too many people up too close that would be detrimental to any still-traditional nomadic Bushman. It might be more like the attention that has been brought to bear on the mountain gorilla in central Africa. The public interest generated by the book and movie *Gorillas in the Mist* has helped to save these animals from extinction, and the public's environmental consciousness has been accommodated by being able to see them on film, without needing to all go themselves and intrude into the gorilla's habitat. No, I don't envision a big safari business, bringing people out to see the Bushmen the way we have brought you. There's too big a risk of not finding any, or, if we did find them, they might break and run, but more importantly, we'd screw them up by contact."

I again remembered the contrast between the Masai I had seen in remote locations in Tanzania versus those on the tourist track in Kenya. The latter had become spoiled by and dependent on their contact with tourists in a way that was demeaning to them. They begged for money, and demanded fees to be photographed. We didn't want that to happen to Qui and his family.

The colorful kaleidoscope of local villagers again turned out en masse for the plane's arrival. We piled in and Andre headed southeast over the very heart of the Okavango delta. During the hour-long, low-level flight to Maun over this unique jewel, Africa's greatest wetland, we saw abundant game, including some of the twenty thousand Cape buffalo reported there, and wildebeest, elephants, zebras, sitatunga, lechwe, and baboons. From the air, the sheer grandeur of the vast delta is beyond one's imagination, too much to absorb. But it, like the Bushmen, is being encroached on by an ever increasing human population and their 'civilized' needs for more land.

Maun had seemed a dusty, rustic, wild west town when we left it ten days before, but after the bush, we now found ourselves considering it a return to civilization. The four of us who had an early afternoon flight for Chobe Park nipped over to Riley's Hotel to visit the craft shop, unfortunately missing Beth Oliver and any further informative save-the-Bushman conversations. We picked up Bushman-made souvenirs—bows, arrows, quivers and hunting shoulder bags, necklaces, tortoise shell compacts, thumb pianos, women's shoulder bags. All of these items had new meaning to us now that we had seen them as they were intended to be used.

We headed for the Duck Inn, Maun airport's unofficial departure lounge, where we were to meet Peter, Salome and Liza for our group's final gathering.

Jack, Tom and Wally were to catch the commercial flight back to Johannesburg about the same time we remaining four headed north for Chobe. Tom was off to the Seychelles, Wally to the States, and Jack to India, Pakistan and Afghanistan.

In the bush, Jack had grown a beard in preparation for his clandestine visit into Afghanistan. Most of the rest of us had followed suit. We were a scruffy lot but not at all out of place in the 'four-wheel-drive-safari-frontier' atmosphere of Maun and the Duck Inn. It was a happy and boisterous finale to our fabulous Bushman experience.

Then it was time for our Chobe flight. It was all the pilot could do to shoehorn all our gunny sacks, bags and artifacts and us four into the single engine Cessna. The flight north-northeast was to Kasane airstrip on the Chobe River just before it runs into the mighty Zambezi at Kazungula, near where Namibia's Caprivi Strip, Zimbabwe, Zambia and Botswana all meet. Some seventy kilometers east and downriver is Victoria Falls. We flew just east of where the Okavango wetlands peter out, over monotonously flat, dry Kalahari bushveld, not too different from the vast expanse we'd flown over between Xai Xai and Tsodilo. We saw herds of elephant, buffalo, giraffe, zebra and wildebeest congregated around isolated pans that still held water.

At the Kasane airstrip we were met by a swank new oversized Landrover cut down for game viewing. It was driven by a blonde European woman and her female Indian assistant, wearing smart khaki uniforms. They immediately opened a bottle of champagne with, "Welcome to Chobe Park and Lodge."

"Don't get spoiled, you lot, at your first African game park," I said. I had been fortunate to visit most of the major game parks in Africa and this was a new, pleasant, experience. Chobe, although in a remote corner of developing Africa, is where Elizabeth Taylor and Richard Burton spent one of their honeymoons.

Chobe Lodge's evening game drives had already begun but, seeing our enthusiasm, the ladies radioed ahead from the airstrip and had a Landrover standing by at the lodge to take us straight out. Chobe has good concentrations of elephant, buffalo and up to eighteen different types of antelope. Hippos and crocodiles are abundant in the Chobe River. Warthogs, down on their knees rooting up the front lawn of the lodge, took little notice of us as we approached to take their pictures.

The best game-viewing occurs along the river where animals are drawn by the water. Chobe Park is a vast area, most of it south of the river, undeveloped and without roads, and thus inaccessible to tourists.

We went and looked at a huge map of the park on the wall of the lodge. I had suggested to our guide that we drive all day to Savuti, the other game viewing lodge, and back the next day.

"Too far, out of the question," he had said.

In Chobe's 4,181 square miles there's a large undeveloped no man's land between the developed game viewing areas surrounding Chobe and Savuti tourist centers. I found myself asking if two or three little bands like Qui's lived there, why couldn't they range over large areas while avoiding encounters with tourists restricted to their vehicles, and the few roads? Bushmen were officially evicted from Chobe in 1952.

The irony is that after whites and Bantu had almost wiped out the animals through over hunting and habitat destruction, authorities then decided to create parks to try to preserve what few animals remained. The animals and Bushmen had lived together for centuries in what were to become parks, but when it was belatedly decided to create the parks, the Bushmen were systematically evicted as if they had been the cause of the animals' demise. Still, the majority of the Bushmen had been dispossessed of their lands inside or out of the reserves, by Bantu or whites, before the reserves were created.

Bushmen could be reinstated in the Central Kalahari and encouraged to continue in Botswana's Gemsbok National Park, a vast area of twenty-four thousand square kilometers which is largely undeveloped and off-limits to most tourists. Joining it at the political boundary with South Africa, is the Kalahari Gemsbok Park, some ten thousand additional square kilometers. When I visited there with Rachel in 1984, I found it to be one of the most stark and beautiful parks in the world.

Botswana has done a brilliant job in creating reserves—over seventeen percent of the land is game parks—but to be questioned is the eviction of the Bushmen as if they were enemies of the animals, when in fact they have been their owners, protectors and conservators for thousands of years. In these areas the nomadic clans could range across the border with the seasons and game movement like they are still allowed to do between Namibia and Botswana. They need land.

The pieces of the puzzle are in place. The big problem is getting the government bureaucracies to go along; and then, find enough unacculturated Bushmen, and next to get them to leave their ancestral ranges to move into these reserves. I do not believe that this, as some would claim, is like putting our American Indians on reservations, or the South Africans relegating many of their blacks to 'homelands.' It would be a case of permitting a few wild Bushmen back into the few natural enclaves called parks—land where they can rejoin their animals. They have survived together for ten thousand years or more, a proven record of pragmatic game conservation, bettering the game animals' long term chances of survival.

In the mythology of the San it is understood that he will only bring destruction to himself if he misuses his animals and environment. God made them together and meant for them to be together, each contributing to the well-being of the other. The San people have never taken from the land more than the land can spare. The parks were established when it became clear that game was being wiped out by overhunting, poaching and habitat loss. The mistake made was in assuming that the San were contributing to game's destruction. In fact they were not. It was only since Europeans arrived on the scene that the game began to suffer. The San as owner-protector of his animals contributes to wildlife's preservation. Wherever game survived there were San, not only in the Central Kalahari Game Reserve but in Makgadikgadi, Chobe, Gemsbok, Etosha, Kaudom and West Caprivi. But unfortunately, as parks were established all over southern Africa, the Bushmen were evicted, leaving only poachers to prey on the game.

Poachers are less likely to try to operate inside the reserves if they have two adversaries. Unfortunately, one of those adversaries, game scouts, are often too thinly spread and too poorly paid to be effective against poachers who frequently tempt them into collusion with the promise of easy money. The Bushmen, the best trackers in the world, who feel the animals are theirs to use and protect, wouldn't cooperate with poachers, and could better observe the poachers' activities and track them down.

Chobe's area could theoretically support four hundred full-time nomadic hunter-gatherers. But it is doubtful whether so many could be found today in all of Botswana. And traditional Bushmen are very territorial, and want to stay where their fathers are buried. Peter questions if a clan like Qui's could be induced to relocate to a haven like Chobe.

The Chobe Lodge ran a video tape presentation in the evening. Filmed mostly in Kenya, the theme had to do with the problem we saw being played out in the Kalahari, of cattle versus wild game in competition for land. The presentation included graphs and statistics indicating conclusively that the wild animals are much less destructive to the environment than domestic animals, especially cattle. Wild animals are naturally adapted to marginal arid areas in Kenya, regions much like the dry Kalahari. The wild animals do not die from tsetse fly which decimates domestic animals, and they can survive on much less water. Wild games produces substantially more high protein, low-fat meat per pound of forage than do domestic animals.

The video chronicled a trend developing in some African countries like Kenya, South Africa and Namibia to commercialize wild animals, rather than to import or expand herds of naturally unfit and environmentally destructive domestic animals. While one identified problem is defining the line betwen game as a protected animal to view, and one to be harvested, some harvesting may ultimately be the best means of species survival. Wild game ranching in South Africa and Namibia shows that overall game populations are coming back in those areas under these controlled conditions. Meanwhile, wild game is fighting a losing battle for survival in some of the countries further north, countries that claim to be protecting the game animals by not allowing their hunting or commercialization. A good illustration is found in recent statistics on elephant populations, down a drastic seventy percent over the last ten years in the countries north of the Zambezi where there is no hunting or cropping, but where poaching is rampant. On the other hand, elephant populations have increased five percent per year in the several countries south of the Zambezi where there are more controls, including organized hunting and even commercialized cropping.

Our second day we made an early morning game drive and then went by boat down the Chobe River to see a large aggregation of hippos keeping cool in a backwater pool, only their backs and sporadically yawning mouths out of the water. Nearby lazy crocodiles sunned themselves on the banks. Along the river were hamerkops and their many impressively large and impregnable nests, fish eagles, and a colony of exotically-colored carmine bee eaters which nest in burrows in the sandy-clay bank.

On our last morning our daylight game drive was rewarded by the sight of a majestic solitary black bull sable coming down to the river to drink with buffalo, elephants and other game. We were content with our short visit to Chobe, but couldn't help thinking of the future. Might it be possible to come here again knowing some nomadic Bushmen were surviving here, even if we were unable to see them?

At mid-morning a bus took us from Chobe Lodge east to the Botswana Zimbabwe border and on along the south side of the Zambezi to Victoria Falls, a trip of some two and a half hours.

We were booked at the Livingstone Hotel, named after Dr. David Livingstone, the first European to view the falls in 1855. It is the oldest traditional hotel, near the falls, within earshot of the crashing water and with a view of the mist from the falls rising to a thousand feet and hanging over lush green tree tops. The original hotel was started in 1904, when the Cape-to-Cairo railroad reached the falls from the south. It has seen many expansions and renovations since and hosted European royalty on many occasions.

Victoria Falls is one of the most magnificent natural wonders of the world. It was here that the character in *The Gods Must Be Crazy* came to pitch the evil Coke bottle 'off the end of the world'. As we viewed the impressive falls, we speculated about the first Bushman who saw the falls five hundred or five thousand or even more than ten thousand years ago. What must he have thought?

We crossed the bridge into Zambia on foot to see the falls from the Zambian side. As I photographed the impressive cataracts a young black African in scruffy attire approached Jim Reed to practice his English.

"You're American? Who are you voting for?" We were surprised that he would be aware of our elections going on half way around the world. "We be for Bush," he continued. "Carter backed sanctions. Sanctions hurt us. Dukakis is for sanctions. We be for Bush."

"We'll have to get that fellow to talk to your firespitting friend, Rachel," Joel said.

The next morning we made our way to the crocodile farm en route to the airport, arriving just as it opened, ahead of the usual tour-bus crowds. The farm raises for commercial use hundreds of young crocodiles in large penned areas, segregated by age. Our interest was drawn to the only full grown reptiles at the farm, a male crocodile and his breeding harem of five females.

We leaned over the fence of the crocodiles' enclosure. "What's happening here?" we asked the uniformed white supervisor, ignoring the lesson we'd learned from the Bushmen of not asking too many questions.

"One of the ole gals was up here when we came this morning. She's laid eggs, we reckon." As we watched, the two black assistants uncovered the first of the white crocodile eggs.

"Whoosh," came a great splashing noise less then ten feet away, from the crocodile pool down under the bank behind the staff digging in the sandy bank. We all instinctively jumped back from our kibitzing

171

over the enclosure fence.

"That's just the bull croc falling back in the water. He can't get up that steep bank but he was making a fake charge trying to scare us off and protect the eggs," said the white supervisor.

We asked where, besides this small breeding group of five female crocs, the crocodile farm got the eggs for the hundreds of small and developing crocs, and learned that they were gathered from crocodiles in the wild out along the Zambezi River. Crocodiles lay forty to eighty eggs at a time. The game department lets the crocodile farm staff go out along the river and gather crocodile eggs to hatch in the protection of the farm provided that when the crocodiles reach one meter in length, which takes about three years, the farm turns five percent back out into the wild along the river. That is the percentage of the small crocodiles that the game department studies have shown would have survived during their first three years out in the open. Birds, fish, and other crocs would have gotten the rest.

"You've got one bull croc for five females. How do you come up with that ratio?" we asked.

"That's a good ratio. He'll cover five females, no problem. In nature the other four males would have been eliminated by battles to the death. That's nature's way of taking care of its excess male crocodile population."

This was another version of what has been happening for eons in nature. "Now why shouldn't the Bushmen be in selected parks living off some of those redundant males," said Joel. "Not crocodiles but impala, kudu or eland."

Our flight took us from Livingstone through Bulawayo to Johannesburg airport. Bud and Joel caught a connection straight out, but Jim Reed decided to stay overnight and joined me in a taxi back to the Santon Sun.

As I checked into the Santon Sun for the third time, the receptionist handed me an envelope from Rachel containing a nice color picture of her smiling face and a brief apology for any overzealousness during that now long ago Sunday evening's heated political discussion with Jim and Joel. Was that really only thirteen days ago?

Later, as Jim and I had a last drink at the Santon Sun, I admonished my friend, "You guys are all leaving a good party too early!" I just could not bring myself to leave until I had scouted Etosha in Namibia and Botswana's Makgadikgadi as potential bush havens for the Bushmen.

I was next off to Windhoek, Namibia's capital, for a four-day drive visiting Etosha National Park to the north. We had wanted to visit Etosha during the Rachel-guided '83/'84 trip, but it was during the Kalahari rainy season, November through mid-March, when the Park closes to visitors.

Starting from Windhoek at daylight, it took most of the day to reach Etosha's east gate at Numatomi, in an Avis Volkswagen minibus rented at the Windhoek Airport. As I traveled north alone through the stark African countryside, I couldn't get my mind off the beleaguered Bushmen. In Namibia the main concentrations of wild Bushmen are in the back country, up against the Botswana border in what's now called Bushmanland, encompassing the Nyae Nyae area visited by the Marshalls in the 50's. The Nyae Nyae Kung Bushmen are the same people as Qui and his clan, but are now separated from one another by the ten-foot border fence installed by the South Africans in 1965, prior to Botswana's independence. The South Africans feared Botswana would be a haven for SWAPO (Southwest Africa People's Organization) terrorists, harassing South Africa for Namibia's independence. The South African administrators did eventually provide stiles every thirty kilometers and have permitted the nomadic San only to circulate back and forth across the border. About mid-way on my trip north I would be passing the latitude of our Hyena Camp, and at Etosha I would be just about due west of Tsodilo Hills.

One cannot become interested in the Bushmen and not run across the Marshalls and their work and efforts. As I traveled north, I thought enviously of the long periods of time over ten years they had spent with the large clans of Bushmen in the 1950's, off to the west, in Nyae Nyae, now Bushmanland.

Laurence Marshall, who had founded the Raytheon Company in 1922, had visited South Africa on business. When he retired in 1950, he and his eighteen year old son, John, encouraged by Harvard anthropologists, began his family search for the lost Kalahari Bushmen, like van der Post a few year later, to see if any pristine hunter-gatherers still survived. Then a man of sixty years, Laurence was as I am, an engineer and businessman, not a scientist.

Laurence, accompanied by John, spent the summer of 1950 scouting for Bushmen in northern Namibia and finally ended up in Xai Xai. It was then decided that they were not properly equipped to pursue their initial contact with the Kung San into remote uncharted country, but that finding them would be the ongoing project for the family. One had to marvel that the Marshalls got as far as Xai Xai in 1950! Thirty-eight years later it was no easy task for us to get there, though we had equipment and resources which had not been available to the Marshalls.

Including the 1950 reconnaissance trip, Laurence Marshall and members of his family made eight expeditions to Africa between 1950 and 1961, living with and studying Bushmen for long periods of time. The family's main emphasis was in the Nyae Nyae area in Namibia, since named Bushmanland. It was there they found the most thriving wild Bushman culture. However, to get exposure to all the main language groups, they also visited other areas, including the southern Kalahari, southern Angola, and the 'tame' Bushmen congregations in Ghanzi and Gobabis farm blocks, in Botswana and Namibia respectively. Their efforts resulted in several films for *National*

A Chobe elephant comes to water. —BG

A herd of hippo bask in the Chobe River as one sounds off. —JP

A thorny bush harbors weaverbird nests. —JP

Below: With a backdrop of social weavers' nests, zebra and wildebeest share an Etosha waterhole. —JP

At an Etosha waterhole, a giraffe semi-kneels to drink. —JP

Etosha springbok search out the meager shade from the mid-day winter sun. —JP

An Etosha pied
crow. —JP

Etosha zebra partially concealed behind a "wait-a-bit" thorn. Impala in the background.
—JP

Gemsbok (foreground) and kudu (center background), like the Bushman, can survive without surface water. —JP

Once home of the Bushman, Etosha, with its abundant wildlife, is a potential haven for the now landless Bushman. —JP

Geographic and other educational television programs filmed by John Marshall, and two books: *The !Kung of Nyae Nyae*, by Laurence's wife Lorna Marshall, and *The Harmless People*, covering both the Gwi of the central Kalahari and the Kung of Namibia, by Laurence's daughter Elizabeth Marshall Thomas.

In 1951 the Marshalls needed over a week to get into Nyae Nyae on their first trip from the west, or Namibia side. They had to break their own trail for the last 150 miles. They were warned by whites and Bantu alike not to risk the danger of visiting the Bushmen, whose poisoned arrows and savage reputation made people give them a wide berth.

These expeditions were the real start of modern, post World War II, investigations of the San. Expeditions and studies by other writers, scientists and anthropologists followed: notably van der Post in 1955-1956, Tobias in 1958, Lee and Devore from 1963 forward, to name but a few.

John Marshall was refused a visa to Southwest Africa after the family's visit in 1958, in what they saw as a move to silence his comments and films that put the cruel apartheid system in the limelight.

John Marshall started the Nyae Nyae Development Foundation in Namibia in 1981. It was partly funded by an endowment left by his father Laurence's estate, earmarked to help some of the remnants of the Kung Bushmen that he and his family had last visited in Nyae Nyae some twenty years earlier.

Today the foundation works directly with the Bushman people out in the bush as well as lobbying in Namibia and internationally to protect them from further dispossession.

In 1962, the state president of South Africa appointed the Odendall Commission to study then Southwest Africa, now Namibia, in order to find ways of promoting the inhabitants' welfare. The commission's report recommended the partitioning of forty percent of Namibia into separate self-governing homelands for the black ethnic groups. An additional homeland was planned for Bushmen, but was not to be self-governing, a reflection of the government's low regard for the capabilities of the Bushmen. The rest of Namibia, the most fertile areas and the mineral-rich Namib desert, was designated as a white area, promoting the welfare of the white minority.

The South Africans' next step, the Development of Self-Government for Native Nations Act of 1968, provided for the creation of six homelands encompassing the northern portion of Namibia: 1) Koakoland in the northwest corner of Namibia, west of Etosha; 2) Damaraland, south of Etosha and Koakoland; 3) Ovamboland, north of Etosha, taking the northern part of what had been the reserve; 4) Kavangoland, east of Ovamboland and north of Bushmanland; 5) Hereroland, south of Bushmanland; and 6) Eastern Caprivi, which would lie just north of Botswana's Chobe Park.

Both Kavangoland and the major part of Hereroland were carved out of the Nyae Nyae area where the Bushmen still roamed free when the Marshalls first made contact with them in 1951. With a single administrative act, the Ju/Wa Bushmen, who reside in the Nyae Nyae area, had lost seventy percent of their territory. Ju/Wa in the local Kung dialect means *ordinary people* or *real people*, their name for themselves. When East Caprivi was created as the homeland for Tswanas living in Namibia, West Caprivi was declared a nature reserve. The Kwe Bushmen, who had always lived in the Caprivi, were henceforth forbidden to hunt, gather, fish, raise livestock, plant crops or even cut reeds to thatch their houses. They lost all their territory. They were dispossessed.

More recently in Namibia there have been attempts to make eastern Bushmanland into a game reserve with a few Ju/Wa people as a tourist attraction. Barred from having any livestock or pets, they would have been required to wear skins and pretend to be wild, what John Marshall calls "The Plastic Stone Age." But that would have resulted in the eviction of about two thousand Bushmen, the majority of whom had made the transition into a mixed economy, away from the former nomadic foraging culture. This move was resisted on behalf of the Bushmen by John Marshall's Nyae Nyae Development Foundation, as creating a park and leaving a few people in it as curiosities, but evicting and then ignoring the rest, is not the answer.

Now is a very crucial moment for all the people classified as Bushmen in Namibia. In the transition from South African rule to independence, Namibian land could be restored to Bushmen. The West Caprivi Game Reserve, for example, could be reopened for people to come back and settle and farm. So too, their reintroduction into the Kaudom Game Reserve, just north of Bushmanland, land taken away in the 1970's, could help thousands of Ju/Wa people to survive and live meaningful lives.

One of the unforgettable sights en route to Etosha is the nests of the social weaver bird. Whole colonies of these gregarious birds build huge, conspicuous nests in acacia thorn trees. The nests resemble big sections of thatched roofs. The straw colonies are divided into individual compartments which are used as nests, but the birds reside in the colony year round as it serves to keep them cool in summer's heat and warm during the cold Kalahari winters. The weavers add to the nests year after year, often eventually breaking down the tree limbs with their ever heavier structures.

Etosha Park is almost eighty-eight hundred square miles, as large as Botswana's Gemsbok National Park or over twice the size of South Africa's Kalahari Gemsbok. It is larger than South Africa's Kruger or the largest parks in Tanzania and Kenya, Serengeti and Tsavo.

Still, conservationists have a problem with Etosha's boundaries in that despite its current relatively large size, the park has been reduced geographically, for political reasons, so that there is no longer a corridor for game to pass around the north side of the huge salt pan, disrupting centuries old game migration routes and the natural ecosystem.

Land that had originally been part of the reserve was taken back to create the Ovamboland native area to the north, and today the area between the pan and the Angola border has one of the highest population densities in all of Namibia. The salt pan by itself is over three hundred square miles. Geologists believe it was once fed by the Kunene River of Angola, which later changed course to bypass Etosha and flow westward directly into the Atlantic. Etosha means the "great white place" in the Ovambo language of the Bantu tribe to the north.

For thousands of years the park was the sole preserve of the Heiqum Bushmen, until this century, when it was made a game park, and the people were evicted. In the 1890's a rinderpest out-break affected all of southern Africa, killing wild animals as well as domestic cattle, and brought German authorities into the area to try to contain the disease. They were stationed at what have become today the eastern two of the three overnight tourist camps in the park. The Germans created the original Etosha Park Game Reserve in 1907 as an area of over four times its present size. In 1967 Etosha was reduced to its present size to accommodate the tribal homelands to the north, when the animals' northern corridor around the salt pan was lost to the reserve.

During my three-night stay in Etosha I was in my car from daylight to dark, but spent considerable time stopped at the waterholes along the south edge of the salt pan wher the animals congregate, observing and photographing the profusion of game. My first night was at the old German fort at Numatomi, a picturesque white structure which is reminiscent of a Sahara foreign legion outpost that has been converted to a tourist hotel with adjoining camping sites.

I camped the second night further west at Halali camp, and the third night at the Okaukuejo camp near the southwest access into the park. As one goes west the park gets progressively more barren, the tree savanna giving way to a sparser thorn-scrub savanna. The last section of the park west of Okaukuejo camp is almost devoid of game, very dry and barren.

The inside accommodations were fully booked at each location, but my Volkswagen combi and I found space in the clean camping areas provided at each site. Most overseas tourists are on organized tours, which will not come unless they can book inside rooms. Generally, only the local European population camp out under the stars, and as Etosha is a long drive from Windhoek, and much further from Johannesburg or Pretoria, camping space is not hard to find. A barbecue pit is provided at each camping site with a bath house nearby with hot and cold running water. I found everything spotlessly South-African-Dutch clean.

Having visited most of the parks in southern and eastern Africa, I don't think you can top Ngorongoro crater in Tanzania for breathtaking beauty and numbers and variety of animals in a concentrated area. But Tanzania can claim three magnificent parks situated back to back, Lake Manyara in the Rift Valley, the Ngorongoro crater, and the Serengeti plains with annual migration of thousands of zebra and wildebeest, with the accompanying lion, leopard and cheetah. Still, Etosha has its own park personality and must rank as one of the world's exceptional wildlife paradises on earth. Conservationists of the world are to be congratulated for setting aside such beautiful reserves as these for posterity.

Though Etosha is noted for its carnivores, in the three days I saw only one lioness lying in ambush around Salvadora waterhole and a leopard at dusk at Nuamses waterhole, just north of Halali rest camp. Too few predators for an artifically-elevated game population? A few clans of foraging Bushmen would right the eons old balance of nature, and put Etosha one up on Tanzania's world class parks.

So what about Etosha as a potential haven or sanctuary for the San? Again the tourists are restricted to their vehicles, and the vehicles to the established roads. Indiscriminate roaming around in the bush is not allowed. The small portion of the park that has been developed with roads for tourists is restricted to the water holes and springs in the narrow strip along the south edge of the huge Etosha salt pan, which is a glaring white expanse stretching off as far as the eye can see, not unlike the Great Salt Lake. Meanwhile, the expanse to the south of the pan and the majority of the area to the west is without roads, inaccessible and off limits to tourists. There is certainly ample unused space for a few small family bands of nomadic San. They would harldy make a dent in the teeming herds of animals; zebra, wildebeest, giraffe, springbok, kudu, gemsbok, black faced impala, ostrich, warthog, and would only add to the allure of Estosha.

As I returned south, leaving Etosha through the southwest gate near Okaukuejo Camp, my thoughts went again to the Kung Bushmen off to the east. In 1960 the Southwest African authorities opened up a government settlement in Bushmanland, at Tsumkwe, encouraging the Bushmen of Nyae Nyae to resettle and avail themselves of government services. This eventually resulted in the concentration of too many Bushmen in one area and led to depletion of the environment, tensions and drunkenness, further exacerbated by the South African army establishing a military base for Bushmen they were using as trackers to fight SWAPO in nearby Angola. Starting in 1982, many of the Ju/Wa Bushmen people have relocated back away from Tsumkwe to thirty or more communities out in the bush, back to where the Marshalls found them in 1951. Today these 'back-to-the-bush' San still hunt and forage, but now a good generation later, they have small subsistence herds of livestock, do some gardening, and have been provided with bore holes to ensure water supplies. A problem for the Ju/Wa Bushmen's livestock is predators. There are an estimated 400 lions in the area which, with diminished wild game, prey on and kill the Bushmen's cattle. San are not allowed guns, while, paradoxically, rich foreign recreational hunters are allowed to shoot lions, and the elephants which tear up the Bushman's bore hole pumps, foraging for water.

When the Marshalls first visited the Kung Bushmen of Nyae Nyae in 1951, they encountered completely isolated, nomadic hunter-gatherers, dressed in animal skins, hunting with poisoned arrows. The Marshalls were able first to make friends with one band, then were introduced to the rest of ten family bands ranging in size from ten to forty members, who each had hunting and gathering territories 'owned' by individual bands through inheritance, centered around natural permanent or semi-permanent water sources or pans with names like Gautscha, Kautsa, Deboragu, Nahtsoba, N!o !go, Keitsa and Khumsa, and included Tsumkwe, which was later chosen by the South African government as their 'civilizing' center for Bushmen. The bands were related through kinship ties of blood, marriage, or 'same name'. The Kung of Nyae Nyae were isolated from civilization in this northwest corner of the Kalahari by a desolate stretch of inhospitable wasteland to the west of them, then an escarpment. These Nyae Nyae Bushmen were related through marriage ties to the Botswana Bushmen in Ngamiland, in the isolated northwest corner of Botswana, and they visited back and forth, using specially provided stiles, even after the ten foot border fence was erected in 1965, leading up to the Botswana's independence in 1966. It was not until the Marshalls broke a track into remote and isolated Nyae Nyae in the early 1950's that white farmers following the Marshalls' tracks first penetrated the area from the west, to shanghai or 'blackbird' some of these largely defenseless Bushmen as workers, slaves and serfs.

In December of 1959 the first Bushman commissioner from the Southwest African government in Windhoek arrived in the Nyae Nyae area and established his administrative post at Tsumkwe. He started introducing people to 'civilized' ways of keeping goats, planting gardens, opening a clinic, a store, and a Dutch Reform Church mission. The commissioner enticed the Ju/Wa to congregate at Tsumkwe, giving up their nomadic hunter-gatherer life in the bush for the 'better life' of gardening, raising goats, working for money.

When the commissioner retired a decade later in 1970, his paternalistic efforts in promoting self reliance, and taking the Ju/Wa Bushmen from the stone age to the modern day, had largely failed, and by this time Bushmanland had been created, securing a homeland for Ju/Wa Bushmen by giving away 70% of the Nyae Nyae range the Marshalls had found them in twenty years earlier! The western two thirds of the much reduced 'administrative' Bushmanland was an uninhabitable waterless area.

In the 1970's Tsumkwe expanded into an administrative complex with roads, boreholes, police station and lock up, with blacks in a segregated housing complex, whites living separately, and Bushmen living in their traditional encampments in a three mile radius. Tsumkwe provided employment for Ju/Wa, expanding from nine persons in 1969 to 85 in 1972, but each employed former hunter-gatherer dragged an average of six dependents into a sedentary life style and unemployment. The local area could not support a foraging economy for so many people concentrated in one place. The bush skills and survival knowledge were being lost, as 800 people were living on top of each other in a rural slum with inadequate means of subsistence or survival. Hunting and gathering had come to be viewed as backward by many of the Ju/Wa.

The rules and values of their hunter-gatherer culture were put under extreme stress. Efforts to maintain goat herds and gardens collapsed under the demands of hungry relatives, following the Bushmen's long ingrained sharing ethic. The administration introduced cattle, and some 47 men bought animals at subsidized prices with their wages, but no model for productive cattle management was provided by the administration. Few Ju/Wa built kraals or milked. Their cattle were killed for food by predators. Poor nutrition and social disintegration contributed to a rising death rate. Genealogies show that the birth rate had risen with sedentization, but that at some time during the early 1970's the population was diminishing because the death rate exceeded the birth rate.

These tensions exploded in 1981 when, with a government loan to the black Kavango shopkeeper at Tsumkwe, a liquor store was opened. Drunkenness turned the incessant arguments into uncontrolled violence, which led to injury and death. As one informant explained, "The fight was always there inside us. Liquor lets it out." In the mid 1980's Little Qui, who with the Marshalls help survived the puff adder bite to continue hunting on a pegleg, was murdered in Tsumkwe by his son-in-law, home on leave from military duty, in an alcohol induced release of violence.

In 1982, when apathy and despair seemed to have a stranglehold on the Tsumkwe population, and the South African administration was still more concerned with infrastructure rather than people, several groups made the effort toward self development by turning their backs on Tsumkwe and returning to their traditional waterholes and foraging territories in the bush. The private fund established by a bequest from the late Laurence Marshall encouraged and assisted the Ju/Wa in a kind of outstation movement. The idea, which came from the Bushmen themselves, was to develop a mixed economy based on cattle husbandry and supplemented by some hunting and gathering. Hunting was still possible if small groups were widely scattered. Some Ju/Wa already owned cattle, bought from the subsidized administration herd, and the Marshall fund provided additional cattle and basic tools. Livestock was individually, not group, owned. Initial attempts to build kraals and milk their cattle at Tsumkwe failed. It was obvious that for any development effort to succeed it would have to be done away from the chaos of Tsumkwe, which the Ju/Wa came to refer to as 'the-place-of-death'!

By this time John Marshall could again obtain a visa into Namibia. There, he administered the funds from his father's estate plus additonal funds solicited from donors, but more importantly aided and encouraged the Ju/Wa Bushmen through the false starts and failures of the Bushmen's own idea of 'going back to the bush'! The 'official' administration at Tsumkwe was indifferent and even hostile to the Bushmen's self-determination efforts, with the Marshall foundation acting as liaison between the government and the Bushmen.

Starting with the 'cattle fund' bequeathed by Laurence Marshall's estate, the incorporated non-profit Nyae Nyae Development Foundation evolved with a board of directors in Windhoek and a sister organization in the United States, the !Kung San Organization, Cultural Survival Inc., Cambridge, Massachusetts. The Nyae Nyae Development Foundation objectives had widened, raising funds in order to assist more Ju/Wa in developing subsistence farming communities, and as a lobbying group to help protect Bushmanland.

It may come as a surprise to many to know that N!Xau, star of the movie *The Gods Must Be Crazy*, was no longer the game skin wearing Bushman, like Qui, he so convincingly depicted in the movie. Rather, he was recruited by the South African movie makers from among the Ju/Wa Bushmen in Namibia's Bushmanland where the film makers found him in tattered European clothes, working as a janitor in Tsumkwe. N!Xau was enticed to dress up in skins to act in the movie. The 'star' is among those who have since turned their backs on Tsumkwe to return to the bush to try to recapture some of their people's happier days and former culture, before they were lured in from the bush to be civilized from 1960 forwards.

On the return south to Windhoek, whenever possible, I left the main paved road and took scenic secondary roads to the.west. In this starkly beautiful country the roads become less traveled. Eventually I had to stop and open wire cattle gates across the road. There were no other cars and not the slightest possibility of a petrol station in this raw African landscape. Like Salome returning to Maun, my fingers were crossed as I approached Windhoek, as the Avis Volkswagen's needle had been on empty for too long!

Back in Windhoek in late afternoon I checked back into the Safari Hotel, exhausted from the four-day trip. The next morning, when I turned in the Avis VW Combi at the Windhoek airport before my flight to Johannesburg, I had logged 2,371 kilometers on the Etosha sojourn, almost fifteen hundred miles, and had seen enough abundantly, even over-stocked park land to satisfy the needs of many nomadic clans.

I left wondering why the threatened Bushmen couldn't be brought up to the same level of attention as the animals and allowed back in Etosha where they once lived. Foraging Bushmen had lived with 'their' animals for centuries before they were thrown out of the parks and conservation areas without due consideration for their unique history and special status as the charter members of God's special wildlife Eden—southern Africa. It is not right for the minuscule population of surviving traditional Bushmen to be lumped together with Bantu and whites who have succumbed to the white man's version of civilization, of anything for the almighty dollar, which has led us to become the true enemies of the animals. But ironically, it is these new black Bantu members of the civilized club, along with their white compatriots, represented in today's governments of southern Africa, who are the real culprits who continue throwing the unrepresented wild Bushman charter members off their land and separating them from their game.

—12—
Makgadikgadi

It was mid-September when I retraced my steps back to Botswana. Santon Sun to Johannesburg airport, changing planes in Gabarone for Maun in the heart of the Kalahari. What a difference, I thought, three weeks make! This Kalahari trip, starting innocently enough as a small adventure, a return to the remote African bush, was now sweeping me along, with our group's questioning if something could not be done for the preservation and salvation of the wild Bushman and his tame kin.

Peter and Salome met me in Maun, where it was almost mid-day. One of the now familiar Toyota safari vehicles was loaded, ready to head out to the Makgadikgadi.

"The drive to the turn-off south to the pan and game viewing area will take about four hours," Peter said.

"No time for the Duck Inn. You're straight off to the bush," Salome needled with a good-natured smile.

We drove east out of Maun on the road toward Francistown. Leaving Maun and the edge of the Okavango Delta, we went abruptly into the flat acacia thorn thirstland.

As we traveled down the gravel road, Peter gave me a rundown. "Paralleling us off to our south is the Boteti River which gets its water from the Thamalakane River flowing through Maun, along a fault of the same name, which limits the southeast flow of the Okavango Delta waters, like an overflow drain. The Thamalakane gets its water out of the Okavango Delta, receiving Angola rainfall through watercourses like the Bora River we traveled to look for the river Bushman."

Only about two percent of the water that enters the Okavango Delta from Angola survives absorption and evaporation to leave the south end of the Delta, to flow beyond it toward the Boteti River as far as Lake Xau, southwest of the Makgadikgadi, or the Nhabe River toward Lake Ngami. In non-drought Kalahari rainy seasons, October through

187

May, half as much volume of water as enters the Okavango is added through rainfall within the Okavango. At these times the outer boundaries of the Okavango flooded areas expand to 5,000 square miles, with the seasonal flooded area adding to those perennially inundated.

Lake Ngami, mostly dry in recent times, is some eighty kilometers south of Maun, and is still fed on rare occasion by waters from the Okavango. Traveling on foot, David Livingstone arrived at an impressive 'wet' Lake Ngami in 1849. He later continued north to the Zambezi River in 1851 and on to discover Victoria Falls in 1855. Livingstone found the area around Lake Ngami and along the Boteti River to be an animal's paradise. Hunters moved in and slaughtered by the hundreds and then thousands, elephant for ivory, and lion, leopards and antelope for skins and meat. There was no law to speak of before Botswana became a British protectorate in 1895.

The Boteti River carrying Okavango water east peters out before reaching the Makgadikgadi, an area of some forty-six hundred square miles made up of two main pans, or shallow depressions, which are dry except when they collect local rain water for short periods seasonally. Ntwetwe Pan on the west and Sowa on the east, constitute the lowest elevations in Botswana and the whole Kalahari basin. Our destination, the sixteen hundred square miles Makgadikgadi Pans Game Reserve supporting wild antelope, is situated on the grass plains west of the pans and south of the Maun-Francistown road. We hoped to see the great herds of zebra and wildebeest before their annual migration north, across the Maun-Francistown road to Nxai Pan, a national park of a thousand square miles made up of forest and savanna. Nxai and Kgama-Kgama Pans provide water for the game during and for a time after the rains.

The Makgadikgadi salt pans are said to be the largest in the world. Authorities think they are the remnant of a fossil lake that once covered 60,000 square kilometers, four times the size of Okavango's present wetland. The game reserve, created in an area where the animals naturally congregate, is predominantly open grass land, flat to slightly rolling with several small but important pans, seasonally holding rain water that attracts the game. The reserve supports large concentrations of zebra, wildebeest and springbok, smaller numbers of gemsbok and ostrich, and accompanying carnivores, such as lion, jackal, hyena and cheetah. The big salt pans attract a profusion of flamingos, pelicans, waders and other water fowl for short periods in nondrought years, when they collect shallow depths of water. Otherwise they are heat-shimmering dry. The huge open grass plains are broken only by the occasional low bush and small groups of vegetable ivory palm, known for the fruit which is used to make decorative items like necklaces and the heads of walking sticks.

We turned south off the gravel road to Francistown onto a two-rutted track leading into Makgadikgadi, and, after a half hour, stopped to

Baines, accompanied by Livingstone in 1862, painted the Baines' Baobabs. Prince Charles, guided by van der Post in 1987, also painted them. —JP

The fallen, but still living, member of the 'Seven Sisters' that make up Baines' Baobabs. —JP

Left: The Makgadikgadi savanna is broken by an occasional stand of vegetable ivory palms. —JP

Below: The close-knit five ambulatory children of Qui's clan. —WT

camp on a slight domed rise in a grove of the vegetable ivory palms overlooking wide open spaces in all directions. The tall palms rustled and rattled in the breeze in this otherwise immense expanse of almost eerie silence. Mansu set about installing our simple camp.

As on visiting Etosha and Chobe, I intended to size up this place as a potential nomadic Bushman haven. Etosha had lots of game; in fact, it gave the appearance of being overstocked, thus overgrazed. As tourists are restricted by the established roads to the waterholes along the south side of the huge salt pan, they have access to only a very small part of the reserve. Chobe is similar. The roads restrict tourist access to only limited areas around the Chobe and Savuti lodges. By contrast the Makgadikgadi is a commercially undeveloped and much less-visited reserve with no lodge or accommodations, no roads to which the tourists are in turn restricted. Still, there is no reason that it would not be suitable for reintroduction of nomadic Bushmen, who might follow the game's annual migrations in and out of the region.

The first afternoon and well into the next morning Peter was perplexed and puzzled, for as we toured around we found no game. The reserve seemed deserted. Had they migrated north to Nxai Pan? Then we met a Landrover loaded down with five whites and three blacks, all bristling with firearms.

"Ghanzi farmers," Peter said in disgust as they pulled away.

"They were looking for zebra?" I asked in amazement. "But why are they hunting zebras in the reserve?" Peter recognized the black in the front seat as the Makgadikgadi game scout in charge of guarding the reserve. Was he moonlighting this day as a hunting guide? Officials throw the Bushmen out and replace them with paid poachers! We were crestfallen and furious.

Peter reported later following up on this incident with Ghanzi farmers. He was told that their aim was to capture game for translocation to their farms, but they did not have permission to do this inside the reserve, and why the guns?

We camped in the Makgadikgadi Pans Reserve for three nights. Finally, late in the second day, after much frustrated searching in the broad open plains, we did spot several large herds of springbok, wildebeest and zebra, but they were extremely skittish! As we approached the herds of several thousand animals, they would break and run in a cloud of dust as soon as our vehicle got within a couple of kilometers.

"That's a pretty good sign that vehicles have been spitting lead at them," I remarked to Peter's grim nod.

The large herds of animals did not mix species. "In the Makgadikgadi the zebra and wildebeest don't mingle like they do in the Serengeti," remarked Peter.

We stopped to observe a large herd of ostrich and counted forty-five, the largest single concentration I can remember seeing anywhere in Africa. Though we heard lions on their nocturnal hunts, we encountered only one lone female out hunting in the daylight.

We drove down to the edge of the dry Ntwetwe salt pan, an immense, blinding white, heat-shimmering expanse, completely devoid of life. The game was all well away, off to the west on the grassy plains around what remained of the small rain-supplied fresh water pans.

Unlike at our calm camp sites at Hyena and Scorpion, there tended to be a brisk wind blowing across this vast open expanse, rattling the palm branches. We had to don jackets for our evening campfire.

We kept coming back to the issue of what could be done for the San. To me the Makgadikgadi Pans Game Reserve seemed another possible home for some clans. There is certainly plenty of game seasonally, and the Bushmen's presence might well keep out the likes of the poachers we had seen.

On our last night, about an hour after the sun had gone down, we suddenly became aware of vehicle headlights flashing around on the plains a couple of kilometers east of our encampment. We got up and stepped away from the light of our fire and stared into the dark.

"Obviously poachers, the scum. This explains the extreme skittishness of the game," I grumbled to Peter with a feeling of revulsion. As a former hunter and sportsman I hated the idea of poaching. Poaching is indiscriminate greed-driven slaughter, a far cry from the legal sport that allows the taking of strictly limited numbers of male trophies and contributes funds to the animals' long-term conservation and survival.

We continued to see the lights roving around the plain southeast of our encampment. It was eerie, seeing the phantom light flashing across the horizon on this vast open space, to the accompaniment of crackling and rustling as occasional strong gusts of wind rattled the palm branches over our heads. As we silently watched the vehicle lights careening in the distance, my hair stood up as a lion roared behind us off to the west. "Probably as disgusted as we are," Peter said. "Those bastards are having a real go at the game."

The lights continued flashing around out on the plains. After an hour of our agonizing, the lights disappeared. It was over; finally it was dark.

The next morning as we broke camp, we could see no game. The previous night's clandestine vehicle activities had pushed the game out of our area. We circled out east to look for the herds before departing west for Maun. Not a trace of the large herds, we saw little except bird life.

A most noisy and conspicuous bird, which we saw here in profusion, was the black korhaan, the pheasant-sized bird that Qui and Noishay were snaring. The male has a black neck and underbelly with splashes of white on a long spindly neck, body and wings, and speckled brown back and wings, a grey bill fusing into red at its base, and yellow legs. What etches them in one's memory is their mating antics. The colorful male launches himself from the ground, like a flushing pheasant, with a harsh cackling screech. He flutters and flies straight up for thirty feet or so, then as suddenly drops straight down with wings outspread and legs dangling, like a pilot parachuting out of a disabled plane. Once back on the ground he speeds off on foot. The raucous mating performance of the male black korhaan must have been repeated a hundred times, with the area heavily populated by this bird.

Another entertaining character was the suricate or grey meerkat, a member of the mongoose family. These are very social creatures living in burrowed colonies of twenty to fifty animals. Their antics were like a troop of serious clowns, some moving on all fours, others standing straight up with arched backs, staring at us from ten meters or closer with their big innocent eyes, without apparent fear. "They are real hams," said Peter. "And those cute little rascals regularly dispatch deadly poisonous cobras with their nimble and quick attacks."

Leaving Makgadikgadi, we went north on the Francistown road to the famous Baines' Baobabs. Baines was an early explorer only slightly less famous than Livingstone. He painted this rather unique grove of baobab trees back in 1862 when he and Livingstone were traveling together, walking and exploring north through Africa. Prince Charles had a go at painting the same trees when he visited the area in 1987 with Laurens van der Post as his guide.

Located on the Kanyu flats south of Nxai Pans, Baines' Baobabs is the name given to a grove of big, old, gnarled baobabs on a slight rise that would become an island in the wet season. Now Kudiakam Pan was an eye-dazzling white salt flat surrounding and framing the cool shade and shadows of the baobab grove. At the center are the Seven Sisters, seven closely clustered baobab trees, one fallen over but still alive.

One can imagine why Baines was attracted to the site, as the grove presents endlessly appealing views that beg to be photographed, and I tried to capture the area in color and black and white. To do it properly one would have to stay around at least a full day to see the subject in the changing direction and intensities of light and shadows.

Continuing west along the old Francistown road took us by the Bushmen's pits where we stopped for a picnic lunch. The Bushmen are reported to have mined iron ore here, which they traded to Bantu tribes for finished products, metallic tips for arrows and spears.

From the Bushman's pits we continued the hundred kilometers back into Maun. I chose to ride in the observation seats in the back of the Toyota with Mansu, enjoying a relaxing remote African Sunday drive.

The next morning I woke up refreshed at first light. I faced up to having to call a halt for now to this southern African sojourn and get myself onto a flight back to Johannesburg and on to the States. 'I have to break Africa's hold on me and get back to civilized things,' I thought, with a feeling of frustration and guilt for succumbing to such mundane pressures.

After an English breakfast at Riley's, I went to visit the Bushman craft shop. Beth Oliver was away, but I picked up more handicraft items, and packed my gear for the early afternoon flight back to Johannesburg. I couldn't leave Maun without a visit to the Duck Inn and lunch with Peter and Salome.

"Peter, you talk about small businesses and industry for this area. Has anyone thought of a taxi service for Maun?" I joked. It was a hike from Riley's with all my gear.

"Progress is coming to Maun fast enough," scowled Salome.

I knew she was right, that the very lack of progress was one of the things that was saving the few nomadic San from extinction. I knew, too, that we had been fortunate to see them at all, that hardly anybody has had such an opportunity because of the very nature of the San, sequestering themselves in remote areas, living nomadically and often moving. They are out of sight and out of mind. But for the special efforts of a few anthropologists, they would be unknown. Unfortunately, the general public doesn't have easy access to anthropologists' findings. *The Gods Must Be Crazy* did capture many people's hearts and brought some attention to the San people. While it was a very entertaining movie, it gave the audience no hint that the culture they were seeing is on the brink of extinction. The movie was not meant to be a manifesto nor have altruistic motives. It was a commercial effort, and a comedy at that, but it may have unwittingly proved a point. In San Francisco it ran for seventy weeks, setting a new record for longest running movie. Through it people discovered and liked the Bushmen. Might they not now be motivated to help them?

I left Maun on that positive thought for Johannesburg. There I left a sleeping bag and camping gear at friend Rachel's house as seed for a return trip. She was still 'out-of-the-country'.

The flight straight through from Johannesburg to Frankfurt and on to San Antonio was long, giving me time to reflect on the Bushmen's plight, and whether to become actively involved. But I had been on a lot of tough construction projects and knew from experience that where there was a will, there was a way. Arriving home jet-lagged, I still had the will. Now to find the way.

—13—
Epilogue

Back at my base camp in the Texas hill country north of San Antonio, the Bushmen were still with me. I watched the last half of the Seoul Olympics, as I sorted through a month of bills and other loose ends. Then I followed that every four year extravaganza, the presidential elections, and the fall football season, my '49ers suffering a letdown at midseason, but coming back to win the 1988 season's Superbowl.

But even back in civilization, the haunting memory of our sojourn with the Bushmen wouldn't go away. I kept thinking of them as *our* Bushmen, as if by virtue of the week we had spent with them they had fallen under our care. "Bush for the Bushman," I kept saying to myself at odd times when out jogging or driving.

But why us? Why the Wheeler mob? Why should we stick our nose in? It always came back to: but who else? The anthropologists are the one group who, in having studied the Bushmen, know first hand of their plight and struggle for survival. But their activities are largely low key, academic studies and papers that the general public never sees. Some anthropologists are doing more—working directly with the people in the bush, and with the Botswana and Namibia governments on the Bushmen's behalf, raising money and developing plans for wells. We wanted to help this latter group, but we wanted to see more people with a broader base working internationally for the San. Why not inform the world at large of the Bushmen's situation and get people off their duffs to help?

I was used to making things happen, getting the pipelines built, moving men and equipment, identifying the problems and solving them. Was this so different? I had always had considerable corporate money and manpower with which to work, as well as the clout of investing foreign governments as clients behind the projects. In this case we were more at sea. In visiting Qui's clan, it became apparent to us that if something wasn't done soon, it wasn't going to happen. The Bushmen, at least the handful of nomadic ones, are just going to fade into oblivion if someone doesn't act for them. NOW!

The only hope is that a public, made more aware of the Bushmen's plight, will not permit them to be doomed.

It is late for the nomadic Bushmen, most authorities have already said 'too late'. But these people are not yet gone. Qui and Noishay and their clan are there and they had said that there were a few others. But when those few are gone, it *will* be too late. Who could question wanting to not let these special people die or be further dispossessed of their land, anonymous and unknown to the world? We believe if more people knew, as we were now privileged to know, they would move to do something.

Doing something for the San is like doing something for our own kin. And if anthropologists are right, they are our kin, the oldest surviving members of man's family tree.

I visited La Jolla to compare notes with Dr. Wheeler. Over the years many acquaintances had said I should write a book, but about my extensive experiences overseas; being charged by a buffalo in Tanzania, working with the headhunters that killed young Rockefeller in Irian Jaya, being the guest at "you-eat-the-eyeball" mutton grabs in the Saudi desert. I had never given it that much serious thought. Jack and the others agreed that maybe this was the time and the Bushmen a deserving topic. Write a book? I quite doubted that I had either the talent or the patience. Pictures and videos offered by my Kalahari mates helped me recapture the detail, and sustain and rekindle my interest.

I approached helping the Bushmen with the same attitude I had assumed when confronted through the years by a difficult beachhead construction assignment: No good waiting around for someone else to do something, have a go at it. Nothing to lose, everything to gain. As fall was turning into winter I gathered reference books at my Texas base camp and started writing.

Then George Bush played his role by winning the election, essential if our adopted "Bush for the Bushman" cry was to be doubly meaningful; *bush* for land and Bush to help them get it. "Dukakis for the Bushman" was not the same.

Bush came out with his 'kinder and gentler world' slogan, which certainly fit the gentle, long-suffering Bushmen. Bush claimed to be the education president. People need to be educated about the Bushmen and their plight. Bush claimed to want to be known as the environmental president. What better pragmatic environmentalists to champion than the Bushmen who frown on anyone cutting a Kalahari tree and reducing their meager shade? Southern Africa's wild animals had survived ten thousand years under Bushman guardianship until whites and Bantu arrived. Could the new president be encouraged into taking up the cause of these close to nature living, nature loving, born environmentalists?

Typed pages were accumulating. I bought a computer and hired word processing help to convert my rough typed sheets into a manuscript. Hang on Bushmen, we're off and running.

The pitch? The public has to be made aware of how the Bushmen have been dispossessed of their land, killed, shanghaied as serfs or slaves to whites and Bantus, forcefully assimilated with the loss of their culture and civilized against their will by the more powerful and materialistically, if not morally, advanced majority. Public interest could lead to developing a workable plan for saving the Bushmen from extinction, possibly borrowing from the recent tangible success of reforms in Australia that in a dramatic turnaround gave the previously dispossessed Aborigines much of their land back in the Northern Territory, or similar moves by Canada for its Inuit.

We would like to think that George Bush and other world leaders could employ gentle persuasion to draw the attention of the young Botswana and Namibia governments to the fact that the San are an unparalleled and irreplaceable resource not only to the Kalahari region but to the whole world. Do not let them die out. And we certainly would not want to see a commercialization of Qui, to put him and his family in parks to perform for tourists. We only suggest putting the people back in the parks as one option to give them land, because it is their own bush, it is where their animals are. Reserves are a place where they might find food and water without having to compete with the cattle or mining interests, where they could have a viable choice between retaining their nomadic lifestyle or making the transition to a more modern and sedentary mixed economy. If the situation of hunter-gatherer peoples worldwide is any indication, it may be naive at this late date to try to do anything for the San. What has happened to the American Plains Indian, the Inuit, Tasmanian man, and most of the Australian Aborigines outside the Northern Territory would not auger well for a happy ending being in the Bushmen's oracle discs. But let's be positive! We will not know unless we try.

One of my first concerns was updating information on the current status of the Bushman's eviction from the Central Kalahari. I had no luck calling information to find someone in the Botswana government in Gaborone. Next I tried Namibia, to inquire about the San in Bushmanland. I asked information for the country code for Windhoek, Namibia.

"Where?" the operator asked in a puzzled tone.

"It's in Africa. The South Africans call it South West Africa, the UN calls it Namibia."

"Never heard of it," she said.

I persisted and after several international calls I reached Jonas Swanepoel, the Bushman Control Officer in Windhoek. He had worked with the Bushmen as a former religious minister and now had the government post in charge of them. Swanepoel confirmed that the Sar were still doing some hunting with poisoned arrows up in Bushmanland. He had inherited the Tsumkwe 'experiment', where the Bushmen have learned first hand what happens to a nomadic people who are concentrated, confined, and made sedentary and dependent on the bureaucracy. They have seen their people turn to alcohol and other modern vices as a result of their cultural breakdown and resulting despair.

At the government post at Tsumkwe there is a school where Bushmen children are being taught.

"In what language?" I asked Swanepoel.

"In Afrikaans," he answered. "That's the only type of teachers we have." A shame, I thought. Namibia is about to be independent of South Africa. Wouldn't it be better to teach in a more universal language like English so that the Bushmen could better speak for themselves in governmental matters that vitally concern them?

Swanepoel reported that the Bushmen were cooperating with government conservation forces in refraining from taking rare and endangered species like the roan antelope.

He suggested I talk to the people of the Ju/Wa Development Foundation (since renamed the Nyae Nyae Development Foundation of Namibia). Texan Dr. Megan Biesele is the current project director, residing mostly outside of Windhoek up in the bush, in what was Nyae Nyae, now reduced to Bushmanland. I eventually got through to her in Windhoek. She was happy to hear of any interest in the Bushmen and quite helpful in answering my questions and sending information for our efforts on the Bushmen's behalf.

"How about John Marshall?" I asked.

"He's in the States at the moment, but still active in the Foundation," Dr. Biesele said.

I called John Marshall at his home in New Hampshire and explained our group's contact with Qui and his clan and how we were interested in trying to do something for the Bushmen. I hoped to enlist his advice on the Central Kalahari eviction and other current Bushman topics.

"If you want to help the Bushman people," said John Marshall after we talked for some time, "work must be done in Botswana to try to reverse this decision by the government to throw them out of the Central Kalahari Reserve. Then help them develop a mixed economy. That is the way you survive in southern Africa. You know what I mean by the mixed economy?"

"Yes," I responded. "That Bushmen still be allowed to hunt, but doing so when the season is right, while making the transition that the rest of us made eons ago from pure hunter-gatherers or foragers to raising domestic animals and food and working for wages by building fences and herding cattle."

"That's right," said Marshall. "Help people to do that in the Central Kalahari or otherwise they will die. They need land. They're continuing to face death by dispossession. You should try to get that 1970s movie from *National Geographic*."

"Death by dispossession." The words rang in my ear, haunted me in my sleep, long after my conversation with John Marshall.

I obtained John's film from *National Geographic*. When it was filmed in 1973 both the Central Kalahari and the Nyae Nyae San had transitioned to wearing European felt hats and cotton clothes rather than the skins they had been wearing when van der Post and the Marshalls had first seen them in the mid 1950s.

"And what about Etosha?" I asked John Marshall. "Couldn't Bushmen be reintroduced on the south edge of it? The tourists are restricted to the roads in a narrow corridor just south of the pan. South of that, within the reserve, is fifty to a hundred kilometers where nobody goes."

"That would be wonderful," John said. "That would be restoring their land to Bushman people."

Before talking with John Marshall, our focus had been more on the few surviving nomadic Bushmen being given land, one possibility being residence and hunting rights within the parks. Again there was a reminder that it was not as simple as that. The majority of genetic Bushmen were beyond returning to surviving by foraging only. As Jack had said, "You can't uninvent the wheel." We must not forget the tame Bushmen majority. Still, until recently the whole Kalahari was their land and all wild game were their animals. Is it unreasonable to ask the powers that be in Botswana and Namibia to give them rights to some small portion of the land they formerly had inside or outside the reserves? Let the Bushmen themselves choose whether or not to remain nomadic or to make a transition to a mixed economy on their own land.

Our 'help the Bushmen' thrust took on a broadened scope after talking to John Marshall. A Bushmen lobby would have to push for land and better conditions not only for the few wild Bushmen like Qui, but also not forget the majority of Bushmen, most of whom are already living in a mixed subsistence economy, like the ones we had seen in Xai Xai and Tsodilo and the people in the Ghanzi farm block of whom we had heard.

Calling Peter in Maun to discuss our effort, I asked his advice on a contact in Botswana, as my calls through information to government offices in Gaborone had not turned up anybody who understood what I was asking about, or who could give information about Basarwa in Botswana, or the current status of their eviction from the Central Kalahari.

"Call the Botswana Society in Gaborone. They should have someone that can help," Peter suggested. "Also, have you heard that Botswana has refused a visa to the Owens of *Cry of the Kalahari*? Their comments about the hoof and mouth disease barrier fences stopping natural migrations to water sources and killing thousands of wildebeest has caused Botswana a lot of flack from conservationists around the world. If you are stirring it up for the Bushmen, you might not get back into Botswana."

"Botswana should consider opening up the barrier fences. The Botswanans didn't put them up and they are a pre-independence idea. As to Botswana having a thin skin, I hear you," I responded.

The Botswana Society put me onto Dr. Hitchcock, an anthropologist at the University of Nebraska who travels frequently to Africa and is active in Botswana on behalf of the San through the Kalahari People's Fund and other avenues. He provided very valuable current information on the San and the government's changing treatment of them, from his involvement in government projects and studies of 'The Bushman Problem.'

The Botswana government under Quett Masire had been under some international pressure on the San's behalf. As early as 1973 when Masire was Vice President, John Marshall helped a group of Central Kalahari Bushmen arrange an audience with him so that they could plead for water and permission to stay in the Reserve. At the time, Masire seemed moved to help them, insuring their tenuous survival until recently. But he is now under pressure from other camps.

Botswana is dependent on the European Community for a market for its beef, which until diamonds were discovered was Botswana's leading export revenue earner. Botswana has a sweetheart contract to supply beef to the EC at above market prices. Greenpeace and others have pressured the EC to use the beef contract as a club to lobby Botswana for eviction of all humans from the Central Kalahari Reserve. On the other side of the coin, Survival International, a group that works for aboriginal people worldwide, has been carrying on a letter-writing campaign to Masire opposing the Bushmen's eviction from the Reserve. Masire is getting it from all sides.

John Marshall suggested that our group write Masire protesting the Central Kalahari ejection, which we did, joining Survival International and their campaign in 1989. For a time it seems that this campaign had some success, keeping in limbo the actual eviction of the San from the Central Kalahari under the 1986 decree, indicating that Masire and the Botswana government can be successfully lobbied by concerned individuals internationally. But in a November 1991 'action alert', Survival International informed its membership that the balance had tilted against the Bushmen. The Botswana government was again making moves to carry out the on-again, off-again eviction under the 1986 decree. Survival International requested a renewed letter writing effort to Botswana on the Bushmen's behalf. Our group's 1991 letter is in Appendix B to encourage readers to follow suit.

It is vital to keep pressure on for the Bushmen, even if it means coming into conflict with the EC and Greenpeace and whoever else might have interests other than saving the Bushmen. Obviously this situation involves many people worldwide. In all the wrangling of

Without land what is this **Bushman child's** future? —JP

The unattached Bushman woman has chosen the arduous hunter-gatherer life with the clan rather than taking her only other option—competing with the cattle at a well site. —JP

The young unattached Bushman woman has chosen the fast-disappearing foraging life with the clan over the "bright lights" of Xai Xai. —JP

opposing forces it is the innocent bystanders, the San, who are in the greater danger of being lost. Their salvation will come only when the majority realizes that the San and the animals belong together, that the San are protectors of the animals, and the saving of these people contributes to the saving of their game, a potential win-win situation.

In June 1989 I was called away to spend two months on planning Chevron's oilfield development in the remote, rugged jungles of the central highlands of Papua New Guinea. I took my manuscript along but found it most difficult to work on it, given the rustic open air accommodations in the damp jungle, over 250 inches of rain a year. Virtually on the equator, mold and fungus appeared overnight!

I thought of the Kalahari Bushmen. Would they have loved some of this *pula*! Before returning home from the planning office in Brisbane, I took the opportunity to go to Australia's Northern Territory to visit the Aborigine homeland, following up on the Jack Wheeler's lead. This included a campout trip into Kakadu Park, where much of *Crocodile Dundee* was filmed, the home of the largest of the world's 23 species of crocodiles. We then continued north into Arnemland, an Aboriginal reserve into which only a very limited number of non-Aborigines are allowed. I found significant parallels to the Bushmen, both politically and culturally. I became more convinced that the progress in the Northern Territory in granting the Aborigines land and self-determination could serve as a tangible example of what could be done for an aboriginal people, and be emulated for the benefit of the Kalahari Bushmen.

Both the Aborigines' dreamtime creation myths and the creation myths of the San in Africa have taught these two peoples that they and all of nature were created together. With both, nature is everything, a religion. They are also similar in their small nomadic clan structure with low population density. Both cultures have created prolific rock paintings dating back centuries. Both have suffered cultural disruption through genocide, massacre, dispossession from their land, and more recently, benign neglect at the hands of more advanced whites in Australia; whites and Bantu in southern Africa.

The parallels go on. Upon dispossession from their land the first step for both cultures has been to become sedentary serfs or underpaid cattle herders for the invading colonizers. Then cattle and other livestock have been joined by mining as the big GNP producers, both aboriginal peoples' ever more powerful nemesis.

About one percent of Australia's fifteen to sixteen million population are classed as Aborigine. About a third of those are full-bloods. The total numbers of people and the small percentage still living in the traditional ways is about the same for Australia's Aborigines as for the Kalahari San. An encouraging indication to be found in these Australian figures is that the number following a traditional 'back-to-the-bush' culture has been increasing since the Aborigines were given land and self-determination starting in the 1970s.

Those traditional Aborigines that survive are in the remote central Australian deserts or on the tropical fringes north of it, Cape York in Queensland or the Kimberly plateau in the northeast corner of Western Australia, but predominantly in the Northern Territory where the Aborigines make up more than one third of the sparse population. Another parallel of sorts is that Darwin is like Maun in being a remote and isolated frontier town, the gateway serving the outback. Darwin is closer by air to Hong Kong than to Sydney or Canberra.

Administrators in the Northern Territory confirmed that the Aborigines have retrieved or will be retrieving something between thirty and forty percent of the land, over which they now have some real control, as a result of the Land Reform Act of 1976. On these lands they now have the power to decide whether mining goes ahead or not, and if mining is allowed they receive their fair share of the rewards. The 1976 Act made the Aborigines the official owners of the Northern Territory's national parks, like Kakadu and Ayer's Rock. The Aborigines now lease the park lands back to the Australian National Parks System, but retain the power to eject people who desecrate their ancestral sites or the parks in general. Why not something similar for the surviving San of Botswana and Namibia?

In Darwin, an Aboriginal Land Administrator pointed out how one of the first successes for the Aborigines in the 1960's occurred when official Australian policy changed. After two hundred years of first officially-condoned genocide including pacification by force, during which the Aborigines were forcefully dispossessed of their lands, there followed a long period of indifference and neglect, when the policy was to assimilate the Aborigine into the white society, while waiting for those still in the bush to die out. Rather than the previous policy to destroy their culture by forced assimilation into the majority's modern white culture and socio-economic structure, the Aborigines were for the first time in the 1960's allowed to integrate into the majority's society with their traditional culture intact or not, as they chose. During the 1972 election the tent Aboriginal Embassy was set up in the capital with the express purpose of attracting world attention to the Aborigines as "foreigners in their own land". The 'Embassy' and 'Australian apartheid' headlines helped embarrass the government, and sway citizens to vote the labor party into power with a mandate to give the Aborigines land, rights and self-determination. Ultimately it was public awareness and public outcry, both in Australia and internationally, that brought about actions that translated to advantageous changes for the Australian Aborigines.

The two centuries of suffering inflicted on the Aborigines were caused more by ignorance of their unique culture than specifically directed wrath. More simply, the early settlers did not care about their culture, they just wanted their land. When the injustices began to draw international attention, the Australian public stood up and voted to give the land and self-determination to the Aborigines. What could be the 'Aboriginal Embassy' that attracts world attention and gets the equivalent of a Northern Territory's Lands Rights Act of 1976 for the Kalahari San?

Botswana has recently passed legislation that would indicate a policy of helping the San, but, sadly, it seems more for publication than implementation. International attention and outcry could bring more tangible results.

It is true that compared to the Kalahari Bushmen the Australian Aborigines are more sophisticated and educated in the ways of the modern world and are thus better able to be politically active on their own behalf. Most Aborigines speak English, so they can communicate and appeal directly to the majority. The Bushmen are much less sophisticated than their Australian or Inuit cousins and they generally cannot communicate with those in power.

Still, there is no reason that an aroused public, once made aware of the plight of these unique Kalahari people, would not be willing to get behind an effort to guarantee them the land and water sources they need and deserve. The public could raise money where needed, but more important, could lobby for the immediate actions that are necessary for the salvation of all the surviving Bushmen, be they acculturated and facing the problems of making the transition into modern society, or unacculturated and nomadic like Qui and his clan, and wanting to stay that way.

Namibia is a newly independent country, providing an opportunity for rapid change. Now is the time for concerted pressure for land for the Bushmen in Namibia. The new black Namibian government has to hear loud and clear from the outside world that this special minority is an irreplaceable asset to Namibia and the world and must be treated accordingly. Are the wild Bushmen less important than the spotted owl?

How do the Bushmen acquire land in Botswana? First lobby Botswana to rescind the 1986 order to eject more than a thousand Bushmen from their traditional lands in the Central Kalahari. Let them practice a transitional mixed economy. Assure the Central Kalahari Bushmen a well, a school and medical clinic at Kade in the Central Kalahari Reserve. Since the 1986 ejection decree, the Botswana government has periodically cut off services to the Bushmen to freeze them out of the Reserve. Services should be restored. But simultaneously, provide land and water elsewhere outside the Central Kalahari Reserve, enticing most of the tame Bushmen out and eventually leaving only a small number of the more traditional nomadic ones as game croppers and game protectors to thwart poachers like the ones we encountered in the Makgadikgadi Pans Game Reserve.

Despite the Central Kalahari issue which casts Botswana in a bad light, Botswana is still a leading example of enlightened African democracy on a continent with an otherwise often sad track record. Recently the San in Botswana have gotten considerable attention, at the political level and in the press.

It would be naive not to acknowledge that there is some conflict and even confusion in Botswana over the Bushman issue. There are certainly powerful voices in government advocating policies of forcefully civilizing the San and assimilating them into the majority mainstream, intentionally obliterating their 'embarrassing' stone-age culture, while turning a deaf ear to the Bushman's own stated needs and desires. There are many powerful self-interest groups—herd owners, miners, and conservationists—all lobbying for their pet interests which are usually contrary to Bushman survival because their interests involve the taking of Bushmen's land. Observers have pointed out that most of the top Botswana politicians are substantial cattle owners, who thus have reasons to keep the Bushmen landless and in poverty, if only to assure their continued availability as a cheap source of herding labor. One wonders, then, if the government is only paying lip service to the Accelerated Rural Area Development Program (ARADP) and the creation of Wildlife Management Areas (WMA's) to benefit the Bushman.

The Accelerated Rural Area Development Plan targets dispossessed people, mainly the Basarwa, for improved conditions. In line with current Botswana policy, over twenty percent of Botswana's remoter areas have recently been re-designated Wildlife Management Areas. This represents land taken back, mostly from tribal lands, for the RAD's (Rural Area Dwellers), a Botswana euphemism for Basarwa, or Bushmen. The idea is for the government to drill wells in these currently uninhabited remote areas away from established villages or Bantu cattle herding posts, and settle small dispersed groups of Bushmen at the newly created well locations, permitting them to have some small subsistence herds of goats or cattle, as opposed to the Bantus' larger overgrazing commercial herds, and an opportunity to forage for wild game and bush food.

The Bushman would have to be protected from encroachment and dispossession by the Herero and Tswana commercial cattle herders should the new wells be drilled. The numbers of domestic animals would be controlled to small numbers for the Bushman's own protection against overgrazing and the sort of ecosystem degradation that drives game away.

Botswana needs to be encouraged to decrease its dependence on commercial cattle herds as an export producer and to develop other uses for the Kalahari bush, like herding wild game. USAID and the World Bank have begun questioning loans for cattle herd expansion, advocating instead aid with a human face. Why not run herds of eland and gemsbok and wildebeest in some of the marginal waterless Kalahari country where they have survived for millennia? Let trophy hunters pay the Bushman owners to harvest a few males. There is precedent for such a system. In the Canadian Arctic the Inuit hold all the licenses for polar bear and may sell their permits if they wish. Let the Bushmen harvest other redundant males for their own subsistence, then some for market, and possibly even some females within sustained yield game cropping practices.

And what of the wells Beth Oliver reported Sweden would drill? There exists a 1987 proposal to the government for a Ngamiland district well drilling project that fits the umbrella of Botswana's ARADP and WMA concept and that would benefit the very Kung we visited ... Qui and his kin. But this proposal seems lost in bureaucratic limbo.

Some six hundred and sixty Rural Area Dwellers are presently dispersed in eight villages, two thirds in seven villages along the Qangwa valley, some 40 to 50 kilometers north of Xai Xai, and about one third in Xai Xai. The proposal involves a grassroots plan to drill wells and support the relocation of small, clan-sized groups of Bushmen to specific locations chosen by the Bushmen themselves. It addresses the needs of individuals who have been personally contacted and have participated in the planning and want desperately to disperse out into remote bush locations, away from their current concentrations around Bantu cattle posts like Xai Xai and Tsodillo. Under the WMA plan and philosophy, only Bushmen would be allowed to make up these communities near the new wells to be drilled in currently uninhabited remote bush.

The plan would relocate a group of thirty-seven Bushmen from Xai Xai, under their self-nominated leader, east to Gcwihaba within three kilometers of the Gcwihaba Cavern we visited. Since 1975 some of these Bushman have, on their own, hand dug fifteen and twenty meter deep dry wells at the proposed location, without finding water. The group would act as custodians and guides to the now unattended Gcwihaba Caves National Monument.

The proposal would permit a second group of forty Bushmen, under their nominated leader, to escape the Xai Xai cattle post and relocate at Xumxgeni, thirty kilometers to the south. Both these locations could provide Qui and his nomadic band a dry season and drought year emergency water source, other than Xai Xai. Another group of thirty-three Bushmen would relocate to a summer pan at Cheracherano, away from Qangwa and away from competing commercial cattle. Qangwa is the district administrative center some fifty kilometers north of Xai Xai.

The plan provides for five other small groups including new wells in the Qainxaho area and in the Aha hills, all within 'Bushman-walking-distance' of where we visited with Qui and his clan.

Success hinges on government approval, then on how the program is implemented, more than on funding sources. Success would require consulting the Bushmen concerned on a regular basis, to ensure their input at all stages of the planning and implementation process. Only through this process of consultation would the Bushman groups involved be truly in control of their own destiny and not bystanders in

Tsumkwe-type experiments that, though well meaning, can go astray.

It would also be necessary to give full consideration to the social problems that would almost certainly arise if the Bushmen were relocated to new bore holes, creating complex relations between those who move and those remaining behind, possibly because they had jobs herding Bantu cattle; those with and those without cattle; and between Bushman and non-Bushman residents of the Qangwa district. Just who would be entitled to graze and water their cattle at the new sites and who and what statutory bodies would have decision-making powers are crucial questions.

Because of the complexities of such issues and given the difficulties that have arisen elsewhere in previous implementations of similar schemes, like Tsumkwe, it would be imperative for individuals or organizations to work in the bush with the Bushman, liaising with the government and keeping non-Bushmen from usurping the wells.

The Ngamiland well drilling program only requires government approval. Sources for funding have been found and are ready to proceed, including but not limited to Beth Oliver's Swedes.

These people's kin, the Ju/Wa Bushman in Namibia's eastern Bushmanland, serve as an example of the hard won success of a program like the one proposed. But for the likes of John Marshall and Dr. Megan Biesele working with the people and fending off bureaucratic problems, the Ju/Wa Bushmen would not have been able to relocate themselves away from Tsumkwe, the "place of death", where many died due to overconcentration and depletion of the environment, along with a breakdown of their traditional culture. If Botswana authorities were to approve the well drilling proposal, it would permit most of the Kung in the Dobe-Qangwa-Xai Xai areas with the demonstrated will, the way to move away from concentrations around the cattle posts and strike out on their own.

This one program could be the salvation of some one hundred and sixty Bushmen. Not a large number, but when one considers that the total population of the remote Dobe-Qangwa-Xai Xai region is less than a thousand people and two-thirds of those are dispossessed Bushmen, it takes on more significance. Compare it to bringing a handful of surviving California condors back from the edge of extinction, gone from the earth forever, to where they can be reintroduced into the wild.

How can it be that such a simple plan that answers the need has not gone ahead? According to press releases, Botswana is looking out for its minorities, yet the San are being pushed out of the Central Kalahari and their plight in the Ghanzi farm block goes largely ignored, while the move to civilize them whether they want to or not goes on.

The well-drilling program has fallen into a bureaucratic crack. The Bushmen want to see it resurrected and pushed to completion. But there are risks beyond the Bushmen's control. Peter for one fears that if the wells are drilled, large environmentally destructive commercial herds of Bantu cattle will move in, and Qui and his nomadic Bushmen mates will just lose the last of their 'only-Bushmen-can-survive-here' bush.

In October of 1991 Botswanan Bushmen of Qui's region crossed the border fence for a two day informal meeting with their Namibian brethren, with the Nyae Nyae Development Foundation of Namibia acting as the catalyst. The Namibian Bushmen shared with their less fortunate, dispossessed Botswanan kin details of the progress they have recently made since Namibia's Independence in having their land rights and self-development efforts recognized and encouraged, up to the level of Sam Nujoma, Namibia's first black President. Below are paraphrases of a few of the comments the reader would have heard, from the Bushmen themselves, a people who until they lost their land, fed themselves and took care of their own problems. Unfortunately, no government representatives were present.

- If you wait for the government to do something for you, you'll die before it's done, you should help yourself.
- In Botswana it is not clear what they mean when they say they will grant you a well.
- In Botswana, Bushmen are people who work with cattle, but always for others. Our land has been taken.
- In Botswana we have two parties, but neither listens to us. I wish we had representatives who would listen to us.
- If only government would at least hear our tears.
- We haven't got an organization in Botswana: The blacks run all the meetings, we Bushmen are like baby ostriches blindly closed in our eggshells.
- We are behind in Botswana because we can't write and because their meetings don't use our language anyway.
- At Dobe (30 kilometers north of Xai Xai) we had a well registered to us but the government changed it to a council well and the Hereros took it over. We dug that well ourselves with our own hands.

Two actual quotes:

- "We don't want a government which treats us like the woman who ate meat but only smeared her child's mouth with fat. When someone came to ask if the child had been fed she said, "Don't you see the fat around his mouth?' But in fact he was hungry."
- "You from Botswana, you should know that if you go to the government to ask for something, they'll tell you to go away and gather others to work with you. You'll be told to wait five years. But where your fathers' fathers lived is the land you should hold fast to."

Could the young Botswanan and Namibian governments send interested envoys to Darwin to see for themselves the results and compare notes with the Northern Territory's Land Councils, the government entities administering the Aboriginal land reforms? This might give the Kalahari administrators some first-hand ideas and help resolve the conflict over the Bushman issue. An Australian visit could give a louder voice to others closer to the needs of the Bushman and to the richness of the culture, as these officials begin to challenge current policies. An Australian visit could cause Kalahari politicians to question their assumption that these people, little changed from prehistoric times, can make the 10,000 year leap forward in a generation or less and survive the cultural shock of the transition.

Or what about a visit to Canada? Late in 1991, after 15 years of negotiation, the Canadian government has announced the creation of a huge new independently governed territory for the Bushmen's Aboriginal and Commonwealth cousins, the Inuit. To be called Nunavut, meaning 'land of the people' in Inuit, the new territory stretches from Manitoba and Hudson Bay north to the Arctic Ocean, comprising a fifth of Canada's land mass. About 17,500 Inuit live there, and will be given a cash settlement, property rights and a share in any mineral wealth. A second Inuit territory, Inuvialuit, is still under negotiation. It covers Canada's western Arctic shore from Nunavut west to the Alaskan border. The tide changed for the Australian Aborigine in the 1970's, for the Inuit in the 1990's, but where are the still suffering Kalahari Bushmen? Sadly they are being quietly evicted from their only reserve in Botswana.

What about the treatment of our two million American Indians and Alaskan natives? No question their individual lives and cultures have suffered in being dispossessed of most of their land like the Bushmen. No one can be proud that 24% of the native American population is living below the poverty line compared to 10% of the overall U.S. population. But still 950,000 native Americans live on or near the 278 reservations, of which 140 are owned outright by some of the 510 federally recognized tribes. Meanwhile the Kalahari San have all but lost their last sanctuary in Botswana, the Central Kalahari Reserve. In Namibia, the San in Bushmanland are threatened, and but for the front line activities of the Nyae Nyae Development Foundation, supported by Survival International, that last scrap of land would have been lost to the Bushmen.

Mankind owes the San consideration on two levels. First, there is the moral issue. They should be treated fairly and compassionately by civilized men and women to atone for the more than three hundred years of genocide and land dispossession perpetrated on them. Secondly, it must be seen that their culture is important to the world for its own sake, an irreplaceable symbol of all our ancestries. We hope that you, the reader of *Bush for the Bushman*, will add your voice and your effort to those too few already raised, and that through your actions we might turn the tide in favor of the San. Once their culture is gone, it is gone forever, the oldest living legacy of all mankind.

The public must be made aware of the grave situation, and through support in voices and letters, let the leaders of Botswana and Namibia know that the surviving Bushmen are important. We all need to be part of the 'Bushman Embassy,' which will initiate a process by which the

Bushman can redress his real grievances with the rest of mankind.

Four principal organizations supporting the Bushman are the Kalahari Peoples Fund in Botswana, the Nyae Nyae Development Foundation of Namibia and Cultural Survival, Inc. in Namibia, and Survival International in both countries. Their mailing addresses are listed in Appendix A.

Failing some immediate 'like Australia' or 'like Canada' turnabout, it is sad to contemplate that with the present direction and pace of change in civilization, current and future generations will only be able to read of the Bushmen in dusty library books or possibly catch fleeting glimpses of what little has been retained of the Bushmen's culture on films like *The Gods Must Be Crazy*.

The last of the world's Bushmen, those few in the Kalahari, are about to pass to a mere footnote in human history, as has long since been the case in South Africa.

Let this not be their epitaph.

Appendix A

The following are organizations actively supporting the Bushman's fight for individual and cultural survival:

Survival International
310 Edgware Road
London, W2 1DY, England
44-71-723-5535

Founded in the early 1970's, Survival International, with headquarters in London, and branch offices elsewhere, is a worldwide movement to support tribal peoples, the two hundred million threatened aboriginal or tribal people in the world, some four percent of the world's population. Survival stands for tribal peoples' right to decide their own future and helps them protect their lands, environment and way of life.

Survival has an active membership of some 12,000 worldwide, whom they alert to write national leaders to protest when indigenous cultures are threatened. This has proved to give them the clout to lobby governments effectively on behalf of threatened minorities like the Bushman. Survival has actively resisted the ejection of the Bushman from Botswana's Central Kalahari Reserve. Survival works on dozens of cases — wherever tribal peoples ask for support; in Brazil, to stop the invasion by goldminers and immunize against diseases which are killing the Yanomami Indians; in Ecuador, to save the Waorani's forest from devastation by oil companies; in Mayalsia, to help the Dayak peoples protect their forest against 24 hour logging. Interested readers who would like more information about Survival's campaigns for tribal peoples, or membership details, should write or call them at the address above.

Cultural Survival, Inc.
53A Church Street
Cambridge, Massachusetts 02138
(617) 495-2562

A non-profit organization founded in 1972 by a group of social scientists from Harvard, this organization with a 20,000 membership concerns itself with the fate of tribal peoples and ethnic minorities around the world. They have a close association with the Nyae Nyae Development Foundation in Namibia, and support their activities on behalf of the Kung San. Interested readers who join will receive their quarterly publications.

*****

Nyae Nyae Development Foundation of Namibia (NNDFN)
P.O. Box 9026, Windhoek 9000
Namibia, Africa
(264) 61-36327

This organization was created in 1981 by John Marshall and Claire Ritchie specifically to support the efforts of the Kung Bushmen in Namibia's Bushmanland, to insure their land rights and cultural survival. The Foundation aids the San in their daily efforts in the *bush*, while fending off efforts of government and other interests that would threaten their land rights and culture. Since Namibian independence in March 1991, NNFDN's continued front line support for the Nyae Nyae Bushmen has resulted in their successfully retaining rights to their remaining land in Bushmanland with the post-apartheid government. NNDFN was instrumental in lobbying with the government for the ejection of Herero pastoralists "poaching" grazing land in Bushmanland. It is largely due to NNDFN's activities since 1981 that the Kung San in Namibia are currently faring much better than their Kung kin (Qui and his clan) across the border in Botswana. Money sent to NNDFN *will* directly benefit the Bushmen (primarily in Namibia).

*****

The Kalahari People's Fund
c/o Dr. James Ebert
3700 Rio Grande Blvd., N.W., Suite 3
Albuquerque, New Mexico 87107-3042

Founded in 1973, this organization is made up principally of anthropologists who have worked with the Kalahari Bushmen, mainly in Botswana since the early 1970's. They simultaneously developed contacts with the Botswana government, helping them deal with the "Bushman problem". They continue to act as a liaison between the Bushmen and government authorities to try to improve the Bushman's lot more in line with progress achieved by NNDFN in Namibia. Funding to this organization is likely to help Qui and his clan because one of their main emphasis is in Ngamiland, Botswana's northwest corner.

Appendix B

December 19, 1991

H.E. The President, Dr Quett Masire
The President's Office
Private Bag 001
Gaborone, Botswana

Subject: Pressures To Remove Basarwa From The Central
            Kalahari Reserve

Dear Mr. President:

This letter is written to you on behalf of a group who consider themselves friends of Botswana. I have personally enjoyed visiting Botswana on several occasions and our group was fortunate to spend several days camped with a small band of nomadic Kung Basarwa hunter-gatherers in the bush east of Xai Xai in Ngamiland in August of 1988.

We are concerned with outside pressures being applied on your government to remove the Basarwa (Bushmen) from the Central Kalahari Reserve, which ironically was created for these very Basarwa in 1961. We feel their ejection would be a grave threat to the chances of survival of these very special minority citizens of Botswana. You have in your care the Basarwa who are truly the wards of all humanity. As the aboriginal inhabitants of the whole of southern Africa, they are one of the last remnants on earth of all mankind's hunter-gatherer legacy.

You will remember in 1973, John Marshall came to you in Gaborone with some of the Basarwa from the Central Kalahari Reserve, to plead for your intervention to avert a grave survival situation they then faced in terms of thirst and starvation. We applaud the positive action you then took on their behalf, assuring their survival up to now.

We are sorry to hear your government has been pressured for the ejection of the Basarwa by the EEC, using the Botswana-EEC Lome II Beef Contracts as a lever. We have good reason to believe the real behind the scenes lobby on the EEC for the eviction of the Basarwa comes from Greenpeace, under the banner of game conservation.

While we are all serious African game conservationists, we feel strongly that the small numbers of game taken by the Basarwa, hunting in their traditional ways, cannot be considered a real threat to the Central Kalahari game's survival. This is only good game management through limited cropping. We support letting the wild animals and the Bushmen survive together, as they did for thousands of years before the rest of us non-Bushmen arrived on the scene in southern Africa.

To quote John Marshall, from his close involvement with the Bushmen in Botswana and Namibia since the early 50's, the ejection of the Bushmen now from the Central Kalahari would lead to their "death through dispossession." Without dedicated land they cannot possibly hope to survive. It is questionable whether alternate land suitable for resettlement is available. We are further concerned that numerous studies of other relocated Basarwa communities have indicated that the disruptions of resettlement 'away from their father's graves' has caused serious cultural, social, economic and health problems.

We ask you not to bow to misguided outside pressures, and to continue to protect the interests of the Basarwa of the Central Kalahari Reserve and elsewhere in Botswana by assuring them ample land and water and a voice in their own destiny. Only then can they freely chose to either continue as nomadic hunter-gatherers, or transition into a more sedentary "mixed economy," cultivating and owning domestic animals with some seasonal foraging. We thank you for your actions toward prolonging this unique culture, benefiting not only Botswana but all mankind.

Sincerely,

John Perrott

*****

To write to Namibia's President on behalf of the Bushman:
  H.E. The President, Sam Nujoma
  State House, Leutwein Street
  Private Bag 13339
  Windhoek, Namibia
  Phone: (264) 61-220010

Bibliography

Laurens van der Post, *The Lost World of the Kalahari*, Hogarth Press, London, 1958
The above book was reissued in 1988 by William Morrow and Company of New York, with many photos by David Coulson.

Laurens van der Post, *The Heart of the Hunter*, Hogarth Press, London, 1961

Laurens van der Post, photos by Jane Taylor, *Testament to the Bushmen*, Viking Penquin Inc., New York, 1984

Lorna Marshall, *The !Kung of Nyae Nyae*, Harvard University Press, Cambridge, 1976

Alf Wannenburg, photos by Peter Johnson and Anthony Bannister, *The Bushmen*, C. Struik Ltd., Cape Town, 1979

P. V. Tobias et al, *The Bushmen*, Human & Rousseau, Cape Town, 1978

Bern Woodhouse, *When Animals Were People*, Chris van Rensberg Publications, Melville, 1984

Paul Augustinus, *Botswana, A Brush with the Wild*, Acorn Books, Randburg, 1987

Peter Johnson and Anthony Bannister, *Okavango*, C. Struik Ltd., Cape Town, 1977

Richard B. Lee and Irven Devore, editors, *Kalahari Hunter-Gatherers*, Harvard University Press, Cambridge, 1976

Elizabeth Marshall Thomas, *The Harmless People*, Random House, New York, 1958

Mark and Delia Owens, *Cry of the Kalarhari*, G. K. Hall, Boston, 1986

Diane Fossey, *Gorillas in the Mist*, Houghton Mifflin, Boston, 1983

Richard E. Leakey, *The Making of Mankind*, Michael Joseph Ltd., London, 1981

John Gunther, *Inside Africa*, Harper, New York, 1955

Ernest Hemingway, *The Green Hills of Africa*, Charles Scribner's & Sons, New York, 1935

Edwin N. Wilmsen, *Land Filled with Flies, A Political Economy of the Kalahari*, University of Chicago Press, 1989

Jack Wheeler, *The Adventurer's Guide*, David McKay Company, Inc., New York, 1976

Charles Darwin, *Origin of Species and the Descent of Man*, Modern Library

Scott Bennett, *Aborigines and Political Power*, Sydney Allen and Unwin, 1989

Graeme Neate, *Aborigonal Land Rights Law in the Northern Territory*, Alternate Publishing Co-operative Ltd. (APCOL), 1989

Henry Reynolds, *The Law of the Land*, Penquin Books Australia, Ltd., 1987.

Index

ORDER FORM

for
BUSH FOR THE BUSHMAN
Need 'The Gods Must Be Crazy' Kalahari People Die?
$14.95

Telephone Orders: Call toll free: 800-345-0096, have your Visa or MasterCard ready.

Fax Orders: (616) 929-3808

Postal Orders: Publishers Distribution Service, 121 East Front St., Suite 203, Traverse City, MI 49684

Sales Tax: Please add 4% for books shipped to Michigan addresses.

Shipping: UPS Book Rate: $2.75 for the first book, $1.00 for each additional book.

Payment:
☐ Check
☐ Credit Card: ☐ Visa, ☐ MasterCard

Card Number: _____

Name on Card: _____

Exp. Date: _____ / _____

Send To:

Name: _____

Address: _____

City: _____

State: _____ Zip: _____